GAY CUBAN NATION

EMILIO BEJEL

THE UNIVERSITY OF CHICAGO PRESS

CHICAGO AND LONDON

Emilio Bejel is professor of Spanish American literature and literary theory at the University of Colorado at Boulder. In addition to seven collections of poetry and five scholarly books in Spanish, he is author of *José Lezama Lima, Poet of the Image* (University Press of Florida, 1990).

The University of Chicago Press, Chicago 60637
The University of Chicago Press, Ltd., London
© 2001 by The University of Chicago
All rights reserved. Published 2001
Printed in the United States of America

10 09 08 07 06 05 04 03 02 01   1 2 3 4 5
ISBN: 0-226-04173-5 (cloth)
ISBN: 0-226-04174-3 (paper)

Library of Congress Cataloging-in-Publication Data

Bejel, Emilio, 1944–
    Gay Cuban nation / Emilio Bejel.
        p. cm.
    Includes bibliographical references and index.
    ISBN 0-226-04173-5 (cloth : alk. paper)—
ISBN 0-226-04174-3 (pbk. : alk. paper)
        1. Homosexuality—Cuba.   2. Socialism—Cuba.
    3. Nationalism—Cuba.   4. Homosexuality in literature.
    5. Homophobia in literature.   I. Title.
HQ76.3.C9 B45 2001
306.76'6'097291—dc21   00-011811

For Greg,
with all my love

CONTENTS

PART III
REVOLUTIONARY NORMATIVITIES
AND THEIR EFFECTS
93

ACKNOWLEDGMENTS

One never really knows when a research project begins. Perhaps I can say that, for all practical purposes, *Gay Cuban Nation* had its inception with my research on the writings of Senel Paz and Reinaldo Arenas back in the early to mid-1990s. Since that time I have become indebted to numerous people for their contributions to this work. First I would like to thank John Gardner, a doctoral student in the Department of Spanish and Portuguese at the University of Colorado at Boulder and my research assistant for most of the research, writing, and rewriting of this book. John's help has been invaluable, and I am indebted to him for not only his skillful editing of the manuscript but also his common-sense advice on the content of some of the chapters and sections.

Among the many other friends and colleagues who contributed in one way or another to this project's success, I must recognize Luis González-del-Valle of the University of Colorado at Boulder as one of the very few people who ventured to read and comment on my entire manuscript when it was still a rough draft. Luis's comments, both general and detailed, were crucial in my decision to revise the manuscript substantially. Also, my department chair, Leopoldo Bernucci, supported me not only personally but in several practical ways as well, including the scheduling of my classes and addressing my request for John Gardner's continued help. Associate Dean Merrill Lessley was generous in granting a one-year extension of John's tenure. Merrill conveyed my petition to Dean Peter Spear, who graciously approved it.

After writing some sections of the book, I decided to send them to Doris Sommer of Harvard University for her opinion; she read and commented on them very incisively. As one of the leading scholars in the field of Latin American studies, her remarks helped me to reshape some of my ideas on the project. Louis Pérez of the University of North Carolina at Chapel Hill, who read the introduction and one of the manuscript chapters, gave me wise advice concerning their historical context and the publication of the book.

Stephen Clark, a friend and colleague at Northern Arizona University, read one of the later versions of the manuscript and provided me with interesting observations and skillful editorial corrections of the entire work. I also extend my thanks to Antonio Isea of Western Michigan University, with whom I have endlessly discussed many aspects of the work. Antonio's intellectual insights and practical advice contributed to the success of the project. I can say the same about my long-time friends Sonia Rivera-Valdés of York College; Maricel Mayor Marsán, editor of the literary journal *Baquiana*; and Ramiro Fernández, with whom I coauthored the book *La subversión de la semiótica*.

I also would like to thank George Chauncey of the University of Chicago, one of the truly great historians of gay issues in the United States, who was the first to put me in contact with the University of Chicago Press. George suggested that I discuss the publication of *Gay Cuban Nation* with Douglas Mitchell, executive editor of gay studies at the Press. A few days later I contacted Doug, and he and I have communicated countless times since that initial e-mail. I can say without hesitation that the professionalism, diligence, and patience he has demonstrated toward me, in good times and bad, is very much a part of the success of this project.

Finally, I wish to acknowledge the support of some of my close friends who are not in the academic field but who have, for some years, suffered through my frequent mentions of the vicissitudes of my work. They are Vinnie, Carol, Blake, Mario, Osvaldo, Christine, Jeff, Kerry, Ken, Janet, Eric, Gina, Vicente, Isabel, and Paul. Of course, nobody has endured the bad moments of this project and enjoyed its good ones more than my life partner, Greg Gibbs, whose patience and love toward me is immeasurable.

Part of chapter 1 originally appeared as "Cuban CondemNation of Queer Bodies" in *Cuba, the Elusive Nation: Interpretations of National Identity*, edited by Damián J. Fernández and Madeline Cámara Betancourt (Gainesville: University Press of Florida, 2000), 155–74.

Part of chapter 4 appeared under the title "Positivist Contradictions in Hernández Catá's *El ángel de Sodoma*" in *Anales de la literatura española contemporánea* 25, no. 1 (2000): 63–76. An earlier version of chapter 8 was published as "Arenas' *Antes que anochezca*: An Autobiography of a Gay Cuban Dissident" in *Reading and Writing the Ambiente: Queer Sexualities in Latino, Latin American, and Spanish Culture*, edited by Susana Chávez-Silverman and Librada Hernández (Madison: The University of Wisconsin Press, 2000), 299–315. Copyright © 2000 by The University of Wisconsin Press; reprinted by permission. Chapter 9 appeared as an article entitled "*Strawberry and Chocolate: Coming Out of the Cuban Closet?*" in *South Atlantic Quarterly* 96, no. 1 (winter 1997): 65–82. Chapter 11 was originally published under the title "The Unsettling Return of the Butterflies" in *Chasqui* (fall 2000): 3–13. I am grateful to the editors and publishers involved for permission to reprint these texts here.

INTRODUCTION

Homophobic discourses articulated as part of modern national precepts have been publicly expounded by Cuban nationalist leaders from the earliest days of modern Cuban history. Their discussions have often defined the homosexual body, implicitly or explicitly, as a threat to the health of the body of the nation.[1] Yet despite this strong and seemingly obvious relationship between notions of Cuban nationalism and homosexuality, studies on Cuban nationalism have dealt almost exclusively with race, class, colonization, the role of women, and U.S. and foreign relations; very few current works address the role of various definitions of homosexuality in Cuban nationalism, or how different transformations of Cuban nationalism have attempted to define homosexuality.[2] *Gay Cuban Nation* examines precisely this

Regarding texts orginally published in Spanish, all translations into English are my own. Nevertheless, in chapter 8 I occasionally consulted Dolores Koch's translation of Reinaldo Arenas's *Antes que anochezca (Autobiografía)* (Barcelona: Tusquets Editores, 1992), which was published under the title *Before Night Falls (A Memoir)* (New York: Penguin Books, 1993).

1. From the point of view of the relationship between modern Cuban nationalist discourse and effeminacy in men, the earliest known text is from 1791. It was in that year that José Agustín Caballero, a Cuban protonationalist cleric, published an article titled "Carta crítica al hombre-muger" (Letter in critique to the woman-man). In *La literatura del Papel Periódico de La Habana, 1790–1805*, introduction and edition by Cintio Vitier, Fina García Marruz, and Roberto Friol (Havana: Editorial Letras Cubanas, 1990), 75–78.

2. The most recent collection of articles and discussions on the topic of Cuban national identity within Cuba that I am aware of is *Cuba: cultura e identidad nacional* (Havana: Cuban Writers and Artists Union and the University of Havana, 1995). None of these works

issue, paying special attention to the ways in which homosexuality and so-called national identity have been intertwined in Cuban texts since the 1880s.

One of the main underlying concerns in this text is the threat that Cuban nationalist discourse sees in homoeroticism and gender transgressions. I will also examine how this perception is dealt with by different discourses of power as they struggle for a stance of authority on homosexual issues. But in addition to studying the conflicts among the discourses of religion, positivism, nationalism, feminism, and socialism on homosexual matters, I also assert that the notion of homosexuality and homoeroticism is inscribed, by negation, in the prescriptive models of the national Cuban narrative. This idea guides most of my readings throughout the three parts of this book: part 1 corresponds to the 1880s, part 2 to the 1920s and 1930s, and part 3 to the period from 1959 to the 1990s. I have chosen these points in time because I see an obvious connection between nationalism and concerns with homoeroticism in texts from these years.

It is precisely to the argument that the trace of homosexuality is imprinted on the prescriptive models of the national Cuban narrative that the title of this book, *Gay Cuban Nation*, refers. This title clearly implies a great measure of irony as well, since the truth of the matter is that Cuban nationhood has been defined, in part, by its rejection of gayness and queerness. It is also important to note that no single *nationalism* exists, nor a single *homosexuality*; that neither *nationalism* nor *homosexuality* is a single entity that has maintained its essence over a long period. Instead, both concepts are evolving, complex definitions that are continually being transformed. This issue is explored in George L. Moose's pioneering study, *Nationalism and Sexuality*,[3] as well as in Sylvia Molloy and Robert McKee Irwin's anthology, *Hispanisms and Homosexualities*,[4] and Andrew Parker, Mary Russo, Doris Sommer, and Patricia Yaeger's anthology, *Nationalisms and Sexualities*.[5]

deal with the relationship of Cuban nationalism and homosexuality. Nevertheless, there has been a recent major publication in Cuba on homosexuality in literature: Víctor Fowler, *La maldición: una historia del placer como conquista* (Havana: Editorial Letras Cubanas, 1998).

3. George L. Mosse, *Nationalism and Sexuality: Respectability and Abnormal Sexuality in Modern Europe* (New York: Howard Fertig, 1985).

4. Sylvia Molloy and Robert McKee Irwin, eds., *Hispanisms and Homosexualities* (Durham, N.C.: Duke University Press, 1998).

5. Andrew Parker, Mary Russo, Doris Sommer, and Patricia Yaeger, eds., *Nationalisms and Sexualities* (New York: Routledge, 1992). Other important major works that deal with

My readings in this book suggest that despite—or perhaps because of—the enormous efforts to expel the queer body, the specter of homosexuality has always haunted Cuban national discourse. Modern "homosexual identity," owing to its rejection from most definitions of Cubanness, becomes necessary in delineating the limits of that discourse. In this sense, that which is marginal becomes central. Homosexuality, as an abject region at the margin of Cuban national narrative, delimits and defines that narrative; it marks its borders, which is precisely why it belongs to its process of symbolization, and as such can return to the symbolic world of the nation with unusual force. The destabilizing effect of the queer explains, at least in part, the negative definition it has been given in the various transformations of Cuban nationalist discourse that seek coherence in a heterogeneous society.[6] As with every ideological field, that of Cuban nationhood contains a structural contingency that assures a permanent state of instability. Consequently, the specter of homosexuality, as part of the construction of modern Cuban nationalism since its beginning, has ironically become a constitutive element of that discourse through rejection and negation. The queer body thus can offer the possibility of a new perspective, leading to a resignification of the Cuban nation.

Discourses dealing with nationality or with gender usually seek to naturalize themselves by anchoring their limits and privileges in essentialist bases. Furthermore, nationalist discourse and heterosexism often support each other, and this alliance has deeply affected the relationship between the definitions of homosexuality and nationalism

concerns similar to mine in this book are Daniel Balderston and Donna J. Guy, eds., *Sex and Sexuality in Latin America* (New York: New York University Press, 1997); James N. Green, *Beyond Carnival: Male Homosexuality in Twentieth-Century Brazil* (Chicago: University of Chicago Press, 1999); Paul Julian Smith, *Vision Machines: Cinema, Literature and Sexuality in Spain and Cuba, 1983–93* (London: Verso, 1996) and *Laws of Desire: Questions of Homosexuality in Spanish Writing and Film, 1960–90* (Oxford: Oxford University Press, 1992); Emilie L. Bergmann and Paul Julian Smith, eds., *¿Entiendes? Queer Readings, Hispanic Writings* (Durham, N.C.: Duke University Press, 1995); Stephen O. Murray, ed., *Latin American Male Homosexualities* (Albuquerque: University of New Mexico Press, 1995); Daniel Balderston, *El deseo, enorme cicatriz luminosa* (Caracas: Ediciones eXcultura, 1999); and David William Foster, *Gay and Lesbian Themes in Latin American Writing* (Austin: University of Texas Press, 1991).

6. This discursive force toward coherence and toward the suppression of subaltern voices is manifested in many forms. For example, in the histories of Latin American literature there has been a persistent effort to suppress any discussion of homosexual issues, even those regarding the most obvious gay or lesbian themes. For an interesting and well-documented discussion of this issue see Daniel Balderston, "El pudor de la historia," in *El deseo, enorme cicatriz luminosa*, 5–17.

in Cuba. This relationship is associated with the precariousness of Cuba's national discourse, resulting in its extreme dependence on practices and definitions that attempt to set its discursive limits by trying to expel its constructed Others. This relational condition of nationalist discourse implies that despite the universality of the modern concept of nation and nationalism's insistence on claiming an essential nature, the concept of nation is a historical artifact, discontinuous and adaptable, whose ideology is neither reactionary nor progressive in and of itself. Due to this precariousness and permeability, many forms of modern nationalism have adapted themselves to liberalism, fascism, and socialism; to projects of war and peace; and to images of the past and hopes for the future in accordance with the circumstances and formative discourses of each specific nation.[7]

In terms of defining nationalism, the arguments presented in this study consider a wide range of ideas, from Benedict Anderson's "imagined community" to Homi Bhabha's "DissemiNation."[8]

The works of Doris Sommer on the effects of some *national romances* in the heterosexist foundation of Latin American nationalisms also form the basis of one of the main arguments of this text, namely that because homosexuality constitutes an integral part, by negation, of the narrative proposed by the national romances, it continually threatens to destabilize those very romances.[9] In this work I also share some of Partha Chatterjee's and R. Radhakrishnan's theoretical concerns regarding the relationship between the politics of nationalism and other subaltern politics.[10] There is little doubt that the "imagined community" of nationalism insists on being the most authentic collective binding, the true defining principle of the political field as such. Perhaps this claim should be radically questioned so that new relationships of mutual accountability with other polities could be seriously considered.

In the first part of the book, "The Building of a CondemNation," I study the subjection of the "homosexual" based on two variations of

7. See Benedict Anderson, *Imagined Communities: Reflections on the Origin and Spread of Nationalism*, rev. ed. (London: Verso, 1991); the first edition is from 1983.

8. See ibid. and Homi K. Bhabha, "DissemiNation: Time, Narrative and the Margins of the Modern Nation," in Homi K. Bhabha, ed., *Nation and Narration* (London: Routledge, 1990), 291–322.

9. See Doris Sommer, *Foundational Fictions: The National Romances of Latin America* (Berkeley and Los Angeles: University of California Press, 1991).

10. See Partha Chatterjee, *Nationalist Thought and the Colonial World* (Minneapolis: University of Minnesota Press, 1986); and R. Radhakrishnan, "Nationalism, Gender, and the Narrative of Identity," in Parker et al., *Nationalisms and Sexualities*, 77–95.

Cuban nationalism: José Martí's romantic-humanism and Benjamín de Céspedes and Enrique José Varona's scientism. The readings of these texts lead me to believe that this subjection is not only part of modern Cuban nationalist discourse and of Spanish colonialism but also of the United States' imperialist discourse of the late 1880s. Moreover, during Cuba's wars of independence against Spain (1868–98) the image of the military hero was at its height, having not yet been displaced by that of the productive, home-dwelling citizen. The transition from a slave-based mode of production to that of wage labor was also occurring at that time, and the United States had by then achieved considerable economic and cultural influence in Cuba and had shown its intentions to acquire the island.[11] Thus Cuba struggled for independence from Spanish colonization at the same time that certain modern capitalist structures were emerging there and as an expansionist threat from the United States was taking form. The problematic image of the queer that was constructed amidst Cuba's struggle for independence from both Spanish colonialism and U.S. neocolonialism is highlighted in two articles from 1889: "Do We Want Cuba?," inspired and written by several prominent members of the Republican Party, and José Martí's "Vindication of Cuba," written in answer to the American politicians' article.[12]

Martí's active participation in constructing prescriptive models of conduct for citizens of the future Cuban nation (Cuba was still a colony at the time) is well known. Accordingly, the first chapter of this book is devoted to studying some of his writings, especially his article "Vindication of Cuba" and his novel *Amistad funesta*.[13] In my readings of these texts I underscore Martí's paradoxical position in trying to construct a Cuban nationalist masculinity amidst the ongoing

11. See Manuel Moreno Fraginals, *El ingenio. Complejo económico social cubano del azúcar*, vol. 2 (Havana: Editorial de Ciencias Sociales, 1978), especially chap. 2, 174–221. Also see Louis A. Pérez Jr., *Cuba: Between Reform and Revolution*, 2d ed. (New York: Oxford University Press, 1995), especially chaps. 4–7, pps. 70–188. For an informative and interesting article on the influence of American popular culture in Cuba during the last thirty years of the nineteenth century, see Pérez Jr., "Between Baseball and Bullfighting: The Quest for Nationality in Cuba, 1868–1898," *The Journal of American History* 81, no. 2 (September 1994): 493–517.

12. "Do We Want Cuba?," Philadelphia *Manufacturer*, 6 March 1889; reproduced, with introduction and notes, in Philip S. Foner, ed., *Our America: Writings on Latin America and the Struggle for Cuban Independence by José Martí* (New York: Monthly Review Press, 1977), 228–30. Also, see José Martí, "A Vindication of Cuba," in Foner, ibid., 234–41. For a discussion of these articles, see chapter one of this book.

13. José Martí, *Amistad funesta* (Fatal friendship), in *Obras completas*, vol. 18 (Havana: Editorial de Ciencias Sociales, 1975), 185–272.

threat from Spanish colonialism and American neocolonialism, as he simultaneously tries to relate such a construct to his idea of modernity. His response to this complex ideological crossroads is a sort of "manly poet," a model of behavior for all Cuban men. Martí's construct includes, albeit obliquely, a negative image of the "effeminate man" as well as of the "manly woman."

In my reading of *Amistad funesta* I argue that the rejection/construction of the "manly woman" forms an integral part of Martí's articulation of his concept of the nation. For Martí, nationhood is based on an idealized family in which the woman is expected to be feminine, having no strong passions other than maternity and a devotion to the fatherland. I base my reading of *Amistad funesta* on the idea that Lucía, the novel's protagonist, represents a sort of spectral lesbianism, highly threatening to the idea of nation proposed by Martí. Here I also argue that Martí's position arises from a nationalist vision that sees gender transgression as part of the social fragmentation caused by rampant modernity. For Martí, this fragmentation can only be counteracted through the homogeneity that a poetic vision like his provides. Within Martí's view, homoeroticism is associated with all that is prosaic and fragmentary, as contrasted with that which is poetic.[14]

Whereas Martí's position regarding homoeroticism is paradoxical and based on a poetic stance, that of positivists such as Benjamín de Céspedes and Enrique José Varona is fiercely unwavering and dominated by a scientistic position that emphasizes the rhetoric of *the homosexualization of the enemy.* Typical of social hygienism, their positivistic discourse attributes social "vices" to other races, classes, and nations. In their rhetoric the homosexual body is seen as dangerous, a contamination of the national body, and something that must be eliminated. The representation and construction of the "pederast" in their discourse share many characteristics with that of the "homosexual" as defined at that time by sexologists from other countries.[15]

The second part of my study, "New Spaces and New Subjectivities," deals with texts from 1920 to 1940, a time of great economic, social, and political crises in Cuba and abroad. This period in the island's history

14. For a discussion on Martí's ideas concerning the relationship between poetry and modernity, see Julio Ramos, *Desencuentros de la modernidad en América Latina. Literatura y política en el siglo XIX* (Mexico City: Fondo de Cultura Económica, 1989), especially pps. 202–43. Also see Ramos, "Trópicos de la fundación: poesía y nacionalidad en José Martí," in *Paradojas de la letra* (Caracas: Ediciones eXcultura, 1996), 153–64.

15. See Jeffrey Weeks, *Coming Out. Homosexual Politics in Britain from the Turn of the Nineteenth Century to the Present,* rev. ed. (London: Quartet Books Limited, 1983), 5–6.

reveals a renewed resurgence of anti-imperialist Cuban nationalism. Feminism also emerges in Cuba during these years as a new discourse of resistance against the patriarchy. This problematic situation leads me to the ideas of several Cuban feminists on lesbianism and its relationship to national values and politics. Here I suggest that radical feminism's resistance to the prescribed models of conduct formed part of the new spaces from which the rigid power mechanisms attempting to control gender transgression could be challenged. As a result, representations of homosexuality quite different from those of previous years were enabled. In addition to feminism's challenge, some representations of homosexuality based on naturalism and on a new transformation of positivism are discussed here. These issues are examined in the context of four important novels: Ofelia Rodríguez Acosta's *La vida manda* (1929) and *En la noche del mundo* (1940); Alfonso Hernández-Catá's *El ángel de Sodoma* (1928); and Carlos Montenegro's *Hombres sin mujer* (1938).[16]

The third and final part of this work, "Revolutionary Normativities and Their Effects," is the most extensive and ambitious. Its seven chapters cover the period from Castro's coming to power during the 1959 revolution to the end of the 1990s. The introduction to this part examines what may be the most homophobic period in Cuban history: the mid-1960s to the mid-1970s, a time that produced the UMAPs (forced labor camps that included many gay men) and the homophobic policies of the First Congress of Education and Culture. Here I also discuss other events and personalities of the seventies, eighties, and nineties, such as the Mariel boat lift, the documentary *Conducta impropia*,[17] and the life and persona of gay Cuban writer Virgilio Piñera. In this introduction I underscore that despite (or because of) the extreme homophobia of the revolutionary years, Cuba's most insistent and articulate representations of homosexuality as a form of resistance emerge at this time. Some of these representations are often accompanied by highly complex cultural theories that seek to explain homosexuality in new ways and to construct new homosexual subjectivities. Accordingly, the chapters of this part are devoted to a critical

16. Ofelia Rodríguez Acosta, *La vida manda* (Life decrees) (Madrid: Editorial Biblioteca Rubén Darío, 1929) and *En la noche del mundo* (In the night of the world) (Havana: La Verónica, 1940); Alfonso Hernández Catá, *El ángel de Sodoma* (The angel of Sodom) (Madrid: Mundo Latino, 1928); and Carlos Montenegro, *Hombres sin mujer* (Womanless men) (Mexico: Editorial Masas, 1938).

17. Néstor Almendros and Orlando Jiménez-Leal, *Conducta impropia* (Improper conduct). The script of this documentary was published by Editorial Playor, Madrid, in 1984.

study of some of the most outstanding representations of homosexuality as a form of marginality in relation to Cuban nationalist discourse.[18]

Among these representations of homosexuality, I discuss the poetic position of José Lezama Lima, especially as revealed in his novel *Paradiso*.[19] Here I argue that, for Lezama Lima, the lack of natural order in the world makes one pursue a *supranatural* solution, free of temporality and reproduction. Within his antirationalist stance, Lezama Lima implies that homosexuality is a form of *supranature* that breaks accepted limits and permits creativity. But I also believe that Lezama's world vision includes a mythic teleology of the Cuban nation that has a genealogical connection to nineteenth-century Cuban nationalist discourse.[20] Other readings in this section include Severo Sarduy's *Colibrí* and his idea of writing and simulation.[21] In contrast with Lezama Lima's providential vision, Sarduy's text offers a spatial aesthetic in which temporality can scarcely be discerned and therefore national teleology is deconstructed. Sarduy's text proposes representation to be an "impulse of simulation," and reality nothing more than masks concealing other masks, simulations that have no true referent or fixed model. Thus, Sarduy's works frequently insist on portraying not homosexual, gay, or lesbian characters, but rather a sort of "queer transvestite" with no stable referent, and his vision denounces nationalism as a delusional myth.

In this section I also include readings of Reinaldo Arenas's autobiography, *Antes que anochezca*; Tomás Gutiérrez Alea and Juan Carlos Tabío's film *Fresa y chocolate*; and Luis Felipe Bernaza and Margaret Gilpin's documentary *Mariposas en el andamio*.[22] In my view, *Antes*

18. Perhaps here we could recall what Stephen O. Murray said about studies of homosexuality: "We know something about how pederasty and gender nonconformity were represented (often by hostile nonparticipants) in a few societies, but practically nothing about how homosexual desire or behavior is or was experienced or represented by/to those actually involved in it." See Stephen O. Murray, *Homosexualities* (Chicago: University of Chicago Press, 2000), 9. In the Cuban texts I study in this book, there are several representations of homosexuality by "hostile nonparticipants," but since the 1980s we find several representations of homosexual desire and behavior by authors who were actually involved in it. Of course, interpretation of representations of homosexuality is always necessary even in these cases, but I want to underscore this difference in some Cuban texts since then.

19. José Lezama Lima, *Paradiso*, 3d ed. (Mexico City: Ediciones Era, 1973). See also my study on this novel in *José Lezama Lima, Poet of the Image* (Gainesville: University of Florida Press, 1990).

20. This is an idea I share with Rafael Rojas. See his *Isla sin fin: Contribución a la crítica del nacionalismo cubano* (Miami: Ediciones Universal, 1998).

21. See chapter 7 of this book. Also see Severo Sarduy, *Colibrí* (Bogotá: Editorial La Oveja Negra, 1985) and *La simulación* (Caracas: Monte Ávila Editores, 1982).

22. Reinaldo Arenas, *Before Night Falls (A Memoir)*, trans. Dolores M. Koch (New York: Penguin Books, 1993; Spanish original: *Antes que anochezca [Autobiografía]* [Barcelona:

que anochezca portrays the Cuban nation as an *epic of the oppressed,* which implies a constant striving for utopian freedom. Arenas's autobiography can be read as a resounding rejection of an oppressive system that censured and jailed him, yet also produced his persona and his subjectivity. Gutiérrez Alea and Tabío's film *Fresa y chocolate* attempts a sort of "rectification" of the homophobic policies of the Cuban government. Through an alliance between a gay man and an open-minded socialist, the film's logic tries to convince its audience of the possibility of integrating gays (and, by implication, lesbians) into the very concept of the nation.

In chapter 10 I continue discussing works with a gay and/or lesbian theme published from the end of the 1980s through the 1990s. Three of the most outstanding writers of this period deal with this issue in Cuban society: Leonardo Padura Fuentes, in his novel *Máscaras*; and Pedro de Jesús López Acosta and Ena Lucía Portela Alzola, in their short stories. In my readings of these texts I offer examples not only of "coming out of the closet" but also of the paradoxical implications of the veiling and unveiling of machismo.

A critical reading of Bernaza and Gilpin's documentary *Mariposas en el andamio* offers yet another example of the changes in the relationship between the constructs of homosexuality and citizenship occurring in Cuba in the 1990s. My study of this documentary deals with the phenomenon of a transvestism, which simultaneously questions and affirms Cuban *machista* values at the end of the twentieth century. Precisely because the main topic of *Mariposas en el andamio* is transvestism, my reading focuses on the paradoxical implications of "gender trouble" as I see them in this documentary.[23]

The final chapter of the book is dedicated entirely to the reading of texts by Cuban-American writers Elías Miguel Muñoz, Achy Obejas, and Sonia Rivera-Valdés. The texts selected often deal with gay, lesbian, bisexual, and queer topics within American society, and their critical readings invite a reexamination not only of issues related to gender roles but also of the prevailing relationship between Cuba and the United States. The characters in these stories frequently cross

Tusquets Editores, 1992]); Tomás Gutiérrez Alea and Juan Carlos Tabío, *Fresa y chocolate* (Strawberry and chocolate), screenplay by Senel Paz (Canberra: Ronin Films,1993); and Luis Felipe Bernaza and Margaret Gilpin, *Mariposas en el andamio* (Butterflies on the scaffold) (New York: Kangaroo Productions, 1996).

23. See Judith Butler's ideas on "gender trouble" in her book *Bodies that Matter: On the Discursive Limits of "Sex"* (New York: Routledge, 1993). See also Marjorie Garber's ideas on transvestism in her book *Vested Interests: Cross-Dressing & Cultural Anxiety.* (New York: Routledge, 1992; reprint, New York: HarperPerennial, 1993).

accepted boundaries between sexual and ethnic "identities" as well as between nationalities, which is why queer readings of these texts are so illuminating.

The implications of the readings of the texts in this book lead me to reflect on my own project. I realize that although there are undeniable sociological and historical implications in each of the chapters, my work and objectives fall under neither category. My readings are critical cultural studies of modern Cuban texts (novels, short stories, autobiographies, books on social and sexual issues, newspaper articles, documentaries, and films) that examine the relationships between the definitions of homosexuality and Cuban nationalism. As may be implied by the readings I have chosen for *Gay Cuban Nation*, the relationship between the representations of Cuban nationality and homoeroticism cannot be defined as progressively repressive nor as progressively liberating. Instead, it forms a twisting and broken path that changes in the light of various discourses and at various points in time. Not only do social, historical, and political circumstances change in relation to a particular representation of homosexuality, but that representation has no stable referent, no fixed, unchangeable, external reality.

Nevertheless, certain common characteristics can be seen in the readings of the condemnation of homoeroticism in modern Cuban society. Similar discursive conditions during the periods examined construct a condemnation of anything that could be considered a *transgression of gender roles*. This rejection is frequently associated with the construction of a nationalist discourse in which the homosexual is perceived as a corrupter of the national body for having transgressed gender roles. I believe that the insistence on prescribed models of behavior and the establishment of rigid boundaries between genders was first seriously challenged by radical feminism in the 1920s and 1930s, and that this challenge facilitated or at least was part of the new interpretations of homosexuality.

The questions posed throughout this study make it a multifaceted work with several threads to follow. With a queer theoretical approach extended to the study of nationality, I hope to destabilize the totalization of ideas not only on sexuality but also on nationality. The critical position in these readings highlights the incoherence found in relationships that demand stability and naturalness among sex, gender, and sexual desire. Accordingly, I take into account the fact that all the works I analyze have various voices, and that some of these voices can be found between the lines of the texts.[24] Following

24. Here I follow Eve Kosofsky Sedgwick's development of Bakhtin's heteroglossia.

Eve Kosofsky Sedgwick's idea in her *Epistemology of the Closet,* the search for underrepresented voices in these texts is vital; it is as if the very survival of the marginalized subject depends upon a reading against the grain.[25] Therefore, these studies could be considered critical deconstructive readings that attempt to give expression to those voices inscribed in the texts but circumscribed by other voices. My studies are doubly deconstructive readings, since the texts chosen frequently demand to go against the grain of societal norms, and at the same time these texts are themselves read against their own logical grain. Thus my readings try to tease out the often contradictory voices of each text with the hope that this method allows readers to reach their own assessments.[26]

In *Gay Cuban Nation* I strongly imply that modern definitions of homosexuality are closely related to those of modern national identity, and that from its beginnings Cuban nationalist discourse has invested great effort in placing a series of controls and normalization mechanisms over certain bodies and their sexualities. But when I speak of the relationship between the representation of homoeroticism and that of Cuban nationality, I realize I am on shaky ground, since each of these terms lends itself to unending and unavoidable questioning. Any closure or effort to fix the limits of these discursive fields leads to new discursive possibilities. As always, language—any language— when carefully examined, is so thoroughly charged with multiple and contradictory meanings and "histories" that any path we follow leads to new crossroads. This is why an examination of the discourse of nationalism reveals many false or arbitrary limits.

From a political point of view, the study of Cuban nationalism is simultaneously confronted with extraordinary stories of liberation and tales of incredible cruelty. I believe, in fact, that the very intelligibility of each nation depends on articulating these practices and definitions, since the concept of nation—more than an identity—is a relational category whose meaning derives from a changeable system of differences. This is why so-called national identity is largely determined as a function of what it is not—or, better yet, of what it *thinks* it is not—at any given moment and from specific discursive formations. Moreover, it must be emphasized, as Homi Bhabha states, that for nationalist discourse to have direct referential validity, a horizontal homogeneous community would have to exist that could express itself through

25. See Eve Kosofsky Sedgwick, *Epistemology of the Closet* (Berkeley and Los Angeles: University of California Press, 1990).

26. For the use of this method and its possible results, see Murray, *Homosexualities,* 15.

time and despite time—that is to say, despite temporal changes and differences, and despite accidents and contingencies. Of course, this would imply a nonarbitrary linguistic sign, a lack of separation between discourse and reality.[27]

Finally, as part of this introduction's reflections on my own positions and concerns, I must add that, given the homophobia and tales of cruelty that have been part of modern Cuban nationalist positions, it is tempting to conclude that Cuban nationalism is an abomination. There is little doubt that the postcolonial subject must produce a critical and deconstructive knowledge about nationalism.[28] But to condemn Cuban nationalism as a whole based on liberal attitudes articulated outside that society and in recent times could perhaps become an ahistorical and hegemonic stance. In spite of the indisputable totalitarian consequences of some nationalisms (the Cuban, for example), we cannot forget the role nationalism has played, especially in developing countries, legitimizing sweeping social change and modernization, providing constitutional reforms, restructuring the economy, and protecting the nation against colonialist and imperialist control by other nations. Nationalist politics, due to its universal appeal and sense of legitimacy, cannot and should not be rejected outright. At the same time, it seems to me that "the gay, lesbian, or queer question" can and should be conceived as a category with its proper historiography and its own politics; it must be part of a rethinking of the Cuban nation in its totality. But in what place can we conceive the so-called category of homosexuality within the national question? Can a resignification of homosexuality radically redefine Cuban nationhood? Can the concept of Cuban nationhood survive a radical transformation away from homophobia and the fear of gender transgression? The answers to these questions are very complex, and the present work is situated precisely at their ideological crossroads. My readings of Cuban texts are not meant to always pursue these issues of nationalism to their fullest extent, but I truly hope that my inquiries will help to initiate a serious reflection on the deeply disturbing relationship between the representations of Cuban nationalisms and homosexualities and on their mutual possibilities.

27. See Bhabha, "DissemiNation."

28. For an excellent study on the national question in relation to gender issues and the postcolonial subject, see Radhakrishnan, "Nationalism, Gender, and the Narrative of Identity."

1

THE BUILDING OF A CONDEMNATION

In studying the construct of homosexual abjection in Cuban nationalist discourse, it is helpful to bear in mind what Doris Sommer argues in
her *Foundational Fictions: The National Romances of Latin America*.[1]
She maintains that the modernist project in Latin America proposes
a coherence of the "imagined community" that is based on the image
of the heterosexual bourgeois family. This family image—with its
symbolism of attraction, jealousy, and loyalty—serves the modernist
discourse to allegorize the building of the modern Latin American
nation: the citizen-father marries the earth-mother, impregnates her,
and protects her from internal and external queer bodies. The earth-
mother (the nation) is the object of desire that the citizen must
possess and impregnate in order to achieve harmony and legitimacy.
Not only the project but also the process of bourgeois consolidation
must be based on marriage, both literal and figurative: production
implies reproduction.[2] Perhaps Cuba has been more complex and
contradictory in this sense than the majority of Latin American countries, since at the end of the nineteenth century it was frequently at
war with its Spanish colonizer. As a result, the image of the military
hero, far from having been displaced by that of the productive, home-
dwelling citizen, was still at its peak during the wars of independence

---

1. Doris Sommer, *Foundational Fictions: The National Romances of Latin America*
(Berkeley and Los Angeles: University of California Press, 1991).
2. Ibid.

against Spain that started in 1868 and did not reach their conclusion until 1898.

It would be difficult to find a better image of the heroic warrior and independence fighter during the second half of the nineteenth century than that expressed in Manuel Cruz's *Cromitos cubanos* (1892).[3] In her excellent study of Cuban biographies from 1860 to 1898, Agnes Lugo-Ortiz explains how Cruz proposes a sort of prescriptive model for war, a model of conduct for the classic male warrior. Such a hero rejects the "unmanly" man (represented, according to Cruz, by the *modernista* Cuban poet Julián del Casal) who does not devote his life to action nor his pen to seducing women.[4] This repudiation and rejection of the "unmanly" man coincides perfectly with my argument concerning how the "effeminate man" (as well as the "manly woman") is constructed in Cuba to delineate the limits of the Cuban nationalist discourse; this is an excluded being that participates (by exclusion) in defining the nation to which it does not belong. For Cruz, the poet Casal displays a pathological behavior because he distances himself from the "man of action" in war and in public activity,[5] and because in his writing "one perceives a scarcity of women."[6] As Lugo-Ortiz states, Cruz pathologizes the "interior"; he pathologizes Casal's character because he is too homebound and avoids what is supposedly the proper space for the "virile man": war and politics.[7] According to Lugo-Ortiz, in Casal there is a "rupture evidenced by the pathology of the body and the spirit, by a transgression of gender and (hetero)sexuality."[8] She adds that in this national model proposed by Cruz, positive characteristics are related to that which is epic, and she insists that in Casal the epic "becomes de-virilized by a process of 'effemination.'"[9] All of these norms regarding virile and aggressive conduct are proposed by Cruz during or between the wars of Cuban independence (the Ten Years' War, 1868–78; the Little War, 1879; and the War of Independence, 1895–98).

3. Manuel Cruz, *Cromitos cubanos (bocetos de autores hispano-americanos)* (Havana: Biblioteca "El Fígaro," Establecimiento Tipográfico "La Lucha," 1892). Revised with prologue by Salvador Bueno (Havana: Editorial Arte y Literatura, 1975).

4. Agnes I. Lugo-Ortiz, *Identidades imaginadas: Biografía y nacionalidad en el horizonte de la guerra (Cuba 1860–1898)* (San Juan: Editorial de la Universidad de Puerto Rico, 1999). For an excellent study on eroticism in the work of Julián del Casal, see Oscar Montero, *Erotismo y representación en Julián del Casal* (Amsterdam: Rodopi, 1993).

5. Ibid., 217.

6. Cruz, *Cromitos cubanos*, 229.

7. Lugo-Ortiz, *Identidades imaginadas*, 217–19.

8. Ibid., 222.

9. Ibid., 224.

As historian Louis A. Pérez explains, Cuba was experiencing a profound transition at this time in several respects: the divisions between country and city were widening, and tensions were mounting between whites and blacks, as well as between *criollos* (Cubans of Spanish ancestry born on the island) and *peninsulares* (Spaniards). A transition in class structure also occurred, and cultural forms were undergoing appreciable change. What is more, as relations with Spain worsened during these years, ties between Cuba and the United States quickly grew stronger. The Cuban people became increasingly disenchanted with the colonial structures, leading to a greater propensity toward adopting new attitudes and values in relation to the society in which they lived. Although wage labor could not completely eliminate the system of slavery (which lingered until 1886), slave labor underwent systematic attacks during this period.

Moreover, it is no exaggeration to say that by the 1880s Cuba had fallen completely under the influence of the United States. From midcentury the Cuban economy had been able to make vital connections with the world market and had used modern production and transportation technologies, as well as such modern means of communication as the telegraph. All this occurred despite the disadvantages of the colonial structures that Spain insisted on maintaining on the island. Then, starting in the midnineteenth century, Cuba underwent substantial changes that placed the country within the dynamics of capitalism. New social classes emerged at this time, and the middle class began to grow. Several thousand Cubans traveled to the United States and brought back new perspectives on Cuban and American society. American influence grew and solidified itself on every front.[10]

The complex opposing political forces and their discursive precariousness seem to have led the Cuban nationalist movement after 1850 to an intensified effort to naturalize itself, and to an attempt at halting the dissemination of its limits, based on an essentialist rhetoric of "national identity." This rhetoric in turn used that naturalization technique to mark those bodies that it believed must be expelled from the interior of the nation. Perhaps the social instability produced by Cuban society's profound transformation during the latter part of the nineteenth century, as well as the growing urgency felt by Cuban nationalism to mark its discursive limits at that time, led to a radicalization of homosexual abjection in relation to the national project.

10. See Louis A. Pérez, "Identidad y nacionalidad: las raíces del separatismo cubano, 1868–1898," *Revista del Centro de Investigaciones Históricas*, 9 (1997): 185–95.

As Cuban historian Manuel Moreno Fraginals explains in great detail, between 1878 (the end of the Ten Years' War) and 1895 (the start of the last War of Independence) the most profound change in Cuba was the transition from a slave-based mode of production to that of wage labor.[11] It is instructive to mention here what John D'Emilio has pointed out: the modern rejection of homosexuality in countries affected by capitalism was radicalized in the second half of the nineteenth century because of the dramatic changes produced by increased wage labor and other social changes emanating from the emergence of this new economic system. The logic of D'Emilio's argument is as follows: as a consequence of capitalism, which was spreading over much of the world, family unity ceased to play its traditional role and became instead a social institution that depended for its survival on the salary of one or more of its members. This change profoundly altered the family structure and the very definition of heterosexual relationships, since procreation no longer had the same economic function that it did in a feudal structure. Moreover, the freedom of family members was considerably increased, because they now depended on wages, not collective work, to directly produce goods once consumed by the family.[12] Thus the growth of capitalism in Cuba in the 1880s and the instability of modernization and migration may have been what caused some leaders of the country's nationalism to worry a good deal about controlling the parameters of the national construct. In Cuba, one of the consequences of this instability was to blame immigrants (especially those from Spain, Africa, and China) for the introduction of sexual "vices."[13]

There is little doubt that both *criollo* nationalists and peninsular colonialists in the 1880s made very negative public statements regarding homosexuality. On the side of the colonialists, we can find examples like that of Eugenio Capriles Osuna, police inspector for the City

11. See Manuel Moreno Fraginals, *El ingenio. Complejo económico social cubano del azúcar*, vol. 2 (Havana: Editorial de Ciencias Sociales, 1978), especially chapter 2, 174–221.

12. John D'Emilio, "Capitalism and Gay Identity," in *The Lesbian and Gay Studies Reader*, ed. Henry Abelove, Michele Barale and David M. Halperin (New York: Routledge, 1993), 467–76.

13. See chapter 2 of this book. Even into the twentieth century certain sociologists and persons of authority in Cuba (Fernando Ortiz, for example) expressed their conviction that Asians had brought homosexuality to Cuba, or at least were one of the "races" responsible for importing that "loathsome vice." See Fernando Ortiz on the *vicios execrables* (loathsome vices) brought to Cuba by Asians in his book *Los negros brujos* (Miami: Ediciones Universal, 1973; first edition of 1906). Ortiz's ideas evolved over the years toward a progressively less racist position.

of Havana, who defines *maricón* (faggot) in the *Diccionario razonado de legislación de policía*(Dictionary of police legislation) of 1889 as follows: "An effeminate and cowardly man; He who does woman's work; Men who imitate women in their mannerisms, insinuations and at time even in their dress, taking their place in the most shameless acts."[14] As for the nationalists, we can quote the following statement from "Los maricones" (The faggots), an article published in the first issue of the Havana newspaper *La Cebolla* (9 September 1888): "Any foreigner who happens to walk down San Miguel street in Havana, or any street nearby, will be most surprised upon seeing some unlikely sorts: from the waist up they are women; from the waist down, men; and yet from head to toe they are neither men nor women." The article concludes, "Ought the faggots of San Miguel and other streets, and of the houses of prostitution, to be tolerated by the authorities? The Spartans did not allow deformed children to live: their essentially warlike and virile organization rejected those useless creatures. Can the law not correct what nature has mockingly created? We are not exactly asking that individuals be eliminated; rather that their vices not be tolerated in any way, shape or form."[15] The implications that these *maricones* constitute a menace to society that must not be tolerated are quite emphatic in both of these declarations. The statements in these texts clearly demonstrate a great social interest in rejecting the homosexual from the main power discourses of Cuban society existed at the time.[16]

14. Spanish original: "El hombre afeminado y cobarde.—El que se ocupa en las faenas propias de las mujeres.—Ciertos hombres que afectan imitar a las mujeres en sus maneras, insinuaciones, y a veces hasta en el vestir, sustituyéndolas en los actos más impúdicos." Eugenio Capriles Osuna, *Diccionario razonado de la legislación de policía* (Havana: Establecimiento tipográfico, 1889). According to Víctor Fowler, Capriles Osuna completely prohibited the "casas de maricones" (houses of faggots), which he did with the force of a law enacted by the Spanish Civil Government on 4 May 1887. See Víctor Fowler, *La maldición: una historia del placer como conquista* (Havana: Editorial Letras Cubanas, 1998), 17.

15. Spanish original: "Cualquier estranjero que se pasee por las calles San Miguel y adyacentes, en La Habana, quedará sorprendido al ver unos tipos inverosímiles: de la cintura para arriba son mujeres; de la cintura para abajo son hombres; pero de los pies a la cabeza no son hombres ni mujeres. . . . ¿Los maricones de San Miguel y otras calles, y casas de prostitutas, deben ser tolerados, por la autoridad? Los espartanos no permitían que los niños deformes vivieran: su organización esencialmente guerrera y viril, rechazaba esas criaturas inútiles. ¿La ley no puede corregir lo que la naturaleza se ha burlado en crear? No queremos precisamente que se supriman a los individuos; sí que no se toleren sus vicios en asociación y mucho menos en expresión." "Los maricones," *La Cebolla*, vol. 1, no. 1, 9 September 1888.

16. Michel Foucault insists that the social conditions of the last three decades of the nineteenth century are what allowed the change from the concept of homosexuality as an "act" to homosexuality as a "species" to take place. See Michel Foucault, *The History of*

In the texts I analyze in this part of the book, it is obvious that by the 1880s the nationalist discourse defined the Cuban citizen not only in opposition to Spanish colonization, American neocolonization, the importation of European social models, the representation of the black and the mulatto, the representation of the woman, and in relation to class struggle, but also in opposition to the homosexual (and other queer bodies), perceived at that time as among the abject of the nation, among the most repudiated constructs of the national body.

Sexuality, vol. 1, *Introduction*, translated by Robert Hurley (New York: Vintage Books, 1978; reprint, New York: Vintage Books, 1980); originally published as *La Volonté de savoir* (Paris: Gallimard, 1976.)

★ ONE ★

An Apostolic Paradox

As leader of the Cuban Revolutionary Party who was distinguished by innovative writing and martyrlike actions, José Martí (1853–95) has been held up as the most important nationalist symbol by a great many Cubans since the end of the nineteenth century, but especially since the beginning of the twentieth. The figure of Martí has, therefore, frequently been sanctified by Cuban nationalists and those of other Latin American and developing nations, and the most frequent epithet bestowed on him is "the apostle of the fatherland." He was undoubtedly a visionary of advanced social ideas who articulated a humanist and antiracist nationalism for Cuba and Latin America, doing so from outside Cuba (Martí lived continuously in his country only until age seventeen, and he died on the battlefield in 1895 shortly after his fateful return to the island). Living in New York City for many years, he spoke from a marginality in relation to the society to which he refers in his nationalist construct.[1]

This marginality gave Martí certain advantages due to his commanding vision, situated as he was amidst the emergence of the great U.S. power. In addition, he had already calibrated more than half a century's worth of problems in Latin American republics (except for Puerto Rico, the Latin American countries achieved independence

1. Julio Ramos, *Desencuentros de la modernidad en América Latina. Literatura y política en el siglo XIX* (Mexico City: Fondo de Cultura Económica, 1989), 202–43. See also Rafael Rojas, "Martí en las entrañas del monstruo," *Encuentro de la cultura cubana* 15 (winter 1999–2000): 34–49.

many years before Cuba). For all these reasons and many others, it can be argued that Martí is not only the most important patriotic figure in Cuban history but also the most important Latin American intellectual of the period.

Colonizing the Effeminate Man

For Cubans in the second half of the nineteenth century, the idea of modernity is mediated by the United States. In fact, Martí's historical significance would be inconceivable without his relationship to the United States, and it was he who first sounded the alarm in the face of the economic, political, and cultural threat posed to Cuba and other Latin American countries by the great emerging power of the north. This is one of the ideological aspects of Martí's thought that gives it a special currency today. It is for these reasons that in order to study Martí's position on homoeroticism and "queer bodies" (women perceived as too passionate and/or as having masculine characteristics; men thought to be weak or "effeminate"; people dressed "extravagantly"), we must begin by relating some of his writings and ideas to the situation of Cuba vis-à-vis the United States at the time.

If Cuba, which was still under Spanish rule, were to modernize and progress, it had to take on the appearance of its northern neighbor. In fact, by that time the Cuban economy depended to a large extent on the United States. Even various elements of American popular culture were imported to the island, including baseball, which became not only a national pastime but also a symbol of American modernity on the one hand and of what some nationalist leaders conceived as a way to help "virilize" Cuban men on the other.[2] It is not too daring to say, therefore, that the modern abjection of the homosexual in Cuba was intertwined with not only the internal social and economic changes on the island, but also the expansionism and "homosexual panic" that was taking place at that time in the United States.

By the late 1800s, the United States was well on its way to becoming a world power with imperialist aspirations, and with them came an intense preoccupation with masculinity and with what some

---

2. See Louis A. Pérez Jr., "Between Baseball and Bullfighting: The Quest for Nationality in Cuba, 1868–1898," *The Journal of American History* 81, no. 2 (September 1994): 493–517. For an extraordinary recent work on Cuban baseball and its meanings for the Cuban society, see Roberto González Echevarría, *The Pride of Havana: A History of Cuban Baseball* (Oxford: Oxford University Press, 1999).

American leaders perceived as the danger of homosexuality. Theodore Roosevelt warned of the dangerous effects of "effeminacy" during times of peace: "The greatest danger that a long period of profound peace offers to a nation is that of [creating] *effeminate* tendencies in young men" (emphasis added). This idea led Roosevelt to glorify war as, among other things, the best way to "virilize" men.[3] The preoccupation with the possible effeminacy of young American men was extended by some U.S. leaders (with contradictory implications and goals) to the men of entire nations, more precisely to those that the United States was considering for annexation. In regard to Cuba, the accusation was both direct and generalized.[4] On 6 March 1889, the Philadelphia *Manufacturer* published an article titled "Do We Want Cuba?" written by several influential Republican politicians. In this article the advantages and disadvantages of annexing Cuba to the United States were discussed. The advantages cited were generally economic and strategic. Insofar as the disadvantages were concerned, the Cuban character was seen as the most problematic:

> What would be the result of an attempt to incorporate into our political community a population such as Cuba's? . . . The Cubans are not much more desirable [than the Spaniards]. Added to the defects of the paternal race are *effeminacy* and an aversion to all effort, truly to the extent of illness. They are helpless, lazy, deficient in morals, and incapable by nature and experience of fulfilling the obligations of citizenship in a great and free republic. Their *lack of virile strength* and self-respect is shown by the apathy with which they have submitted to Spanish oppression for so long, and even their attempts at rebellion have been so pitifully ineffective that they rise little above the dignity of a farce. To invest such men with the responsibility of directing this government, and giving them the same degree of power as that possessed by the free citizens of our northern states, would be to call upon them to perform duties for which they have not the slightest ability.
>
> As for the Cuban Negroes, they are clearly at the level of barbarity. The most degraded Negro in Georgia is better prepared for the presidency than is the ordinary Cuban Negro for American citizenship.

3. Quoted in Joe L. Dubert, *Man's Place: Masculinity in Transition* (Englewood Cliffs, N.J.: Prentice-Hall, 1979), 167. Also see David Greenberg, *The Construction of Homosexuality* (Chicago: University of Chicago Press, 1988; paper edition, 1990), 393.

4. For an extraordinary account and analysis of the relationship between sexuality and U.S. aspirations of annexation of Cuba, see Peter Hulme, *Rescuing Cuba: Adventure and Masculinity in the 1890s* (College Park: University of Maryland, 1996).

> Our only hope of qualifying Cuba for the dignity of statehood would
> be to Americanize her completely, populating her with people of our
> own race; and there would still remain unresolved at least the question
> of whether our race would not degenerate under a tropical sun and
> under the conditions necessary to life in Cuba.[5]

The U.S. politicians, with an obviously positivist rhetoric (as seen in
their repeated insistence on race as well as on concepts of degradation
caused by the tropical climate), make all of Cuba out to be a nation of
"effeminates," which implies not only a gender-based condemnation,
but also one based on race and imperialism. On the one hand, since
the Cubans are effeminate, they might contaminate the Americans;
on the other, their effeminacy shows them to be an inferior race and
therefore a people who need to be "Americanized," an idea that implies
whitening and virilizing the island's population. This annexation must
be accompanied by a masculinization of the effeminate bodies. This
type of accusatory thinking obviously influenced Martí's nationalist
rhetoric in his response to the Americans' article and in his defense
of Cuban manhood. The United States, the modern country par
excellence that Cuba was supposed to emulate, described Cubans
with a racist and imperialistic discourse that was very disturbing to
Martí. Here Martí's nationalist position has to face a complex political
problem in which there is confluence of imperialism, racism, homophobia, and modernity. From the American politicians' perspective,
the accusation established a direct relation between the "effeminate
man" and barbarity or racial and social inferiority, while civilization
is associated with the "virile" modernity of the United States. As I
will elaborate, from Martí's perspective one of the implications of the
Americans' article is that the modern civilizing country is trying to
fulfill the role of a barbarian expansionist who accuses all Cuban men
of being effeminate.

It must be stated from the outset that Martí's position on homoeroticism and queer bodies is quite paradoxical. When writing on
this subject, he does so in a quite oblique and evasive manner. Let

5. "Do We Want Cuba?" Philadelphia *Manufacturer*, 6 March 1889, reproduced in *Our
America: Writings on Latin America and the Struggle for Cuban Independence by José Martí*,
ed. Philip S. Foner (New York: Monthly Review Press, 1977), 228–30; emphasis added. The
rhetoric in "Do We Want Cuba?" is clearly colonialist. For an examination of the rhetoric of
colonialism and "sissification," see José Piedra, "Nationalizing Sissies," in *¿Entiendes? Queer
Readings, Hispanic Writings*, ed. Emilie L. Bergmann and Paul Julian Smith (Durham, N.C.:
Duke University Press, 1995), 370–409.

us examine first his 25 March 1889 *New York Post* response to the *Manufacturer* article:

> We have suffered impatiently under tyranny; we have fought like men, sometimes like giants, to be freemen. ... But because our government [the Spanish government] has systematically allowed after the war [the Ten Years' War of independence] the triumph of criminals . . . because our half-breeds and city-bred young men are generally of delicate physique, or suave courtesy, and ready words, hiding under the glove that polishes the poem the hand that fells the foe—are we to be considered as the *Manufacturer* does consider us, an *"effeminate"* people? These city-bred young men and poorly built half-breeds knew in one day how to rise against a cruel government . . . to obey as soldiers, sleep in the mud, eat roots, fight ten years without salary, conquer foes with the branch of a tree, die—these men of eighteen, these heirs of wealthy estates, these dusky striplings—a death not to be spoken of without uncovering the head. They died like those other men of ours who, with a stroke of the *machete*, can send a head flying, or by a turn of the hands bring a bull to their feet. These *"effeminate"* Cubans had once courage enough, in the face of a hostile government, to carry on their left arms for a week the mourning-band for Lincoln.[6]

Clearly, Martí's response is extremely defensive; he appears perturbed by the direct accusation of the powerful Americans. And yet, although he does not attack the "effeminates" with injurious terms, Martí adopts the strategy of directing the guilt for that wrong against the Spanish government: the Spanish colonialists are the ones who have corrupted our society with their bad government. Also, the Cubans' supposed effeminacy remains suspended in Martí's text by means of a rhetorical question ("are we to be considered as the *Manufacturer* does consider us, an 'effeminate' people?") and an implicit negative ("These 'effeminate' Cubans had once courage enough . . .").

Martí's article has other noteworthy implications. He states that the Cubans, far from being effeminate, are highly virile, since both the *mestizos* ("half-breeds") as well as the urban youth ("city-bred young men") make sacrifices in their struggle for freedom ("to obey as soldiers, sleep in mud, eat roots . . ."); also, other Cubans (due to the abilities Martí attributes to them, his text seems to imply here that those "other men of ours" are revolutionary farmers) perform great

6. José Martí, "A Vindication of Cuba," in *Our America*, ed. Foner, 234–41; emphasis added.

physical exploits typical of strong, "virile" men ("with a stroke of the *machete*, can send a head flying, or by a turn of the hands bring a bull to their feet"). But, if the Cubans are so masculine as Martí implies, what does it mean that "our half-breeds and city-bred young men are generally of delicate physique, or suave courtesy, and ready words, hiding under the glove that polishes the poem the hand that fells the foe"? To a reader unfamiliar with Martí's ideology and rhetoric, this part of his article may seem quite disconcerting.

In his text, Martí uses an almost inconceivable contrast: the highly virile Cubans are not only of "delicate physique," "suave courtesy," and "ready words," but also hide the hand capable of overthrowing the enemy beneath a "glove that polishes the poem." In other words, these Cubans, in addition to being virile warriors ready for sacrifice, are also delicate poets. However unusual this may seem to the reader of today, it responds to the construct of the *new* Cuban/Latin American man that Martí had already articulated in several of his previous essays. This man wants to distance himself as much from the so-called decadence (with its homoerotic implications) at the turn of the twentieth century as from American utilitarianism; as much from the sensuality of the decadent Europeans that could lead to a rise in queerness supposedly contributing to social fragmentation, as from the materialism that rejects and distances culture and poetry.[7] The nationalism articulated by Martí seems to be a construct that attacks Spanish colonialism while it distances itself from American neocolonialism and utilitarianism. It is a nationalism that cannot ignore the West with its ideology of change and progress (after all, the modern idea of nationalism is a Western creation), but at the same time is unwilling to capitulate to it entirely.

In several of his writings, Martí rejects the emergent mass culture of the United States. His articulation of this idea is based on a cultural concept in which Latin Americans (including Cubans, of course) are, or should be, the offspring of that antiutilitarian counterculture that has poetry as its center. This romantic culture is represented by Martí as the only contemporary discourse capable of unifying the social fragmentation and instability that utilitarian modernization

---

7. See Enrico Mario Santí, "*Ismaelillo*, Martí y el modernismo," in *Pensar a José Martí: Notas para un centenario* (Boulder, Colo.: Society of Spanish and Spanish-American Studies, 1996), 19–50. See also Ramos, *Paradojas de la letra* (Caracas: Ediciones eXcultura, 1996), 160–61; and Fina García Marruz and Cintio Vitier, *Temas martianos* (Havana: Biblioteca Nacional José Martí, 1969), especially 174–91, 195–214.

was rapidly producing.[8] The poetic conception is central to Martí's worldview at the time of his rebuttal of the *Manufacturer* article.

Moreover, like many other nationalisms, Martí's formula partakes of the nationalist inner/outer dichotomy that identifies social roles by gender: the inner space is associated with the feminine and homely, while the outer space is the dominion of the masculine, the political, and the public.[9] Nevertheless, we must clarify at this point that for Martí the woman's place is the inner space of the home except if she is responding to the call of the *patria*, or homeland, in times of war. Within this ideological framework, Martí's nationalism attempts to answer the woman question and the question of gender transgressions. Therefore, the construction of this *new* Cuban/Latin American subject finds itself in a bind between different ideological forces, and the position of the "effeminate man" and the "manly woman" in this construct is often very negative. Both the "effeminate man" and the "manly woman" transgress the gender boundaries that are so much a part of the inner/outer parameters established in the nationalist discourse.

For all these reasons, I argue that Martí's apostolic leadership in the formation of a model for the future Cuban nation is very paradoxical in terms of the modern (homo)sexual construct that such a model implies. And it could not be otherwise, since Martí's modernity, like that of the majority of Latin American *modernistas*, is highly contradictory in relation to certain basic aspects of modernity itself.[10] As Julio Ramos puts it so well, for Martí the modern city, which had been a symbol of the modernity desired by Domingo Faustino Sarmiento and the first Latin American nationalist projects, is often the place of violence and fragmentation. Martí often implies that homoeroticism and gender transgression is a negative consequence of certain modern urban instability. All these implications are part of Martí's attempt to make of his writings and his actions a national project situated at the

8. See Ramos, *Desencuentros de la modernidad en América Latina*, 202–43; and Ramos, "Trópicos de la fundación: poesía y nacionalidad en José Martí," in *Paradojas de la letra* (Caracas: Ediciones eXcultura, 1996), 153–64.

9. See Partha Chatterjee, "The Nationalist Resolution of the Women Question," in *Recasting Women: Essays in Colonial History*, ed. Kumkum Sangari and Sudesh Vaid (New Delhi: Kali for Women, 1989; reprinted under the title *Recasting Women: Essays in Indian Colonial History*, New Brunswick, N.J.: Rutgers University Press, 1990), 233. See also R. Radhakrishnan, "Nationalism, Gender, and the Narrative of Identity," in *Nationalisms and Sexualities*, ed. Andrew Parker et al. (New York: Routledge, 1992), 84–85.

10. See Oscar Montero, "*Modernismo* and Homophobia: Darío and Rodó," in *Sex and Sexuality in Latin America*, ed. Daniel Balderston and Donna J. Guy (New York: New York University Press, 1997), 101–17.

margin of modernity (or, at least, of a certain modernity); he insisted on proclaiming the autonomy of his style as a guarantee of his position as the new Cuban/Latin American man.[11] It seems that within Martí's ideology, the "effeminate man" is in a paradoxical position between materialist modernity (the effeminate man appears as a consequence of materialism and fragmentation) and inherited traditional values (the Spanish colonialists are to be blamed for the condition and increase in the number of "effeminate men"). For Martí, the only possible solution to this dilemma seems to be the concept of the *hombre natural* (natural man). It is the ethico-poetic imperative of nature that serves as the ideological basis for Martí's rejection of the "effeminate man" and, as I will explain next, of the "manly woman" also.[12]

The Specter of the Manly Woman

In spite of Martí's efforts to avoid the thematization of homoeroticism in his writings, the homoerotic question not only appears in his journalistic work in a negative light with relation to the ideal of masculine virility, but also springs forth like a specter on the feminine characters he creates. In the representation of homoeroticism between women, Martí's most noteworthy treatment of the matter is his only novel, *Amistad funesta* (Fatal friendship).[13] If in his "Vindication of Cuba" Martí refers to the question of the "effeminate man," in *Amistad funesta* his interest lies in what could be called the dangers of the "manly woman." Published in installments in the 1885 *El Latino Americano* (The Latin American), a short-lived bimonthly newspaper published in New York, *Amistad funesta* is one of Martí's most paradoxical texts.[14] As a cultural background for this novel, at this point it seems pertinent to cite the opinion of Yolanda Martínez-San Miguel, who affirms the following with regard to the Spanish American novel of the late nineteenth century:

11. Ramos, *Desencuentros de la modernidad en América Latina*, 202–43.

12. For Martí's elaboration of his concepts of the natural man and the natural statesman, see his famous essay "Our America," in *Our America*, ed. Foner, 84–94.

13. José Martí, *Amistad funesta* (Fatal friendship), in *Obras completas*, 2d ed., vol. 18 (Havana: Editorial de Ciencias Sociales, 1975), 185–272.

14. Ibid. Among the numerous studies on this novel, see Fina García Marruz, "*Amistad funesta*," in *Temas martianos*, by García Marruz and Vitier, 282–91; Aníbal González, "El intelectual y las metáforas: *Lucía Jerez* de José Martí," *Texto crítico* 12, nos. 34–35 (January–December 1986): 136–57; and Yolanda Martínez-San Miguel, "Sujetos femeninos en *Amistad funesta* y *Blanca Sol*: el lugar de la mujer en dos novelas latinoamericanas de fin de siglo XIX," *Revista Iberoamericana* 62, 174 (January–March 1996): 27–45.

La novela de fin de siglo XIX latinoamericano confronta una serie de dificultades representativas que se reflejan en la multiplicidad de prácticas discursivas que se exploran. El realismo, el naturalismo y el modernismo se acercan al problema de la representación a partir de diferentes perspectivas, pero en los tres predomina la expresión de una ansiedad ante un espacio nacional en crisis frente a las experiencias de modernización y urbanización latinoamericanos. . . . [U]no de los personajes nacionales que experimentó múltiples transformaciones con la llegada de la modernidad: [fue] la mujer latinoamericana. La experiencia urbana y de modernización implicó una total refuncionalización de los roles sexuales dentro del espacio nacional.[15]

[The late nineteenth-century Latin American novel confronted a series of representative difficulties that are reflected in the multiplicity of discursive practices that are explored. Realism, naturalism, and *modernismo* approach the problem of representation from different perspectives, but in all three there is a predominant expression of national anxiety in the face of modernization and urbanization. . . . One of the national characters that experienced multiple transformations with the arrival of modernity was the Latin American woman. The modern urban experience implied a total re-functionalization of sexual roles within the national sphere.]

In other words, the national project appears as a discourse in which spaces are distributed based on sexual roles.[16] Such a distribution is most evident in *Amistad funesta*, since women in this novel are completely homebound while men take care of public and political matters. This division of space according to sex roles also implies that within the home the female subject possesses a voice and a subjectivity that at times appears to be dominant. When this happens, the female characters in this text are *sujetos deseantes* (desiring subjects) and therefore, as Martínez-San Miguel says, "monstrous and threatening figures that must be controlled," because their unbridled desires threaten the patriarchal stability dictated by the masculine subject.[17]

One possible interpretation of the work is that of a tragic or ill-fated love story between Juan and Lucía Jerez because Lucía has certain "not very feminine" characteristics along with uncontrollable

---

15. Martínez-San Miguel, "Sujetos femeninos," 29.
16. See the introduction of Parker et al., *Nationalisms and Sexualities*, 5–7.
17. Martínez-San Miguel, "Sujetos femeninos," 29.

jealousy, all of which are at odds with the symbolism of Martí's national project. Lucía, Juan Jerez's fiancée, is a highly "queer" woman in this sense because of her excessive and unbridled passion, which frequently manifests itself as jealousy over Juan. But besides the theme of Lucía's "excessive passion" (the ideal woman ought not to have excessive desire in the carnal sense, according to Martí's way of thinking), this story allows for a reading of homoeroticism between women, and certainly for a reading of the attempt by the text to represent Lucía as a monstrous queer who destabilizes the formation of an idealized nation as conceived by Martí. Lucía feels jealousy (love, hate, and envy all at the same time) for a poor, timid, and very beautiful young woman named Sol del Valle. Lucía's feelings for Sol supposedly arise because Sol could be seen as attractive by Juan, but Martí's text puts great emphasis on Lucía's obsessive physical admiration toward and uncontrolled ravings about Sol. The text also praises Juan's personality, mainly his emotional, ethical, and artistic characteristics. Notably, Juan gives Lucía no motive for her jealousy; in fact, the theme of jealousy really appears in this novel without any real motivation. At the end of the story Lucía kills Sol in an uncontrollable attack of passion (jealousy? attraction-hate?).

In typical fashion, Martí uses his text as a pedagogical allegory of nationalism and Latin Americanism in that Martí symbolically presents in the novel his vision of how Cuban society and the "great Latin American family" should behave. The novel insists on the need to follow certain models of conduct and to avoid pernicious acts that threaten the new nations (the future nation, in the case of Cuba). Therefore, I contend that *Amistad funesta* is an allegory of virtues and faults that Latin American societies (Cuban society is included in a privileged manner as Martí's homeland) should take into account for their formation, and of the symbolic sociopolitical relations that Martí proposes as a better path for the countries of "our America."[18]

The very fact that Juan and Lucía are from the same social class (the upper class, to be sure) and the same family (they are cousins) implies that this marriage is not ideal, since it would constitute a sort of sociofamilial incest. Martí would prefer that the future nation, allegorized in the familial relations of the novel, establish an alliance between certain rich and certain poor people, provided that the

18. José Martí refers to Spanish America as "our America." He developed this concept in several of his works, but the clearest articulation of this idea can be found in his essay "Nuestra America" (Our America) (for an English translation of this article, see *Our America*, ed. Foner, 84–94).

moral- and gender-based principles and roles are properly maintained. Such an alliance could have occurred between Juan (the spiritual and kind-hearted rich poet and supporter of land reform for the Indians), and Sol (the pure, beautiful young woman), who in her goodness is innocent and must therefore be cared for by society so that she does not stray from the proper path of her gender role. But Lucía, within the ideology of the novel, exhibits what can be called an "antinatural" behavior, and *Amistad funesta* does not end with a wedding but rather with disaster and crime. Through Lucía's murder of Sol, the novel indicates a fundamental failure between Martí's ideals and the type of woman Lucía is or represents to be in this text; Martí's ethical and familial values have been defeated by modern "madness."

Gonzalo de Quesada, Martí's disciple and the discoverer of the serialized publication of this text by Martí, insists in his introductory note to the novel that it is "autobiographical, since Martí's personality is clearly expressed in Juan Jerez, and even in other protagonists of the work."[19] I would argue that Quesada is both right and wrong in this opinion. It is clear that Juan's character represents some of Martí's ethical ideals. In fact, Juan possesses some of the characteristics of the self-image that Martí insistently projects in his writings: that of the very honorable person, extremely honest, martyrlike, generous, and of exquisite taste who often tries to resolve conflicts through love. These are the qualities generally attributed to Juan in *Amistad funesta*. Nevertheless, it is difficult to see Martí—the political activist intellectual of humble birth who never achieved any great fortune but who had to constantly struggle against economic impoverishment—in Juan Jerez, a rich aristocrat living an elegant life with every conceivable amenity. Also, it is well known that Martí's life was one of constant political activism, a quality typical of the "man of action," and one that led him to direct the political party of the Cuban Revolution against Spain and ultimately to die on the battlefield. Such a life is far removed from the luxury and comfort enjoyed by the aristocrat Juan Jerez, whose activism in favor of land reform only merits a brief mention in the last chapter of the novel.

In the introductory note to his novel, Martí says that in real life he met characters like Manuel, Manuelillo, Andrea, and the headmistress of the girls' school. He adds that in order to write this story, "he remembered an event that occurred in South America in those days, which

19. Spanish original: "autobiográfica, ya que la personalidad de Martí queda expuesta claramente en Juan Jerez, y aun en otros protagonistas de la obra." Gonzalo de Quesada, "Nota preliminar," in Martí, *Amistad funesta*, 188.

could be the basis for the Latin American novel he wanted" (191).[20] Nevertheless, in his note Martí contradicts Quesada's assertion about the "autobiographical" nature of the story, stating that, besides the aforementioned characters, everything else was a novelistic invention that he largely belittles:

> El autor [Martí se refiere a sí mismo en tercera persona], avergonzado, pide excusa. Ya él sabe bien por dónde va, profunda como un bisturí y útil como un médico, la novela moderna. El género no le place, sin embargo, porque hay mucho que fingir en él, y los goces de la creación artística no compensan el dolor de moverse en una ficción prolongada. (Ibid.)

> [The author (Martí refers to himself in the third person), ashamed, begs your pardon. Well he knows where the modern novel, deep as a scalpel and useful as a physician, is going. Still, the genre does not agree with him, because much must be made up in it, and the pleasures of artistic creation do not compensate for the pain of moving around in a prolonged fiction.]

Martí, in his *modernista* aesthetics, prefers poetry to the novel, since the former seems more directly connected to the author's emotions and more removed from the emergent utilitarianism. For Martí, as for several other Latin American *modernistas*, the novel is not a privileged genre. His ideology perceives in the dialogic aspects of the novel a fragmentation that did not contribute to the coherence and harmony that he wanted to obtain (recover?) through a poetic discourse (poetry conceived here as a discourse that leads to homogeneity and which therefore can correct the ills of modern fragmentation). That is why we can say that *Amistad funesta* is as much an allegory of the virtues and dangers confronted by the new Latin American nations as a critique of the genre of the novel itself. Also, the literary genre and sociosexual roles appear as something unsuccessful in this novel, as if Martí were implying that the destabilizing effects of modernity (represented in literature by the genre of the novel and in society by the gender transgression of the "manly woman") threaten the harmony that could be achieved through poetry.

But let me elaborate on the political and ethical allegory of *Amistad funesta*. Juan Jerez is the rich but generous *criollo* who does not flaunt

---

20. Spanish original: "recordé un suceso acontecido en la América del Sur en aquellos días, que pudiera ser base para la novela hispanoamericana que se deseaba."

his wealth but rather uses it to help the honest poor, such as the family of Don Manuel del Valle and the Indians, who are losing their land to the unscrupulous rich (in Martí's allegory, a binary opposition exists between good and bad rich people). It should be remembered here that for Martí there is no class struggle, merely classes, which should love and understand each other. Therefore, Juan is loving, honest, generous, liberal, nationalist, and, of course, a poet. In order to bring about the national project that is symbolically proposed in the novel, Juan, the pater familias, must find the ideal wife: a beautiful woman of loving disposition who knows that her role in marriage is one of subordination to her husband. This ideal woman should not have extreme passions and should dedicate herself to her husband without jealousy or suspicion. But in the story, Juan is engaged to his cousin Lucía, who is far from being the ideal woman Martí wants for the political and ethical symbolism of the Cuban and Latin American nation.

Lucía's characteristics are disturbing from the beginning of the novel: "robust and deep, she didn't wear flowers on her crimson silk dress, 'because the gardens still didn't have the flower she liked: the black flower!'" (191)[21] Typical of Martí's writings, here in this novel it is style, the way of dressing and the language of the flowers, that dictates much of the political and moral symbolism of the characters.[22] In *Amistad funesta* the color crimson and the black flower symbolize excessive passion and a foretelling of disaster. Since the black flower doesn't really exist, its symbolism points to something queer or strange, something falling beyond the realm of the natural, the comprehensible, and even the possible. The young lady who is always well dressed, that is, who always dresses in accordance with those tastes that indicate feminine virtue in Martí's symbolism, is Sol del Valle. She likes to wear white or pale-blue muslin, along with camellias and other delicate flowers in her hair or dress. In *Amistad funesta*, the characters' feelings are often expressed through fashion. Thus the dances and processions are of great importance, since in them the characters (above all the women) show great care in their dress and adornment.

The two eventful dances in the novel take place at the beginning and end of chapter 3. At the last dance, Lucía's "queer" passion toward

---

21. Spanish original: "robusta y profunda, que no llevaba flores en su vestido de seda carmesí, 'porque no se conocía aún en los jardines la flor que a ella le gustaba: la flor negra!'."

22. For the language of the flowers in José Martí's work, see the classic study of Ivan Schulman, *Símbolo y color en la obra de José Martí* (Madrid: Gredos, 1970).

Sol is expressed almost completely through fashion. Moreover, the relationship between Lucía, Sol, and the camellias had been established some pages earlier, in the same chapter. In that section the text plays with a mix of narration, dialogue, and a sort of subjective narration identified with one of the characters, in this case Lucía:

> Un día antes de la procesión Lucía había vuelto a la casa de Sol. Que la perdonase. Que Ana estaba muy sola. Que Sol estaba más linda que nunca. "Mira, mañana te mandaré la camelia más linda que tenga en casa. Yo no te digo que vengas a mi balcón, porque. . . . Yo sé que tú vas al balcón de la directora. Pero mira, vas a estar lindísima; ponte la camelia en la cabeza, a la derecha, para que yo pueda vértela desde mi balcón." Y le tomó las manos, y se las besó; y conforme conversaba con Sol, se pasaba suavemente la mano de ella por su mejilla; y cuando le dijo adiós, la miraba como si supiera que corría algún peligro, y le avisase de él, y cuando fue hacia el coche, ya se iban desbordando las lágrimas.[23]

> [A day before the procession Lucía had returned to Sol's house. Please forgive me. Ana was very lonely. Sol was prettier than ever. "Look, tomorrow I'll send you the most beautiful camellia I have at home. I don't ask you to come to my balcony because . . . I know that you're going to the headmistress's balcony. But look, you're going to be gorgeous; wear the camellia in your hair, on the right, so that I can see it on you from my balcony." And she took her hands, and kissed them; and as she spoke with Sol, she ran her hand softly over her cheek; and when she said good-bye, she looked at her as if she knew she was running a risk, and had to warn her about it, and as she went towards the carriage, the tears were already flowing.]

It is worth noting that the symbolism of fashion in *Amistad funesta* is not limited to the women in the story; there is also a whole series of specifications for how men should dress and wear their hair, and what type of harmony they should achieve sartorially. Furthermore, Martí's symbolism is extremely rigid, since the characters are defined from beginning to end as good or evil based on an enormous accumulation of Manichaean symbols. In regard to the men in *Amistad funesta*, the most emphatic fashion criticism is directed at hairstyle. The text says the following about María Vargas (in spite of the character's name, he is indeed a male), who was "a traditional politician" (203): "Elegant

23. Martí, *Amistad funesta*, 248.

he is indeed. His hair is ridiculous, with the part in the middle of the head and the forehead hidden beneath the waves. It isn't even good for women to cover their foreheads, where the light of the face lies" (ibid.).[24] And from here on there follows a whole diatribe about the error of men's and even women's hair covering their foreheads. For Martí, this style or fashion was disquieting and disharmonious because it covered the forehead, the "mirror over which lovers lean to see their own souls."

Martí does not limit this symbolism of fashion to *Amistad funesta*. For example, men's hairstyles, physical appearance, and the necessary harmony to be demanded in fashion are themes that come together in his critique of Oscar Wilde. Sylvia Molloy has analyzed "Oscar Wilde," an article written by Martí based on the Englishman's visit to New York City in 1882. Wilde gave a lecture in Chickering Hall that Martí attended as a member of the audience and as a journalist. Wilde's topic, "The English Renaissance of Art," dealt with a theme beloved by Martí: a "new imagination" that would counteract modern fragmentation.[25] Nevertheless, the differences between Wilde's and Martí's social and artistic ideas are truly emphatic: the Englishman proposed a total subversion of the fundamental values of modern Western culture, such as those of authenticity, legitimacy, and truth; while the Cuban, much closer to romanticism, preferred to place these values at the service of a new vision of the Latin American man, creating a culture of honesty that would articulate a harmonious and coherent meaning in response to modernization and utilitarianism. In his article about Wilde, Martí prefers, on the one hand, to praise Wilde for his devotion to art and beauty and, on the other, to criticize his manner of dress for its perceived lack of stylistic harmony:

> Look at Oscar Wilde! He does not dress as we all do but in a singular manner. . . . His hair falls over his neck and shoulders, like that of an Elizabethan courtier; it is abundant, carefully parted down the middle. He wears tails, a white silk waistcoat, ample knee breeches, black silk hose and buckled shoes. The shirt collar is cut low, like Byron's held together by an ample white silk cravat knotted with abandon. A diamond

24. Spanish original: "Elegante sí es. El peinado es ridículo, con la raya en mitad de la cabeza y la frente escondida bajo las ondas. Ni a las mujeres está bien eso de cubrirse la frente, donde está la luz del rostro."

25. See José Martí, "Oscar Wilde," in *Obras completas*, 15:361–68. For an incisive study of Martí's article on Wilde, see Sylvia Molloy, "Too Wilde for Comfort: Desire and Ideology in Fin-de-Siècle Spanish America," *Social Text* 31–32 (1992): 187–201.

stud shines on the dazzling shirtfront; an ornate watch-chain hangs from the fob. Beauty in dress is imperative; of this, he is the perfect example. But art demands of all its works temporal unity, and it hurts the eye to see a handsome man wearing a waistcoat from this period, breeches from another, hair like Cromwell's and a foppish turn-of-the-century watch-chain.[26]

For Martí, the spirit of a person is reflected in his or her clothing and personal style; Wilde simply reflects something distorted and queer that Martí can neither accept nor comprehend. Wilde's fashion is somewhat like Lucía's black flower: both fall beyond the natural, the comprehensible, the acceptable, and the desirable. Martí's insistence on a nationalist imagination—which unites the fragments of modern incoherence via the allegory of a national family, thereby recovering the harmony upset by a galloping modernity—vanishes before the figures of Wilde and Lucía, before their character, style, and manner of dress. In Martí's ideology, Wilde's and Lucía's fashion and moral characteristics frankly represent much of the queerness that the new nations of the continent should avoid. Although he does not say so openly, what seems to bother him most is the homoeroticism implicit in Wilde's and Lucía's figures, a certain queerness that carries with it a disquieting difference. Although without being directly insulting nor using new medical terminology such as that employed in Havana by his contemporary Benjamín de Céspedes and Enrique José Varona (see chapter 2), Martí shows his disgust at what he conceives as a hindrance to the national and continental project of the "new Cuban/Latin American man." Within the semantics of *Amistad funesta*, Lucía's passion for Sol (and, to a certain point and to a lesser degree, that of Sol for Lucía) is not only excessive but also unhealthy and unnatural.

The novel tells us that Lucía behaves toward Sol with the sensuality that dishonest men feel for beautiful young women. In its account of the first big party, during one of the moralizing digressions that Martí frequently employs, we are told that most men don't know how to appreciate a woman in any way other than to satisfy their basic carnal appetites:

> No es para la mayor parte de los hombres una obra santa, y una copa de espíritu la hermosura; sino una manzana apetitosa. Si hubiera

26. Martí, "Oscar Wilde," 15:363.

un lente que permitiese a las mujeres ver, tales como les pasean por el cráneo los pensamientos de los hombres, y lo que les anda en el corazón, los querrían menos.[27]

[Beauty is not a sacred work for the majority of men, nor a crown of the spirit; but rather an appetizing apple. If there were a lens that would permit women to see how thoughts pass through the heads of men, and what lies in their hearts, they would love them less.]

But the following sentences are truly surprising:

Pero no era un hombre, no, el que con más insistencia, y un cierto encono mezclado ya de amor, miraba a Sol del Valle, y con dificultad contenía el llanto que se le venía a mares a los ojos, abiertos, en los que se movían los párpados apenas. La conocía en aquel momento, y ya la amaba y la odiaba. La quería como una hermana; ¡qué misterios de estas naturalezas bravías e iracundas! y la odiaba con un aborrecimiento irresistible y trágico. . . . Lucía Jerez . . . era quien de aquella manera la miraba. (Ibid.)

[But it was not a man, no, the one who with greatest insistence, and a certain bitterness mixed with love was looking at Sol del Valle and could scarcely contain the tears that came in waves to her eyes, open, her eyelids barely moving. She was getting to know her at that moment, and loved her and hated her. She loved her like a sister; so mysterious these wild and raging natures! and she hated her with an irresistible and tragic loathing. . . . Lucía Jerez . . . was the one looking at her that way.]

From the moment that Lucía meets Sol, she loses "all color" (237)[28] from the emotion she feels when she is with Sol. At times Sol's hand trembles in Lucía's and she looks at her "full of hope and tenderness" (ibid.).[29] On one occasion, Lucía tightly embraces Sol after placing a rose on her bosom:

Oh, dijo Sol de pronto ahogando un grito. Y se llevó la mano al seno, y la sacó con la punta de los dedos roja. Era que al abrazarla Lucía se le clavó en el seno una espina de la rosa. Con su propio pañuelo secó

27. Martí, *Amistad funesta*, 234.
28. Spanish original: "a Lucía se le desvanecía el color."
29. Spanish original: "llena de esperanza y ternura."

Lucía la sangre, y de brazo las dos entraron en la sala. Lucía también estaba hermosa. (238)

[Oh, said Sol suddenly, stifling a cry. And she raised her hand to her bosom and took it away with the tip of her fingers reddened. In hugging her Lucía had stuck one of the thorns of the rose into her breast. With her own handkerchief Lucía dried the blood, and arm in arm the two entered the room. Lucía was also beautiful.]

In a certain sense, Lucía's passion for Sol is requited, since a few days after the rose incident we are told that Sol is very much under her influence, although the narrative tries to excuse Sol's feelings by saying that she is "timid and new" (ibid.).[30] Here the text warns us of the danger posed to the nation (Sol) by unbridled passion and, symbolically and indirectly, by homoeroticism between women. This danger appears throughout the whole work as the opposite of virtue, approaching the limits of transgression:

Lucía se había entrado por el alma de Sol, desde la noche en que le pareció [a Sol] sentir goce cuando se clavó en su seno la espina de la rosa. Lucía, ardiente y despótica, sumisa a veces como una enamorada, rígida y frenética enseguida sin causa aparente, y bella entonces como una rosa roja, ejercía, por lo mismo que no lo deseaba, un poderoso influjo en el espíritu de Sol, tímido y nuevo. (236–37)

[Lucía had entered into Sol's soul since the night in which she (Sol) seemed to feel pleasure when she (Lucía) stuck the rose's thorn in her breast. Lucía, ardent and despotic, at times as submissive as a girl in love, then rigid and frenetic with no apparent reason, and beautiful then like a red rose, wielded, even though she didn't want to, a powerful influence over Sol's spirit, timid and new.]

All these contradictory and "unnatural" feelings between the two female characters lead me to assert that the representation of the "national family" in *Amistad funesta* projects an image of a truly monstrous family. The queer element of homoeroticism and gender "deviation" that forms, by negation, part of the definition of Cubanness, has not been assimilated but rather abominated, negated, and rejected in this novel. Nevertheless, Martí's text tries to represent

30. Spanish original: "tímida y nueva."

Lucía's passion in nonsexual terms: despite the references to physical attraction between the two women, the narration insists on describing such a relationship as a spiritual and moral deviation more than as something carnal. Different from the positivist discourse of his time (see chapter 2 for examples), Martí's text is uninterested in analyzing the psychological and physiological symptoms of "deviate" individuals, instead insisting on marking the limits and definitions of what Martí considers ethical.[31]

Amistad funesta establishes a complex dichotomy between the interior home space assigned to the female role and the exterior political or public space associated with the male. Lucía appears within the novel's ideological framework as a monstrous threat that obliterates this interior/exterior dichotomy: she inserts masculine elements into the home, the feminine space, while at the same time interrupting, from the interior space, the external arena pertaining to the political activity of men. Furthermore, the murder of Sol by Lucía occurs in the countryside (at a country estate), which can be read as a destabilization of the most basic natural order and of Martí's worldview in which poetry, ethics, and politics harmoniously coexist. If the ultimate cornerstone of Martí's ideology is the concept of nature, the "unnatural" attraction of Lucía to Sol along with the homicide at the end of the work signify the destruction of the only elements capable of harmonizing the madness of the frenzied modern world.

According to the implications in Martí's text, the "new Cuban/Latin American man" should be the center of phallic power in the national family, and should be a virile yet generous man, strong but spiritual and refined, masculine yet also poetic. His female counterpart should be exactly the opposite of Lucía Jerez: she must be loving, maternal, not very passionate (except in terms of national obligation and maternity), dedicated to her husband, sweet, and aware of her subordinate position to the man. The danger to this ideal "national family" comes from the transgression of the established gender limits, from the "effeminate man" and the "manly woman." As I have already argued, these warned-about "deviations" from the ideal national family, these monsters amidst the desired harmony, are always lurking like ghosts in the reverse of every definition of the national character, hence their imminent and constant danger.

---

31. See Jeffrey Weeks, *Coming Out: Homosexual Politics in Britain from the Turn of the Nineteenth Century to the Present*, rev. ed. (London: Quartet Books Limited, 1983), 95.

★ T W O ★

The Positivist Production of the Pederast

Martí's writings were not the only ones competing to become the dominant discourse on homoeroticism and many other issues in the new (and, in the case of Cuba, future) Latin American nations. In fact, the discursive and ideological position that emerged in a progressively dominant fashion in late nineteenth-century bourgeois culture was scientific positivism.[1] It is not in the name of poetry (as in Martí's case) but rather in that of science that the emergent positivism claimed its position of primacy in sexual matters within the nationalist discourse. Positivist doctors, sociologists, and intellectuals spoke out on many national issues of the period, especially in relation to the project of social hygiene and sexual issues. Several Cuban leaders had positivist ideas; in this sense they are the opposite of Martí, an avowed antipositivist. The Cuban construct of homosexuality at the end of the nineteenth century became much more sharply defined in the sociological and medical treatises of the day and in the commentaries on those treatises made by positivist intellectuals. In this regard the years 1888 and 1889 are of special interest, as we shall soon see.

As Oscar Montero has researched so well, in those two years a revealing event that could be called the Havana Centers of Clerks

---

1. See Leopoldo Zea, *El positivismo en México* (Mexico City: Ediciones Studium, 1953). In his introduction, Zea discusses the emergence of positivism in Latin America in general, not just in Mexico.

Scandal took place.[2] Based partially on this event, Dr. Benjamín de Céspedes published a study in 1888 titled *La prostitución en la Ciudad de La Habana* (Prostitution in the city of Havana). In a section on male prostitution, the Cuban physician and intellectual presented the results of his research on homosexuality in certain neighborhoods of Havana, and in the Centers of Clerks.[3] Young, recently arrived Spanish immigrants, for the most part unemployed and in desperate financial circumstances, lived temporarily at these centers. Céspedes's study concludes that these young Spaniards were corrupting the Cuban nation because they supported themselves by selling their bodies to other men (presumably wealthy Cubans). In his representation of homosexuality, Céspedes mixes positivist comments with a strident homophobic morality while paradoxically including elements of religious rhetoric:

> Y aquí en la Habana, desgraciadamente, subsisten con más extensión de lo creíble y con mayor impunidad que en lugar alguno, tamañas degradaciones de la naturaleza humana; tipos de hombres que han invertido su sexo para traficar con estos gustos bestiales, abortos de la infamia que pululan libremente, asqueando a una sociedad que se pregunta indignada, ante la invasión creciente de la plaga asquerosa; si abundando tanto pederasta, habrán también aumentado los clientes de tan horrendos vicios; si habremos retrogradado hasta los bochornosos días de la Roma decadente, revolcados en el lodo de esas ciudades sodomíticas que nos describen los archivos bíblicos, alcanzados por la cólera y el fuego celestes. (190)

> [Unfortunately, here in Havana, there exist in greater numbers than can possibly be believed, and with greater impunity than in any other place, enormous degradations of human nature, abortions of infamy that freely swarm, sickening a society that indignantly asks itself, before the growing invasion of this disgusting plague; if there abound so many pederasts, then the numbers of clients of such horrendous vices must have increased; if we have regressed to the shameful days of Roman decadence, wallowing in the slime of those Sodomitic cities touched by heavenly fire and wrath.]

2. Oscar Montero, "Julián del Casal and the Queers of Havana," in *¿Entiendes? Queer Readings, Hispanic Writings*, ed. Emilie L. Bergmann and Paul Julian Smith (Durham, N.C.: Duke University Press, 1995), 92–112.

3. Benjamín de Céspedes, *La prostitución en la Ciudad de La Habana* (Havana: Establecimiento tipográfico O'Reily, Número 9, 1888): 190–95.

As is well known, scientistic rhetoric often tries to acquire its authority based on classifications. In other words, its logic implies that by using classification its discourse will sound scientific and therefore true. Céspedes "scientifically" classifies the "pederasts" in association with the "races": "Three classes of pederasts abound: the black, the mulatto, and the white, living together indiscriminately in houses and outbuildings, scattered throughout all the neighborhoods of Havana, where they stay out all night and keep appointments with their clients" (198).[4] Regarding the racially marked with the gender-marked identities, Céspedes classifies the "pederasts" according to "the black, the mulatto and the white," and also with the Chinese, whom he calls a "wretched race that vegetates . . . like a vegetating plague of mushrooms on a rotten organism" (ibid.).[5] Céspedes delights in stereotyping the Chinese as drug addicts and weak people, and proposes expelling all of them to China, and the Africans to Africa, so that Cuba may be rid of these ills. Céspedes also describes two Chinese drug addicts who "approached each other, came together, and squeezed each other like females" (202).[6]

But later on in Céspedes's text the classification of *pederasts* goes from racial-sexual to active/passive, maintaining that "they are not always passive in their sexual relations, and on demand, although not for the pleasure of their clients, they take the active role, resulting in the cohabitation of two pederasts" (192).[7] According to Céspedes, these pederasts have no sense of ethics whatsoever ("They are born without moral instinct" [191]),[8] and they are unaware that their "aberration" is "genetic." They support themselves through prostitution, since they are "incapable of other work" (ibid.)[9] Céspedes attempts to naturalize the division of the gender roles by assuring that the pederast "comes to modify the consciousness of his [the pederast's] personality and his sex in such a way that in his tastes, occupations and character, he

4. Spanish original: "Abundan tres clases de pederastas: el negro, el mulato, el blanco, viviendo indistintamente juntos en casas y accesorias, repartidos en todos los barrios de la Habana, donde pernoctan y dan cita a sus clientes."

5. Spanish original: "miserable raza que vegeta, como una plaga vegentante de hongos en un organismo podrido."

6. Spanish original: "se acercaron, se juntaron y se oprimieron como hembras."

7. Spanish original: "no siempre son pasivos en sus relaciones sexuales, y por exigencias, aunque no por gusto de sus visitadores, se prestan a ser activos, resultando el contubernio de dos pederastas."

8. Spanish original: "Han nacido sin instinto moral."

9. Spanish original: "incapacitados para otro trabajo."

unconsciously imitates feminine traits" (191–92).[10] As a typical social hygienist of the period, Céspedes insists that these individuals are carriers of every sort of venereal disease, which he associates with a certain symbolic contagion: he correlates the illness of the pederasts with the moral illness of the city of Havana, and by extension the entire nation. To further distance these "types of men" from positivist values, Céspedes says that, besides being perverted, vice-ridden, inverted, and sick, the pederasts are "*superstitious,* to the degree that several neighbors adjacent to one of these houses complain of the disappearance of cats, which they exterminate in the belief that they scare off their customers" (192).[11]

Moreover, in a seeming contradiction to the scientism and positivism implicit throughout the work, Céspedes's text also calls on religious imagery such as "heavenly fire and wrath" and biblical terms such as *sodomite.* This positivist treatise, which repeatedly makes negative implications about superstition and religion (usually regard these as expressions of an inferior phase in human social evolution), resorts to religious images to reaffirm the social control it proposes for the Cuban society. Notably, in the Cuban society of the period, homosexuals "exist . . . with greater impunity than in any other place" (ibid.), according to this treatise. Although Céspedes is probably exaggerating to alarm his audience, his statement implies that the Spanish government was not very effective in repressing the Havana homosexual subculture, or at least that the homosexuality discussion was constantly intertwined with political struggles (as discussed in chapter 1, Martí also accused the Spanish government of whatever "effemination" may exist in Cuban men).

Céspedes's treatise provides us with relevant information on various aspects of homosexual life in Havana at that time: it offers irrefutable proof that a homosexual subculture existed in the Cuban capital, and that such activity was seen by some—at least by those in a position to publish their studies in the national press—as an abomination, both in the individuals who engaged in such practices and in the nation as a whole. Céspedes does not limit himself here to reporting

10. Spanish original: "llega a modificar de tal manera la conciencia de su personalidad y de su sexo, que en sus gustos, sus ocupaciones y su carácter, remedan inconscientemente los rasgos femeninos."

11. Spanish original: "*supersticiosos,* hasta el punto de que varios vecinos colindantes con una de esas casas se quejan de la desaparición de los gatos, que ellos exterminan por creer que ahuyentan a sus parroquianos."

on behavior, for he also classifies it and endows those individuals who engage in it with an identity based on their sexual activities. Moreover, he constructs this identity as part of racial, class, gender, and delinquency issues.

Perhaps without being aware of it, Céspedes is acting as the agency of rhetorical power that most typifies the moment of emergence of the modern Cuban society: the doctor with positivist ideas who researches, classifies, names, and morally judges men who have sexual relations with other men, thereby contributing to the formation of a certain Cuban modernity that identifies the homosexual as the abject of the nation. Céspedes also distinguishes between "active" and "passive" pederasts, lending support to a defining binary that has continued in Cuban society up to the present day.

But Céspedes's writings did not go unanswered. In 1889, a few months after the publication of *La prostitución en la ciudad de La Habana*, the Spaniard Pedro Giralt also published in Cuba a rebuttal to Céspedes's work.[12] In this rebuttal, Giralt basically rejects Céspedes's accusation against the Spaniards, flipping this logic to accuse the Cubans (specifically the rich *criollos* who supposedly picked up young Spaniards from the Centers of Clerks) of being the true corrupters of society. According to Giralt, the entire matter had to do with class differences: the Spaniards engaged in this behavior out of economic necessity, whereas the *criollos* did it out of perversion (Giralt not only uses the term *pederasts* in reference to homosexuals, but also *maricones* (faggots), a term still used in Cuban society). It should be underscored here that Giralt insists on considering the homosexual matter a class-related problem. As the critic Oscar Montero says, "[In] Giralt's response to Dr. Céspedes, homosexuality, particularly as it affected the relationship between the urban elite and the working class, is the talk of the town."[13] Montero adds an astute commentary that refers to the relationship between sexuality, social class, and the young Spaniards in the Centers of Clerks to whom Céspedes attributes the city's corruption:

> The setting described by Dr. Céspedes is absolutely marginal. Homo-sexuals live in dens, and although they cruise the heart of the city, they confine themselves to the periphery of its square and to the late evening

12. Pedro Giralt, *El amor y la prostitución. Réplica a un libro del Dr. Céspedes* (Havana: La Universal, 1889).
13. Montero, "Julián del Casal and the Queers of Havana," 101.

hours. Dr. Céspedes's pederasts are marginal not only because of their sexual preference but because of their social class, which he hastens to define by lumping together career criminals, "dirty alcoholics," and hairdressers and "maids" of prostitutes. The clerks of the guild residences are foreigners for the most part and dangerously close to the class in question; besides, the doctor asserts, their living conditions tend to foster aberrant same-sex practices. Except in the passing, though alarmed, mention of the clients, the class of intellectuals and professionals, such as the doctor himself, is beyond the reach of the marginal group, thus reified in the name of science and presented as an object of study, a monstrosity in a natural history museum.[14]

Céspedes, in his activism as a social hygienist, proposes several "remedies" to control "masculine homosexuality," which he perceives as a true physical and moral epidemic. Curiously, in another of his works, he proposes baseball as one of those "remedies."[15] Imported from the United States in the 1860s, the sport soon became a symbol of American-style modernity in Cuba, since it came from the powerful, modern neighbor to the north and was seen as the antithesis of the Spanish bullfights, which now symbolized everything backward and barbarous. Céspedes took an active role in the new social meaning of baseball in Cuba, and came to represent it as an effective way of distancing young people from all sorts of bad habits and vices, as well as a means for them to overcome poverty and ignorance. Baseball, despite its recent introduction, was represented as an affirmation of the national anticolonial consciousness, and also as a method for virilizing young Cuban men. Accordingly, the Cuban writer Carlos Loveira, in his somewhat autobiographical 1920 novel *Generales y doctores* (Generals and doctors), says that the protagonist Ignacio García, recalling a Sunday afternoon in Havana before 1895, compares baseball with bullfighting: the former is a civilized sport, moral and manly, while the latter appears as a savage activity that would attract no civilized Cuban.[16]

It is also important to point out that Céspedes's *La prostitutión en la Ciudad de La Habana* contains a preface by Enrique José Varona, one of the most distinguished Cuban intellectuals and supporters of Cuban

14. Ibid., 103.
15. See Pérez, "Between Baseball and Bullfighting."
16. Ibid.

independence of that period and perhaps the most important positivist in Cuban history.[17] Varona's preface rails against what he regards as vices brought from Europe. Employing a highly racist rhetoric (and referring to all the "vices" studied by Céspedes), he states that Cuba has received from Europe "the virus of its pestilent corruption,"[18] and he expresses his conviction that this entire problem is also related to "decrepit" races and "demoralized" economic situations:

El autor de este libro [Céspedes] ha querido estudiar uno de los más pavorosos problemas sociales de la hora actual, mas no solamente para acumular datos y preparar conclusiones, sino para proceder científicamente, es decir, para hacer obra de higienista social. . . . [E]l que lea estas páginas se convencerá pronto de que, si Cuba participa imperfectamente de la cultura europea, en cambio ha recibido sin tasa el virus de su corrupción pestilente. A los ojos del lector atónito se descubre una nueva faz de la colonización europea; y penetra en el fondo sombrío de estas sentinas donde la codicia y la concupiscencia humanas han amontonado los detritus de las viejas civilizaciones, revueltos y mezclados con los elementos étnicos más disímiles. Allí verá lo que han dejado los piaras de ganado negro, transportadas del Africa salvaje, los cargamentos de chinos decrépitos en el vicio, arrancados á su hormiguero asiático, y los cardúmenes de inmigrantes europeos sin familia, desmoralizados por la pobreza y la ignorancia, dispuestos á vivir como en aduar ó campamento, regido todo por el burócrata soberbio y licencioso, hinchado de desdén por la tierra cuyos despojos se reparte, dispuesto á ser pregonero de su atraso y de su inmoralidad, que él mismo en primer término fomenta, y de que él exclusivamente es responsable.

Así la corrupción, que señala con tan terribles caracteres el estado de podredumbre de las sociedades del Viejo Mundo, toma nueva forma entre nosotros, sin perder su gravedad, antes bien, aumentándola, por cuanto, socialmente, es más grave encontrar corroído por el cáncer un organismo nuevo y en vías de crecimiento.[19]

[The author of this book (Céspedes) has tried to study one of the most dreadful social problems of our day, not only to accumulate data and draw conclusions, but also in order to proceed scientifically, that is to say, to do the work of a social hygienist. . . . [H]e who reads these pages will

17. Enrique José Varona, prologue to Céspedes, *La prostitución en la Ciudad de La Habana.*
18. Spanish original: "el virus de su corrupción pestilente." Ibid., x.
19. Ibid.

soon become convinced that, while Cuba participates only partially in European culture, it has nevertheless received the virus of its pestilent corruption without measure. A new facet of European colonization is revealed to the astonished eyes of the reader; and he penetrates into the darkest reaches of these degradations where human greed and concupiscence have piled high the detritus of the old civilizations, stirred up and mixed with the most dissimilar ethnic elements. There he will see what the herds of black cattle, transported from darkest Africa, have left, and the burdens of the Chinese, corrupt in their vices, torn from their Asian anthill, and the human shoals of family-less European immigrants, demoralized by poverty and ignorance, willing to live as in dowars or camps, governed by the arrogant and licentious bureaucrat, full of disdain for the land whose spoils he distributes, ready to be spokesman for its backwardness and immorality, which he himself has fomented first and foremost, and for which he is exclusively responsible.

Thus the corruption, which makes manifest with such terrible char-acters the state of poverty of the Old World societies, takes new form amongst us, without losing its gravity, but rather increasing it, insofar as, socially, it is graver still to find a new and growing organism corroded by cancer.]

As may be gathered from these statements, Varona severely con-demns sexual "vices" because they corrode the "new organism" of the emerging Cuban society, and he believes that this corruption was inherited from Europe. Varona does not clarify what part of Europe he is referring to here: just Spain, the rest of Europe, France? It seems that his intention is to insist on accusing that the vice comes to Cuba both as a product of Spanish colonialism and as part of the modern corrup-tion from the rest of Europe, thus supporting the construction that homosexuality and other ills come from other countries and societies (at times accused of being too backward and at others too progressive). But Varona also strongly suggests that although in Cuba the edifying European models have not been widely adopted, the importation of their negative elements has indeed been acquired and is increasing. With this idea he implies that although the European models were generally desirable for the new Latin American nations, it remained for the Latin Americans to sanitize them or extract from them certain characteristics (homosexual behaviors among them) that seemed to detract from the beneficial aspects of European culture. Varona adopts a negative position that radically classifies bodies considered queer in relation to the national body. Moreover, his writings imply that homosexuality is a condition not only of foreign import but also of the poorer classes.

It is worth mentioning here that the abjection of queer behavior in Cuban society at the end of the nineteenth century is not limited to marginal characters and/or foreigners such as those described by Céspedes and Varona. The accusations of homoeroticism were also leveled at the most distinguished classes of the country and at the most illustrious persons. Perhaps the most outstanding case of the latter is the one involving Julián del Casal (1863–93), regarded by many critics as the second-most important Cuban *modernista* poet at the turn of the twentieth century, after Martí. His stylistic sensuality and what some critics have considered his general "queerness" sparked long debates over his orientation even before his early demise. Moreover, several critics have tried to deny or even to ignore any sort of "deviation" in Casal. That is why we are so indebted to the critic Oscar Montero, who has published a groundbreaking book that addresses the theme of Casal's eroticism and his possible homosexuality.[20] Montero's research has had a liberating effect in that until its publication, commentaries and opinions on this subject in relation to Casal were frequently very evasive. In one of his articles, Montero in effect summarizes his study of the poet in relation to his eroticism: "any reading that mentions or skirts, as is often the case, the question of sexuality in Casal, or more properly the question of its textual representations, is predetermined by the ambiguous character of Casal's open secret."[21]

Varona himself expressed reservations in regard to the sensuality in Casal's literary work. It should be clarified, nevertheless, that it is not known with certainty whether Julián del Casal was homosexual. Irrefutable proof has yet to be found, although this is perhaps unimportant, since what counts for our purposes are these *representations* in relation to homosexuality and queer bodies at the turn of the twentieth century. Whatever Casal was or did in his life, he was never forgiven for not leading a "normal" life or using a less sensual and erotic literary style. All these condemnations of homoeroticism suggest that such a "deviation" was seen as dangerous to social stability. The gender role differences were equated to the biological differences between the sexes and to the social and patriotic role of the citizen.

20. See Oscar Montero, *Erotismo y representación en Julián del Casal* (Amsterdam: Rodopi, 1993).

21. Montero, "Julián del Casal and the Queers of Havana," 98.

Varona, like his positivist teachers, August Comte and Herbert Spencer, assumed that social life and the differences between the sexes could be explained through biology.[22] Spencer, for example, maintained that the differences between the sexes were due to an imperfection in the evolution of women and the need to conserve vital energy for the demands of reproduction. That is why, he maintained, a woman's lesser energy will not allow her to reach the intellectual level of a man.[23] As I also pointed out, Varona's positivist position carries with it a series of similar associations that are mixed with racial-, class-, and gender-based constructs.

By the end of the nineteenth century, male homosexuality had begun to have some voices in the western European countries, with Oscar Wilde being the most notable example. In Cuba, however, it seems that this was not the case. If is true that by that time in Cuba the preoccupation with certain "deviant" behaviors (effeminacy in men and sexual passions and masculinity in women) already constituted a very grave matter in the dominant discourses, it nonetheless seems that there was no voice in literature or journalism that clearly dealt with the matter from an alternative perspective. Those who progressively dominated the modern field of sexual discourse were the positivists, who sharply denounced and negatively defined this behavior. Cuba had no Oscar Wilde, no Walt Whitman. Those who could speak, perhaps Julián del Casal, were most likely intimidated into silence. Discussing the homosexual issue and its representation in a less negative light seemingly did not occur in a systematic way in Cuba until the 1920s and 1930s.[24] Several of the postulates and attitudes of positivism will be radically questioned by some Cuban feminists of those decades, as we shall see in the next section.

22. See Elio Alba Bufill, *Enrique José Varona. Crítica y creación* (Madrid: Hispanova de Ediciones, 1976).

23. See Jeffrey Weeks, *Coming Out: Homosexual Politics in Britain from the Turn of the Nineteenth Century to the Present*, rev. ed. (London: Quartet Books Limited, 1983),

24. Here I must make the proviso that in 1914 Miguel de Marcos, a Cuban author and journalist, published a short story collection titled *Lujuria: Cuentos nefandos* (Havana: Jesús Montero, 1914) that included "Sodoma in excelsis" (Sodoma in Heaven), which dealt openly with the gay theme: a narrator who feels extremely attracted to a "sodomite" (a term used in the text to mean a very effeminate man). Despite the brevity of this story, the openness of the gay theme in this text written and published in Havana undermines the reiterated statement by scholars insisting that the first gay-themed text in twentieth-century Spanish American literature was Augusto D'Halmar's *La pasión y muerte del cura Deusto* (The passion and death of Father Deusto) (3d ed., Madrid: Editora Internacional, 1924). I would like to thank Carlos Espinosa Domínguez for providing me with information about de Marcos's short story collection.

//

NEW SPACES AND
NEW SUBJECTIVITIES

The period from 1920 to 1940 was one of great social and economic turmoil in the Cuban republic, which had been established in 1902. In the 1930s there occurred what has been called the *revolución del 30* (thirties revolution) to reflect the deep economic, political, and social crises of those years. Social and political struggles dominated Cuban society, ending the relative political stability of the republic's early years. In addition, national capitalism could not take hold, and the island's reliance on sugar as the only cash crop remained a constant obstacle to national control of the economy. In fact, the wars of independence at the end of the nineteenth century caused great poverty and devastation in the early twentieth. Cubans had little real control over the means of production in industry and commerce. Unlike other Latin American nations, Cuba did not expel the Spaniards after it achieved independence, and the Spanish businessmen who remained on the island after the Spanish-American War retained their property.[1] Nonetheless, those who actually controlled the Cuban economy at the time were primarily American. Not surprisingly, Cuban political life during the 1920s and 1930s was dedicated to contending with the thorny question of dependence and political honesty, and nationalist discourse reemerged with a renewed force. The 1920s brought the shrinking of the world sugar market

1. Louis A. Pérez Jr., *Cuba: Between Reform and Revolution*, 2d ed. (New York: Oxford University Press, 1995), 189–228.

and finally the Great Depression, which plunged Cuban society into another crisis.

It is well known in Cuban history that the struggle against the dictatorship of Gerardo Machado galvanized many of the country's political forces in the 1930s. The commotion of those years was caused by the country's abnormal rate of modernization. The struggle of the liberal and leftist groups centered predominantly around the protest against U.S. imperialism, the denationalization of the country, and political dishonesty. But organizations also sprang forth from the *economic classes*, particularly the industrialists, who were worried about the nationalist question.[2] In addition, the relatively large middle class (around one-third of the population) represented another important force against the status quo.[3]

Moreover, from the beginning of the twentieth century, an impressive feminist movement had developed that can be seen as an expression of the relative modernity of Cuban society in that period in spite of the country's impoverishment. The women forming these movements lobbied for legal reforms such as the right to vote, and for improved laws concerning marriage, property, divorce, and labor rights.[4] Although several of the feminist activists tried to keep the movement from being branded as a fomenter of *garzonas* or lesbians, a certain sector of Cuban feminism in the 1930s publicly discussed and debated the issue of lesbianism (or *garzonismo*, as it was called at that time) in the media as well as in literature.[5] Instead of the almost complete negativism of earlier notions of homosexuality, in these years we find more complex representations of "homosexual identities," both of and by men and women alike.

I should note here that the debate on the family, marital relations, and the role of women in Cuban society began in earnest at the start of the twentieth century in essays and writings by Miguel de Carrión

2. See Marifeli Pérez-Stable, *The Cuban Revolution: Origins, Course, and Legacy* (New York: Oxford University Press, 1993), 17–35.

3. Ibid.

4. See Lynn K. Stoner, *From House to the Streets: The Cuban Women's Movement for Legal Reform, 1898–1940* (Durham, N.C.: Duke University Press, 1991). See also the recent book by Catherine Davies, *A Place in the Sun? Women Writers in Twentieth-Century Cuba* (London: Zed Books Ltd., 1998).

5. See Nina Menéndez, "No Woman Is an Island: Cuban Women's Fiction in the 1920s and 1930s" (Ph.D. diss., Stanford University, 1993) and *"Garzonas y Feministas* in Cuban Women's Writing of the 1920s: *La vida manda* by Ofelia Rodríguez Acosta," in *Sex and Sexuality in Latin America*, ed. Daniel Balderston and Donna J. Guy (New York: New York University Press, 1997), 74–189.

(1875–1929), José Antonio Ramos (1885–1946), Carlos Loveira (1881–1928), and others.[6] These men were in a sense predecessors to the feminist movement of the 1920s and 1930s, which was led by such women as Ofelia Rodríguez Acosta, Irma Pedroso, Dulce María Loynaz, Lesbia Soravilla, and Mariblanca Sabas-Alomá. In Miguel de Carrión's famous novel from 1919, *Las impuras* (The impure ones), the character of Rogelio is described as follows:

> Ninguno de los vicios que atormentan la naciente virilidad de los escolares dejó de hacer presa en él. Tuvo aventuras amorosas entre sus mismos compañeros que le valieron una terrible reputación; y como era osado y jactancioso, él mismo se encargaba de abultarlas, completándolas con toda clase de mentiras. Después, cuando terminó el bachillerato, los amores fáciles de lupanar y algunas criaditas de su casa, cazadas al descuido, se encargaron de encauzar sus ardores por otros derroteros.[7]

> [None of the vices that torment the budding virility of students left him untouched. He had amorous affairs with his own male classmates which earned him a terrible reputation; and since he was daring and boastful, he took charge of padding them himself, filling them out with all sorts of lies. Afterwards, when he had finished his degree, the easy loves of the brothel and some of the little housemaids, pursued nonchalantly, served to channel his passion down other paths.]

In this passage, it is implied that Rogelio's homosexuality has been a somewhat transitory phenomenon, typical of "the vices that torment

6. See Menéndez, "No Woman Is an Island," 2–3. In his recent book on homosexuality in Cuban literature, Víctor Fowler mentions that in 1922 (presumably in Cuba, but it is not clear) Graziela Garbalosa published a novel titled *La gozadora del dolor* (The pain lover) in which there is "a formidable chapter on lesbianism." I have been unable to obtain this novel nor to confirm this information. See Fowler, *La maldición: una historia del placer como conquista* (Havana: Editorial Letras Cubanas, 1998), 6. On the same page, Fowler speaks of the "magnificent poems by Mercedes Matamoros in *El último amor de Safo* (Sappho's last love) (1901)." I have also been unable to confirm this bibliographical information. Another important gay Cuban writer whose work has been part of the "open secret" about his homosexuality is Emilio Ballagas. For an interesting essay on Ballagas by Virgilio Piñera, see Piñera, "Emilio Ballagas en persona," *Ciclón* (September 1955): 41–50. In addition, Miguel de Marcos's short story collection *Lujuria: Cuentos nefandos* (Havana: Jesús Montero, 1914) includes "Sodoma in excelsis" (Sodoma in Heaven), in which there is a clear representation of a man who demonstrates a great physical attraction toward another one. Other stories in this collection represent lesbian sexual encounters.

7. Miguel de Carrión, *Las impuras* (The impure ones) (Havana: Librería Nueva, 1919).

the budding virility of students," but the open and almost casual references to his homosexual practices are still significant due to the direct and matter-of-fact tone in which the novel narrates them.

In my opinion, however, it is Cuban feminism that opened a radical new perspective that not only benefited women's rights, but also questioned patriarchy and gender roles in general. In doing so it chose a new way to represent homosexuality. In fact, starting from the Cuban feminist movement of the 1920s and 1930s, one can perceive some degree of success in the creation of a discourse in which the homosexual's defense is not uncommon. In many ways, the discourses struggling for authority on sexual issues at this time were the religious, the positivist, and the feminist. Feminism (especially the radical feminism that I discuss in chapter 3) frequently questioned the naturalization of the sex-gender relationship, gender roles, and the status quo of the traditional family and of patriarchal society. Yet all of these discourses often were under the umbrella of nationalism—that is, all of them declare their principles and practices in the name of some sort of national morality. The homophobic foundations of nationalism were not systematically and directly questioned.

Everything dealt with in this study thus far seems to lead to the idea that different social and political forces in Cuba—especially with the radicalization of Cuban nationalism, which started in the midnineteenth century and was renewed in the 1920s and 1930s—joined to form complex homophobic discourses (challenged briefly by the radical feminism of the 1920s and 1930s) that articulated a sort of homosexualization of the enemy (along with racial, class, gender-based, political, and nationalistic implications) to suit their own ends. This put the homosexual in a highly indefensible position, declaring him an Other of the nation.

It seems that Cuban feminists' insistence on publicly debating their ideas during the 1920s and 1930s (even in widely circulated magazines such as *Carteles* and *Bohemia*) affected the new interpretations and representations of homosexuality in their society. During those years, in spite of the public repudiation of homosexuality, there also emerged a debate that was occasionally favorable to homosexuals. For example, in a public letter responding to Mariblanca Sabas Alomá's homophobia, Dr. Flora Díaz Parrado writes that lesbianism is "a type within human incongruence,"[8] and that this behavior "is more acceptable than that

8. Spanish original: "un tipo dentro de la incongruencia humana." See Mariblanca Sabas Alomá, *Feminismo: cuestiones sociales—crítica literaria* (Havana: Editorial Hermes, 1930), 106–108.

of the servile woman." (ibid.).[9] She adds, "I believe that the *garzona* [lesbian] is a sort of transition from the woman of 1914 [before the First World War] to the woman of the future" (ibid.).[10] Díaz Parrado states that all of society's beliefs change, and just as it now seems laughable that people once believed epileptics to be morally deviant, so too will popular ideas about lesbianism seem equally ridiculous (ibid.). This probably was the first time in Cuban history that there had been such a debate. Díaz Parrado adopted a historical and cultural stance concerning the question of homoeroticism, a position that is not found in past discussions on this subject. Even literature, which up until then had maintained an almost absolute silence about the open representation of homosexuality, now joined journalism and sociomedical treatises to form another battleground where these issues were represented, frequently in contradictory terms but at times opening a serious dialogue on this issue.

I should note, however, that most Cuban feminists of the period did not see the question of homosexuality as something positive or even acceptable. Regarding the discussion on lesbianism, I can refer first to the negative opinions that Mariblanca Sabas Alomá, one of the most distinguished leftist feminists of the period, expresses in her article published in the popular weekly magazine *Carteles* in April 1928 (ibid.). Sabas Alomá, in spite of being considered very progressive on social issues, especially women's rights, insists on completely disassociating feminism from lesbianism. She accuses lesbianism of being a crime against nature and a behavior reflecting an excess of sexual passion and a deviation in terms of sex-gender roles (the author does not distinguish between sex in the chromosomal sense and gender in the sense of sociosexual roles, something that other Cuban feminists of the period, Ofelia Rodríguez Acosta above all, are at times able to articulate somewhat in their work). In her statements Sabas Alomá unknowingly mixes arguments from diverse discourses that are at odds with each other. For example, her concept of "crime against nature" seems to combine the traditional religious morality of sin against nature and the scientific argument that sees homosexuality as a deviation of instinctual desire. What is even more paradoxical in Sabas Alomá is her accusation that lesbianism stems from an "excess of sexual passion" (ibid.), which is the same traditional argument used against

9. Spanish original: "es más aceptable que la de la mujer servil."
10. Spanish original: "creo que la garzona es un tipo de transición entre la mujer de 1914 y la mujer del porvenir."

women who don't strictly follow the behavior prescribed by patriarchal society (for example, Lucía from *Amistad funesta*, as I mentioned in chapter 1).

But the most noteworthy aspect of Sabas Alomá's arguments is not the repetition of traditional concepts as part of her feminist positions, but rather the combination of these ideas with leftist and historicist conceptions of homosexuality. Sabas Alomá blames capitalism for the oppression of women—that is, she explicitly places this issue within a Marxist-Leninist framework: women ought also to occupy themselves with the problems of poverty, administrative corruption, education, health, and the search for "a future without borders," as Lenin put it (ibid.). From her leftist position she considers lesbianism a product of this capitalistic oppression, and once capitalism is eliminated, women will enjoy full rights and equality and lesbianism will disappear. Nevertheless, in spite of these statements, Sabas Alomá asserts that women and their rights cannot be completely subsumed under a proletarian ideological umbrella that does not take gender differences into account.

In light of these ideas, we must ask ourselves: if lesbianism is a historical product of capitalism, how does this historicist concept relate to that of "crime against nature"? Is this a historically constructed phenomenon, an eternal essence of "nature," or both? Adding to her contradictions, Sabas Alomá engaged in a public debate with the influential positivist doctor and intellectual Gregorio Marañón, since she thought that the Spanish physician placed too much emphasis on the biological and physiological causes of homosexuality (ibid.). In spite of this debate with Marañón, Sabas Alomá, as it is easy to ascertain from her arguments about lesbianism being a crime against nature, cannot avoid brandishing positivist arguments when referring to it. Also, at times she adds religious expressions to her leftist feminist discourse. Nonetheless, Sabas Alomá's argument that homosexuality is caused by the abuses committed by capitalism has been repeated by many Cuban leftists since then—even and especially after Castro's revolution took power in 1959. I will elaborate on this issue in the third section of this study.

★ THREE ★

The Feminist, the Garzona,
and the Gay Man

O f all the known feminists who embodied a renewed representation of homosexuality during the 1920s and 1930s, Ofelia
Rodríguez Acosta (1902–75) was the most radical. Although she was
one of the most important literary figures of the period, histories
of Cuban literature frequently omit her work or only mention it in
passing. I maintain that Rodríguez Acosta was an important feminist
writer of her day; what is more, her literary work, articles, and interviews
express ideological positions and political insights on the state of
society that were perhaps unsurpassed in her country at that time.

Rodríguez Acosta published seven novels, several stories, some
books of chronicles, and a play, in addition to a great many articles
on the most burning issues of the time. She lived what was then
termed an "independent life," frequently a euphemism for *garzonas*
(lesbians), especially those of certain economic means who remained
single, were not amorously associated with any man, traveled, and
participated in social and political activities. She frequently adopted
leftist political positions, although these ideas evolved toward a kind
of existentialism. She visited many countries, and in 1940 moved to
Mexico, where, according to some accounts of her life, she lived until
the mid-1960s, when she returned to Cuba. These same reports inform
us that Rodríguez Acosta died in Havana in 1975. Nevertheless, it
should be noted that such little attention has been paid to this author
that in biographical notes on her life both the date of birth and place
of death are inconsistent (some accounts say she was born in 1906,

and others say 1902), and there is also some confusion as to whether she remained in Mexico beginning in 1940 or returned to Cuba in the mid-1950s or 1960s. It is known that she died in a home for the mentally ill, but it is unclear whether this occurred in Santovenia, a hospital in Cuba, or in a mental institution in Mexico. In spite of all this confusion, the center of her life and work was indisputably feminism.[1]

The sociopolitical positions of Rodríguez Acosta should be classified as radically feminist in order to differentiate her stance from that of revolutionary feminists with a more leftist posture, like that of Mariblanca Sabas Alomá, which does not radically question the traditional position on homosexuality. Rodríguez Acosta's feminism has at least five radical characteristics: redefinition of the traditional family; a separation of sex, gender, and sexual object; a denunciation of inequality, especially that of class; and a progressive representation of homosexual relations, that is, a representation that shows the possibility of homosexual desire and love to be as authentic as that of heterosexual relations, a love that is not a mere derivation of heterosexual love and desire. Rodríguez Acosta radically redefines the family, conceptualizing it as "the spiritual relationship between people who are closer—by their life circumstances—to each other, than to other more distant people."[2] She adds that "love is the only basis of the home, although church and courthouse archives may say otherwise."[3] In other words, for her the family ceases to have the exclusive connotation of a union between

1. See Susana A. Montero, *La narrativa femenina cubana, 1928–1958* (Havana: Editorial Academia, 1989), 39–57. See also Elena M. De Jongh, "Feminismo y periodismo en la Cuba republicana: Ofelia Rodríguez Acosta y la campaña feminista de *Bohemia* (1930–1932)," *Confluencia* 11, no. 1 (1995): 3–12; and "Gender and Controversy: Cuban Novelist Ofelia Rodríguez Acosta," *Journal of the Southeastern Council on Latin American Studies* 23 (March 1992): 23–35.

2. See De Jongh, "Femenismo y periodismo," 8. In spite of the fundamental ideological ruptures of Rodríguez Acosta and other feminists of the 1920s and 1930s, Víctor Fowler affirms that "the moment of greatest opening in terms of [homosexuality] in our literary history is the short period during the mid-1950s when the magazine *Ciclón* was founded and directed by José Rodríguez Feo and Virgilio Piñera." See Fowler, *La maldición: una historia del placer como conquista* (Havana: Editorial Letras Cubanas, 1998), 8–9. It seems that Fowler bases his opinion on some articles on homosexuality published in *Ciclón* in 1955. I believe that the rupture of *Ciclón* was much more brief and limited than that of the 1920s and 1930s, and spearheaded by radical feminism. Also, I think that it is impossible to compare the national impact of a few articles published in 1955 in a magazine of very limited circulation to the public discussion of the 1920s and 1930s in magazines such as *Carteles*, *Bohemia*, and *Revista Social*, to which must be added works on homoerotic themes by Ofelia Rodríguez Acosta, Lesbia Soravilla, Flora Díaz Parrado, and others, as well as works by male authors such as Miguel de Carrión, Alfonso Hernández Catá, and Carlos Montenegro.

3. Ibid.

a man and a woman. Rather, a family is a group of people united by mutual love who have come together thanks to "life circumstances."

It seems that by the 1920s and 1930s a transformation of positivist scientism opened a limited public space for the discussion of homosexuality as something not necessarily criminal (although still deviate and sick), but radical feminism had opened it in a more radical way through its antipatriarchal stances. For radical feminism the matter to be resolved was not the clear delimitation of gender differences. Rodríguez Acosta's feminism implied that marking gender role differences would not solve "the problem," and besides, the questioning of "the problem" is what needed to be radically rethought. The radical feminist discourse tries to acquire authority by attacking the patriarchal system at its core. It is worth noting that even with this radical posture, the majority of feminists, including Rodríguez Acosta, placed feminism under the umbrella of nationalism. Indeed, in the course of her tumultuous life, Rodríguez Acosta supposedly participated in an armed confrontation against the women's wing of dictator Gerardo Machado's paramilitary forces.

Now I must point out that Rodríguez Acosta's radical feminist position is not always coherent with itself, nor is it bereft of multiple contradictions. It should also be noted that her position on homosexuality and other matters was not the same in 1929 (when *La vida manda* [Life decrees] was published) as in 1940 (the year in which *En la noche del mundo* [In the night of the world] appears.) In those twelve years, Rodríguez Acosta modified her ideas toward a more coherent stance, at least in sexual matters. That is why a reading of *La vida manda* leads me, on the one hand, to distinguish some aspects of the text that can be called progressive, and, on the other, to emphasize an internalization of the homophobia and machismo of the period along with unresolved ideological contradictions. Nevertheless, and in spite of the notable differences and paradoxes inherent in both novels, *La vida manda* and *En la noche del mundo* both possess some noteworthy similarities.

La vida manda as well as *En la noche del mundo* are highly pessimistic stories, gloomy actually, like the products of someone extremely displeased with society and life in general. Everything in these two novels ends in disaster, suicide, or murder, most persistently represented in the uncontrolled sadness of their characters (especially those who seem to embody the author's alter ego). We must not forget that Ofelia Rodríguez Acosta finished out her days in a mental institution and that the social ruptures she attempted were highly threatening to the status quo of the time. She frequently proposed free love, homosexuality as a marital option, political honesty, the equality of social classes, the liberation of women from the yoke of machismo, the radical reinterpretation of the traditional family, and the rejection of the utilitarianism of the modern world. It was too radical a revolution for her society and time, and the characters of her novels reflect her great disillusionment. Moreover, feminism was possible in and through modernity, but Rodríguez Acosta's posture was that of a feminist who frequently scorned modern life, who took delight in denouncing the world that surrounded her in almost all its aspects. This is why her characters don't progress from failure to victory but experience failure after failure.

Life Decrees

All of these social, psychological, and ideological dead ends in Rodríguez Acosta's thinking explain the tremendous pessimism that overcomes Gertrudis, the main character of *La vida manda* (Life decrees), first published in 1929. Almost the entire novel deals with her failures. Gertrudis, a young Cuban woman in Havana toward the end of the 1920s, lives with her uncle and godfather, Don Esteban. As a poor orphan with a rebellious character, she tends to lead an ever more independent life: she works as a clerk in a bank, saves money to achieve economic independence, and lives her life in relative freedom. Notably, Gertrudis's space is often the outdoors, whereas previous female characters lived mainly within the home (Lucía in *Amistad funesta* is a typical example). Don Esteban is a benevolent patriarch who represents someone Gertrudis can always count on, and he frequently exhibits tolerance of her ideas and behavior. Don Esteban is also a sort of national symbol, since he is a veteran of the Cuban War of Independence. This aspect of his character makes him an allegorical national figure from the start.

Gertrudis's relationship with her uncle-godfather is extremely important in the novel. It implies, within the logic of the first part of the narration, that the Cuban patriarchal influence over women is quite benevolent, that a woman like Gertrudis can free herself from that oppressive past, and that such oppression can be breached. But later in the narration this is seen to be untrue, since just the opposite happens: social forces punish the feminist woman mercilessly, and Gertrudis is unable to break with *machista* rules.

As the novel opens, it is said of the protagonist that she "was born with wings, and that the wings, in her adolescence, had grown, become wider, stronger."[4] Gertrudis is leaving her boyfriend, Antonio, because she is not in love with him, going against the advice of everyone, including Don Esteban, for Antonio is a good man. It is also said that Gertrudis has "a masculine ambition" and that she is "strong and rough" (46). In fact, the narrative in the first third of the novel seems to indicate that Gertrudis is not interested in men. Fonseca, one of the characters who works with Gertrudis at the bank, says, "I've never seen you look at a single man," (47), to which Gertrudis replies, "None has awakened any interest in me yet" (48). Nevertheless, some time after having left Antonio, Gertrudis meets Damián Varona, who becomes the love of her life, her central passion. Damián's last name also makes his character a possible national allegory; this symbolism is reinforced when moments before Damián and Gertrudis first meet, Gertrudis sees Enrique José Varona in the street, and refers to him as "wise elder" and "teacher of three generations of Cubans" (45). Clearly, Enrique José Varona (1849–1933) appears in *La vida manda* as Gertrudis's idea of a Cuban national treasure.

Despite being a rather controversial figure in Cuban history, Varona, with his long and prolific political and intellectual life, had become a living idol to many young Cubans by the time Rodríguez Acosta wrote her novel. His notoriety probably stemmed from not only his many national, political, and intellectual activities, but also his civic opposition to the dictatorship of Gerardo Machado (who was deposed in the year of Varona's death, 1933), which perhaps explains why Rodríguez Acosta singles him out as the only historical character to appear in the novel. That Gertrudis's true love shares the surname of this very important Cuban intellectual does not appear to be a coincidence, especially if we consider the appearance, some pages before Damián's first mention in the novel, of the character Enrique José Varona walking down a Havana street. If this symbolism is valid, the novelistic construction of Gertrudis would be a sort of Cuban feminist who finds the love of her life (and by symbolic association, the love of her country) in the masculine idealization of Enrique José Varona, the civic Cuban intellectual who led the Cuban Revolutionary Party at the end of the nineteenth century, after José Martí's death; shown support (contradictory, to be sure) for the Cuban feminist movement of the period; and displayed a strong civic resistance against Machado's dictatorship.

4. Spanish original: "había nacido con alas, y las alas, en la adolescencia de la mujer, se habían engrandecido, ensanchado, vigorizado," Ofelia Rodríguez Acosta, *La vida manda* (Madrid: Editorial Biblioteca Rubén Darío, 1929), 20–21.

There can be no doubt that in *La vida manda*, as is the custom in many Cuban and Latin American novels, a national allegory is embedded in the narrative's plot. There are frequent references to the republic, the socialist ideals of the main character, the political ethics that she wants for the nation, her preferred symbolism for referring to the national situation, and so on. Other references directly attack the government of Machado, who was still in power at the time of the novel's publication. But the paradox of the symbolic association between Damián Varona and Enrique José Varona is that the former, although seeming at first to be Gertrudis's ideal man, later turns out to be an opportunistic liar. He promises her eternal love, only to confess later that he is a husband and father. Gertrudis loses her virginity with him, which in the novel and in Cuban society of the day was seen as the complete surrender of a woman to the ideal man, and thus was of great significance and social symbolism. She eventually discovers that even his marriage is a lie, since he lives with the other woman out of wedlock and had claimed to be married simply to escape from his relationship with Gertrudis. Therefore, the symbolism of the figures of Enrique José Varona and Damián Varona, as with so many other aspects of the novel, is highly contradictory. Perhaps this contradiction symbolizes some of the text's logical tensions in general, since a constant ambivalence toward its "feminist revolution" can be noted in Gertrudis: she constantly oscillates between rupture with phallic power and falling desperately in love with it.

Almost the entire core of the story is dedicated to Gertrudis's failed love for Damián Varona. Her suffering on behalf of this love is of such magnitude that it increasingly worsens. Once separated from Damián, she seeks various solutions to alleviate her suffering, among them working, having a child with her former boyfriend, the now-divorced Antonio (the baby dies shortly after birth), and also having a love affair with a lesbian named Delia. The end of the story ends on a terribly gloomy, pessimistic note, for Gertrudis shoots herself in the head. Instead of dying, however, which for her at that moment would have been a liberation from what she calls the "Imperative of Life," she is blinded by the wound to her optic nerve.

The novel's depiction of the relationship between Gertrudis and Delia is truly ambiguous. It is not completely clear that they ever have a physical relationship, but Delia is clearly a lesbian who has assumed her sexuality and is in love with Gertrudis. When Gertrudis is disconsolate over her problems with Damián, Delia offers her a ride home in her car and takes advantage of the occasion to talk about her sexual orientation. The first sign of Delia's lesbianism is revealed in a conversation between the two characters. Gertrudis begins:

—Yo puedo tratarla a usted cuantas veces la vea. Me siento un poco comprendida por usted; pero si fuéramos amigas, quizá se echara todo a perder. Usted sabe que yo sé quién es usted.

—¿Y me lo censura?

—No.

—Me compadece?

—Tampoco.

—Soy así de un modo inevitable.

—Sea usted como usted quiera y por lo que quiera. Lo único que a mí me interesa de usted es su corazón.

—¿Lo cree usted capaz de amar?

—En un sentido pagano, humano y divino.

—¿Hay otro sentido?

—Para mí, sí.

—Explíquelos todos. Pagano, ¿por qué?

—Porque es usted amante del placer en todas sus variaciones.

—Bien. ¿Humano?

—Porque es usted generosa para todos los seres. Comprensiva y compasiva. Porque a usted le inquieta el sentido de la muerte.

—¿Y el cuarto?

—Es que usted no tiene, o mejor: su corazón. El del sacrificio, el del afecto directo, personal, íntimo. El que nace del centro, del núcleo mismo del corazón: del que no es sólo pagano, porque no busca el placer principalmente; ni abstractamente humano, porque va derecho al hombre en su individualidad; ni divino, porque no es homogéneo ni místico: el que lleva todos estos espejismos, sufre todas estas influencias, pero triunfa de todas ellas: el amor absoluto, sin principio ni fin.

—¿Ama usted?

—Tengo esa gloria.

—Quiera Dios no la pierda: me dolería demasiado.

—¿A usted?

—Amiga mía—déjeme llamarla así por un momento—quizá esté usted despertando el cuarto sentido de mi corazón. (107–109)

["I can talk to you whenever I see you. I feel somewhat understood by you, but if we were friends, maybe everything would be ruined. You know I know who you are."

"And do you condemn me for that?"

"No."

"Do you feel sorry for me?"

"No, not that either."

"I can't help being this way."

"You can be however you want and for whatever reason. The only thing I care about is your heart."

"Do you think it's capable of love?"

"Yes, in a pagan, human, and divine way."

"Is there any other way?"

"For me there is."

"Tell me about them all. Why pagan?"

"Because you love pleasure in all its variations."

"All right. Human?"

"Because you are generous with all beings. Understanding and compassionate. Because the feeling of death bothers you."

"And the fourth?"

"You don't have it, or rather, your heart doesn't. It's the love of sacrifice, personal, intimate, direct affection. It comes from the center, from the very core of the heart; it isn't only pagan, because it doesn't seek mainly pleasure, nor is it abstractly human, because it goes straight to you in your individuality; nor is it divine, because it isn't homogeneous or mystic: it bears all these illusions, bears all these influences, but overcomes them all: absolute love, without beginning or end."

"Do you love?"

"I have the pleasure."

"God willing you won't lose it; it would hurt me too much."

"You?"

"My friend, let me call you that for a moment, perhaps you are awakening the fourth sense of love in my heart."]

A few months later, after the breakup with Damián, Gertrudis finds Delia alone again, and Delia declares her love:

—¿Cuánto sufre usted!

—Gracias, Delia. Es usted muy bondadosa conmigo.

—Porque la quiero, Gerturdis, hasta el sacrificio. No lo olvide usted; recuérdelo siempre, si es que pueden flotar mis palabras en su memoria, sobre este mar de fondo de su corazón.

—¿Me quiere usted, me ha dicho? . . .

—Hasta el sacrifio, sí.

—No la entiendo, o quizá es que no puedo entenderla en este momento.

—Yo nunca he amado a una mujer como a usted, hasta la renuncia, hasta la pureza de los sentidos, con estar los sentidos tan pendientes de ella . . .

Delia, calle usted. ¡Calle usted, por favor! Me trastornan sus palabras, porque no puedo ahora razonar. Ha hecho usted mal en elegir este momento para decírmelas: estoy indefensa. Pero de todos modos, creo no ha debido hacerlo nunca. ¡Qué lástima! Pierdo su casi amistad. Porque, usted sabe, yo no soy mujer que soporta estas situaciones. Le ruego me deje usted en la próxima esquina.

—Como usted quiera. Usted no puede comprender como yo la respeto y la estimo. ¡Oh, si usted supiera! Es aburrido. Quiero hacer de este amor una pequeña obra de arte, acaso una virtud moral . . . ¡Oh, si lo lograra! Yo creí que no había más sensaciones nuevas, y las hay, sí. En lo erótico, lo agoté todo; en lo lírico, estoy haciendo sorprendentes descubrimientos . . . (150–51)

["You're suffering so!"

"Thank you, Delia. You're very good to me."

"That's because I love you, Gertrudis, to the point of sacrifice. Don't forget it; remember it always, if my words are able to float in your memory, on that deep sea of your heart."

"You love me, you say?"

"To the point of sacrifice, yes."

"I don't understand you, or maybe I can't understand you right now."

"I've never loved another woman like I love you, to the point of abandon, to the purity of the senses, with my senses so dependent on her . . ."

"Delia, be quiet. Please be quiet! Your words are driving me mad because I can't think now. You picked a bad time to tell me this: I'm defenseless. But anyway, I don't think you ever should have done it. What a pity! I'm losing your almost-friendship. Because, you know, I'm not the kind of woman who can bear these situations. Please just let me out at the next corner."

"Whatever you want. You don't know how much I respect and admire you. Oh, if you only knew! It's boring. I want to turn this love into a little work of art, perhaps a moral virtue . . . Oh, if only I could! I thought there were no new sensations, but there are. In the erotic realm I went through them all, but in the lyrical realm I'm making surprising discoveries."]

Later, at a party where Gertrudis becomes terribly drunk, someone has sex with her. At first she doesn't know who did it: "Was it Damián? Félix? Antonio? Delia? Her desires were physically calmed, without her knowing how or by whom" (200).[5] It turns out to have been the person she least suspects: Fonseca, her friend from the office with whom she frequently converses. Nevertheless, the relationship between Gertrudis and Delia continues. In fact, once Gertrudis recovers somewhat from her constant melancholy and returns with renewed dedication to her job as a clerk, gossip about her personal and sexual life begins to circulate: "She even likes women. She lives with Delia. Don't you know who Delia is? Well Delia is . . ." (212)[6] Fonseca, the friend who essentially raped Gertrudis, says that "the worst things are said" about her: "That you live with Delia" (213).[7]

The text does not make completely clear if this comment has any truth to it, but this entire matter of lesbian desire and lesbian love remains significant. It seems that *La vida manda* is one of the very first Cuban novels to deal with this issue in such a clear fashion and with such sexual and romantic implications. Although Gertrudis seems to have a somewhat negative opinion of these relationships, she does not condemn them completely. It is important to point out here that the text of *La vida manda* mixes the question of lesbian relations with concepts of ideal love and sacrificial love. The narrative attempts to distinguish between erotic desire and ideal love. Love seems to acquire its greatest significance within this logic when it reaches "total sacrifice"—an obvious effort by the author to dematerialize the love between two persons, especially homosexual love.

In spite of the emphasis the text places on this vision of a dematerialized love, near the end of the novel is a section in which this romantic answer seems to be clearly negated:

> La Biología y la Fisiología venían poniendo los puntos sobre las íes en las relaciones sexuales de los hombres. Venían rajando el terrón, azúcares y sales, de la moral. Venían absorbiendo tanta lágrima tonta y explicando tanto conflicto pueril. Venían destruyendo el sentido falso, convencional, endeble, hipócrita de la virtud.
>
> Los hombres y las mujeres de la nueva generación, los niños aquellos que ella [Gertrudis] estaba viendo jugar, amarían con más valor y verdad,

5. Spanish original: "Era ¿Damián? ¿Félix? ¿Antonio? ¿Delia? Sus deseos fueron calmados físicamente, sin que ella supiera cómo ni por quién."

6. Spanish original: "Hasta le gustan las mujeres. Vive con Delia. No saben ustedes quién es Delia? Pues Delia es . . ."

7. Spanish original: "Se dice lo peor . . ." "Que vive con Delia."

y darían su vida a cosas más altas, serias y trascendentales que el amor. (231–32)

[Biology and Physiology were making things clear in men's sexual relations. They were breaking the back of sweet and sour morality. They were soaking up so many silly tears and explaining so much puerile conflict. They were destroying the false, conventional, weak, hypocritical sense of virtue.

The men and women of the new generation, those children that she [Gertrudis] was seeing at play, would love with the same valor and truth, and would give their lives to higher things, more serious and transcendent than love.]

Up to this point the text seemed dominated by a romantic logic. Now it seems to take up scientism.

La vida manda contains an ideological subtext that permeates the entire novel and constitutes a complication that is extremely contradictory and difficult to unravel. According to the (il)logic of this text, "life" is frequently a negative force culminating in destruction at the hands of the passions, but at other times the text seems to suggest that this "life" is a positive force, because it leads to events as sublime as childbirth and self-sacrificial love. This life is an imperative, which in the end "decrees" on account of its unstoppable, natural, and omnipotent power. At the end of the novel Gertrudis's misfortunes seem to be attributed to the force of life that she has been unable to avoid. This (il)logic becomes even more complicated when the text tells us that she must achieve a "salvation through art." Is this art the opposite of life? Everything would seem to lead to the conclusion that this art would be somehow opposed to the negative force of Life, but the text also tells us that art should come from nature. Although it is not clarified in the novel, if we follow this way of thinking, nature, more than brute force, is an ethical and esthetic idealization of a whole series of romantic principles and ideas. What is certain is that for Gertrudis, the negative force of life has somehow taken possession of social forces, since in the text the current state of society is spoken of disparagingly—a position seemingly at odds with much if not all of modernity.

All this leads us to conclude that Gertrudis's feminism fails precisely because it is riddled with unresolved contradictions: the imperative of life as a natural negative force that controls all of reality; the (failed) desire for salvation through art; (con)fusion between the "natural," the "esthetic," and the "ethical"; social antimodernist positions in spite of aspirations to a feminist modernity; an understanding of love between women coupled with a condemnation of that love; a rejection of machismo and the social roles imposed on women along with the desire to have a child (the solution by means of maternity) as last hope of salvation; and a historical yet biological response to sexual matters and the "human condition." In the face of this ideological knot the only escape seems to be death, and Gertrudis carries out this solution at the end of the novel with a botched suicide attempt. Here death is held up as a sort of utopia, a liberation from all problems, from life. In novels dealing with homosexuals, radical feminists, and others living outside the social norm, death is the typical solution to their plight, as it is in *La vida manda*. Gertrudis cannot overcome the social and psychological forces opposed to the radical change of society, so her "life decrees" are a complete failure.

In the Night of the World

Some twelve years after the publication of *La vida manda*, Ofelia Rodríguez Acosta published *En la noche del mundo* [In the night of the world], a novel featuring, a gay male couple. This text displays a greater ideological coherence regarding homosexuality than does *La vida manda*. Published in Havana at Manuel Altolaguirre's Verónica Press in August 1940, *En la noche del mundo* presents certain values and opinions that make it one of the most progressive literary texts—in terms of (homo)sexuality, above all—written in Cuba in the early twentieth century. The novel is actually a very complex text that attempts to represent a great many problems in an all-encompassing manner. Ironically, its broad coverage of so many issues is perhaps its greatest merit and its greatest failure. But the representation of gay relationships is somewhat coherent and worth studying with some attention.

Although many of the problems dealt with in this novel seem to be taken from the time of Machado's dictatorship, Rodríguez Acosta does not identify precisely the city in which the story takes place. All we do know is that it is a great modern city in a climate in which it snows, at the time of Hitler's invasion of Czechoslovakia. The characters of *En la noche del mundo* represent different types of individual and social issues, but they all react in various ways to the extreme and rapid modernization of their city and their world. Several, but not all, of the characters are related by family or by friendship. At the end of the text the enigmatic notation "Madrid-Paris" appears, but we do not know if the author had these two cities in mind when she wrote the novel or if that is where she wrote it.

One immediately notes the extreme class differences among the characters of *En la noche del mundo*. Almost all of them seem to be Hispanic, but several are poor, others are of the middle class, and a few are rich. They also represent a great variety of political orientations, since some are communists conspiring against the government, while others are wealthy defenders of the system, and several speak contemptuously of fascism as the greatest threat in the world. In these descriptions one notes much antipathy directed toward the wealthy characters. There is also a gay male couple. If there is such a thing as main characters in this far-reaching novel, one of them is certainly Pablo, a poor laborer who is thoughtful, extremely pessimistic, and enamored with existentialist ideas. His favorite philosopher is Nietzsche. Another very sui generis character is a girl who seems to be a visionary or soothsayer called *La Visionaria* (The visionary). Her behavior and comments are always highly idealistic, and her entire way of thinking goes against the materialistic stance of the modern world, the lack of poetic understanding it is governed by, and its fragmentation and alienation.

At one point in the narration Pablo tells La Visionaria that what she says are dreams, and if she were to write them in verse "no one would read them," because "romanticism is dead."[8] I read these statements as a semantic indication that any poetic or idealistic vision of the world is frequently associated in this novel with romanticism. Romanticism is viewed as pertaining to a poetic world that has almost completely disappeared as a horrible consequence of modernization, yet is perceived as perhaps a value worth recovering. This is why La Visionaria represents a poetic space within modernity as she tries to somehow resist this same modernity. In other words, she is a product of modernity who aspires to be a space of resistance to a certain kind of utilitarian modern life. In this sense, the novel is geared toward an anti-utilitarian romanticism that can be considered a possible solution to the ideological tensions of the text. In fact, perhaps this solution represents one of the ideological paradoxes of Rodríguez Acosta's worldview in this and other works.

En la noche del mundo is also full of allusions to consumerism and the logic of modern fragmentation. According to the novel, mass culture is invading every aspect of society, and its characters almost always react

8. Ofelia Rodríguez Acosta, *En la noche del mundo* (Havana: La Verónica, 1940), 24.

negatively to this phenomenon. As far as writing style is concerned, the text's descriptions frequently employ a language typical of Spanish American *modernismo*, but the narration of the events lies mainly within the realm of literary realism. In the midst of this atmosphere, two characters named Emilio and José Luis appear. They are a gay couple in the present-day sense of the term. Emilio is very much in love with José Luis, and, at least at first, José Luis seems to have quite a bit of affection for Emilio. In their first scene, José Luis has a very bad case of the flu, and Emilio watches over him with extreme tenderness and care. This initial representation of the gay couple in a nonsexualized situation is significant, since it immediately implies that the relationship is not based solely or principally on sexual contact but rather on love and attention to emotional and other needs. This is why such a representation impairs even the term *homosexual*, since it affirms the possibility of homosexual desire yet places it on a level of love and tenderness apart from an exclusively carnal situation. The relationship between Emilio and José Luis, therefore, is not only homo-sexual but also homo-tender, homo-loving, homo-attentive, homo-nurturing.

The gay couple of Emilio and José Luis is represented in a domestic atmosphere very different from the jail of Carlos Montenegro's *Hombres sin mujer* (to be studied in chapter 5) or the complete rejection and isolation of Alfonso Hernández Catá's *El ángel de Sodoma* (see chapter 4). It is also significant that Rodríguez Acosta chooses a gay male couple and not a lesbian one. As we saw in the first section of this chapter, although *La vida manda* features a lesbian who assumes her homosexuality, the lesbian couple is never described explicitly as such, and much about this relationship is quite hidden and ambiguous. In contrast, the gay male couple in *En la noche del mundo* appears in a much more defined, open, and positive fashion. Their situation is also significant because it differs from the deterministic atmosphere of naturalism (as in *Hombres sin mujer*) or the scientist implications of that naturalism (as in *El ángel de Sodoma*). Indeed, they are situated within a whole global, political, and social context that puts their relationship into historical perspective.

In the first scene featuring Emilio and José Luis, a heterosexual character named Gabriel visits them. Through Gabriel and Emilio's conversation we learn much about all these characters. Gabriel, followed by Emilio, says:

> —¡Bah! Lo pasa uno bien [se refiere a una fiesta a la que ha asistido]. Para ti, que no hay en el mundo más que José Luis y tus pinceles, no

tiene eso interés. Tú te has hecho una vida, pudiera decirse, al margen de la vida.

—Es verdad; el amor de José Luis primero, y mi arte después, y nada más . . . ¿para qué otra cosa?—y miró al enfermo fervorosamente—. Tenemos nuestro mundo—continuó, arrellanándose en la butaca con movimientos reposados,—y nada fuera de él nos importa. La gente se agita en afanes vulgares, incomprensibles: la política, el dinero, las diversiones. . . . Todo estupideces y groserías . . .

—¿Ves, Gabriel? Ya es de día; un día extraño y seco, de un invierno caprichoso. Hemos visto amanecer muchas veces aquí: alejados de todo y de todos. Solos, plenos de nuestro querer. A veces ni apagamos la luz eléctrica. Insensibles al paso de las horas conservamos aquí dentro de nuestro ambiente personal, mientras allá afuera dos hombres luchan tonta y baldíamente. Amigo, lo que se llama amigo, eres tú el único . . . el único que nos comprende.

—Si ustedes quieren vivir así no veo por qué se les ha de encontrar mal. Yo lo acepto todo: nada me asombra ni me esclaviza. Todo lo encuentro posible y natural. Cada cual debe hacer lo que le da la gana, y ya está. (39–40)

["Bah! I just had a good time (at a party he has attended.) For you, there's nothing in the world but José Luis and your brushes, so that's not interesting. You've lived your life, you could say, at the margin of life."

"It's true; first comes José Luis's love, my art next, and then nothing . . . What do I need anything else for?" He looked ardently at the sick man. "We have our world," he continued, sitting back in the armchair with restful movements, "and nothing outside of it matters to us. People get all worked up over vulgar, incomprehensible things: politics, money, amusements. . . . All idiotic and vulgar things . . ."

"You see, Gabriel? It's daylight now; a strange dry day in a fickle winter. We've seen the sunrise many times here, far away from everything and everyone. Alone, full of our love. Sometimes, we don't even switch off the lights. Unaware of the passing of the hours we keep our personal atmosphere safe inside here, while out there two men struggle, stupidly and in vain. My friend, my true friend, you're the only one . . . the only one who understands us."

"If you want to live this way I don't see why they should find it reprehensible. I accept it all: it doesn't shock or overburden me at all. I think it's entirely possible and natural. Everyone should do what they want, and that's that."]

This dialogue shows that Emilio adores José Luis, and that his love is sincere and powerful. It is also obvious that from Gabriel's point of view, gays have the right to do whatever they want with their desires, and that he perceives this relationship as something natural. What we are witnessing in this conversation is basically the description or representation of a marriage between two men, not a *homosexual* relationship in the scientistic sense of the term. In this novel the stereotype of homosexual relations has been overcome or at least redefined. Nevertheless, it seems that Rodríguez Acosta limits the life these gay men have together to the closet (at least partially) and that she has them represent a form of private resistance to social norms. At any rate, this representation is really quite radical for a culture in which virtually all other representations of gays and lesbians are monstrous: the pervert, the prostitute, the degenerate, the carrier of venereal diseases, the sinner, the traitor to his/her country, the deviate, the "woman-less man," the overbearing killer. Now we have two lovers who care for each other deeply and who are represented as dignified beings who have the right to live out their relationship without any outside interference.

Other interesting aspects about the gay couple are described in the novel. Emilio is an artist, a painter, thereby establishing an association between the gay male and artistic sensibility that can be read in some other Cuban texts (see, for example, my study of the character Diego in chapter 9). In fact, Emilio insists that his art is an anti-utilitarian "pure art" that scorns the "vulgar" world of consumerism. In this sense, Emilio's art comes to be an esthetic realization of some of Gertrudis's ethical ideals in *La vida manda*. The implication of this association of gay men with an anti-utilitarian artistic sensibility is quite telling: in Rodríguez Acosta's *En la noche del mundo* the esthetic and poetic aspects of culture are associated with gayness. Here I can notice the contrast between this vision and Martí's, for example, where the poetic, ethical, and esthetic social values are contrasted with homoeroticism. In *En la noche del mundo* alienation is associated with vulgarity and intransigence, and gayness with the artistic and the poetic. This novel pairs the alienation of the modern artist with marginal homosexuality, and both are constructed in a poetic space from which utilitarian and "vulgar" modernity is resisted. The image of the gay man in this novel is quite different from those of the *pederasta* or the *maricón* (faggot) as portrayed in other Cuban texts.

The narrative of *En la noche del mundo* is full of negative comments about the city: "in this morning of the city, an oppressive fever and anxiety floated in the air. Synthesis of a civilization in which the last trace of human personality was lost. . . . This dissatisfaction was a general phenomenon: perhaps the most important thing about the symptomology of the times" (149–51).[9] In spite of these basic ideological tensions within the text, the narrator's statements can be read as an attempt to construct a modern romantic reaction that contrasts itself with utilitarian modernity and that tries to create an antipositivist space of resistance where the poetic vision can hold sway. In fact, Emilio's painting clearly symbolizes an artistic vision that tries to fill the void left by modern life.

But the character who seems to be Rodríguez Acosta's alter ego in the novel is a female lawyer named Natalia. This character is represented in a very positive fashion, in sharp contrast with Gertrudis in *La vida manda*. Natalia says that she is preparing a book on sexual matters. She finds, however, that not only men are opposed to her ideas, but also the women who reject her feminism. For example, Leticia, Gabriel's wife, reproaches Natalia for her feminism: " 'Your devotion to the feminist cause is astonishing . . . that faith you have in women: I don't believe in them, nor in the 'woman' you defend' " (80).[10] Natalia embodies the ideals of radical feminism, since she has no intention or desire to marry. Moreover, it is implied that she sees nothing wrong with lesbian relations. In the face of Gabriel's insistent declarations of love, Natalia replies, "I don't believe in marriage; I don't want to marry you or anyone else," (190)[11] and she adds, "I don't want to get married or engaged at all" (191).[12] Gabriel, who is renowned as a Don Juan and is on the verge of divorcing his wife, feels very hurt by Natalia's rejection and tells her angrily that "no woman has resisted me" (ibid.).[13] At this point in the story Gabriel is represented as an incorrigible *macho*, although he seems understanding of the gay relations between Emilio and José Luis. This paradoxical behavior

9. Spanish original: "en esta mañana de la ciudad, flotaba en el ambiente una fiebre y una inquietud opresoras. Síntesis de una civilización en la que se perdía la ínfima personalidad humana. [. . .] Esto de la insatisfacción era un fenómeno general: quizá más importante de la sintomatología de la época."

10. Spanish original: "Es asombroso su devoción por la causa feminista—agregó Leticia —esa fe que tiene usted en la mujer. Yo no creo en ella: en la 'ella' que usted defiende."

11. Spanish original: "no creo en el matrimonio, que no quiero casarme ni con usted ni con nadie."

12. Spanish original: "no quiero casarme ni comprometerme en forma alguna."

13. Spanish original: "ninguna mujer me ha resistido."

seems to imply that Rodríguez Acosta's ambivalence toward machismo has not been completely resolved.

In *La noche del mundo*, Rodríguez Acosta's political position is a socialist democracy that aspires to social and economic justice and in which the rights of marginal groups are advanced. Above all, this novel criticizes nascent fascism, "economic imperialisms," and "the white terror" (ibid.). A proletarian vision of the world is affirmed, but with certain objections, since at various times in the novel the author expresses her distrust of the dictatorial characteristics of the communist world of the period. In reality, the novel does not progress toward an optimistic vision but rather an apocalyptic end of the world, hence its title. It also prophesies the Second World War, which occurred shortly after the work was published. The novel foretells and itself moves toward the terrible holocaust produced by the encounter of the political and ideological forces that buried the social achievements of the previous decades.

Following this apocalyptic progression, José Luis separates from Emilio because he has fallen in love with a woman and plans to marry her, implying that José Luis is basically bisexual. Significantly, despite this estrangement between the gay lovers, their final destiny is far from the suicide or murder of the representations of homosexuals in most of the works analyzed in the first and second sections of this study. Next, Gabriel kills Natalia out of *machista* (male-oriented sexism) frustration for not wanting to marry him, and Pablo commits suicide over the senselessness of the war and life; there is a series of strikes, university riots, killing of citizens by security forces, and radios announcing the showdown with fascism, communism, and the "economic oligarchies." Finally, the war that causes everything to collapse arrives. The last voice heard in the novel is that of La Visionaria, who speaks highly idealized and poetic words of hope.

From the national point of view, Rodríguez Acosta suffered through the struggles against Machado and the disillusionment in the aftermath of the dictator's fall. In the international arena, Hitler, Stalin, Mussolini and Franco had come to power in Europe by 1940, with all the political and social consequences that those forces represented. In the novel, however, Rodríguez Acosta prefers to take the road to an apocalypse that in the end is weakly contained by La Visionaria's utopic vision, an extremely idealized solution. La Visionaria is a rather alienated woman who views the world optimistically because she lives only to interpret her own dreams in a crazed fashion. Although this is an absurd solution to the ills around her, her utopia opens a small glimpse or space that enables a form of resistance, from which other alternatives to a historically hopeless situation can be conceived.

In the end, this final solution presented by *En la noche del mundo* is not the only possibility the text suggests. For example, the solution could have been a feminist utopia, with Natalia guiding the process in which feminism would lead the world to a better future, a world in which the abusive systems based on false gender, race, and class differences have been overcome. Or, the text could have taken the route of Emilio's artistic solution, an anti-utilitarian cultural utopia having queer overtones and allying with feminism. The text also could have taken Pablo's solution, existentialism paired with a panoramic vision that sees everything from a distance and from the point of view of a failed worker. These feminist, queer, leftist, and other alternatives are reading possibilities that occur in this novel at different points in the story, contributing to making it a text with other possible horizons. Rodríguez Acosta's radical feminism can make new associations that allow for new spaces for gay men and lesbians, and it does so from an anti-utilitarian, antipositivist, and antireligious position. But even in this radical feminism, nationalism remains the umbrella under which all these social and political possibilities are situated. What is never questioned is nationalism itself.

★ F O U R ★

Another Positivist (Trans)Formation

Some of the earliest representations of homosexuality in the role of a protagonist in Cuban literature come from the pen of Alfonso Hernández Catá (1885–1940). The insistence and centrality with which his representations treat the question of queerness in the Hispanic world of the early twentieth century are significant. Hernández Catá's first novel on this matter, *La juventud de Aurelio Zaldívar* (Aurelio Zaldívar's youth), was published in 1911.[1] This work appeared in Madrid rather than Havana, and is a very ambiguous text that addresses homosexuality obliquely. Some of his later works, especially *El ángel de Sodoma* (The angel of Sodom) from 1928, lose this ambiguity to demonstrate a central and sustained interest in the homosexual theme.[2] Also indicative of the social and discursive changes occurring during the 1920s and 1930s in the Western countries is the fact that the English-speaking world received Marguerite Radclyffe-Hall's influential novel, *The Well of Loneliness*, in 1928—the

1. Alfonso Hernández Catá, *La juventud de Aurelio Zaldívar* (Aurelio Zaldívar's youth) (Madrid: Biblioteca Renacimiento, V. Prieto y Compañía, 1911).
2. Alfonso Hernández Catá, *El ángel de Sodoma* (The angel of Sodom) (Madrid: Mundo Latino, 1928). Here I should remind the reader that Ofelia Rodríguez Acosta's novel *La vida manda* (Life decrees), which I studied in chapter 3, was also written in 1928 (and published in 1929). Although it deals with the theme of lesbianism briefly, homosexuality does not assume a leading role in the text.

same year that *El ángel de Sodoma* was published and Ofelia Rodríguez Acosta's *La vida manda* was written.[3]

There are special circumstances in Hernández Catá's life, however, that may explain his literary precociousness. He was born in 1885 of a Spanish father and a Cuban mother in the Spanish province of Salamanca, his father's homeland. A few months after his birth the family moved to Santiago de Cuba, where Hernández Catá lived during the War of Independence and at the age of nine witnessed the burial of José Martí. His only formal schooling was in the Colegio de Don Juan Portuondo and the Instituto de Segunda Enseñanza de Santiago de Cuba. In 1901, having barely reached the age of sixteen, he was sent by his family to Toledo, Spain, to attend the School of Military Orphans; his father, a lieutenant colonel in the Spanish army, was now dead. Hernández Catá left the military academy for Madrid, and from that point onward his life was a constant journey through and between Europe and Latin America. In 1907 he married and also published his first book, *Cuentos pasionales* (Passional stories).[4] By 1911, when *La juventud de Aurelio Zaldívar* was published, he had written other novels.

Hernández Catá returned to Cuba on several occasions, keeping in touch with its writers and intellectuals and serving as a diplomat for the republic for many years. In 1940 he died in an aviation accident in the Bahía de Botafogo near Río de Janeiro.[5] These biographical data are important to our study, since they show that Hernández Catá, who was legally Cuban, proud of his nationality, and in constant contact with the island's culture, can also be considered a Spanish writer: almost all of his extensive work was published in Spain, even though many of his texts were also read with interest in his homeland. Moreover, it can be argued that his cosmopolitan upbringing gave him the advantage of an early familiarity with the European opinion on homosexuality and other related matters.

Although Hernández Catá touches on the theme of homosexuality in several of his writings, I will limit my study to his novel *El ángel de Sodoma*. As the best known of his works, it has also brought him the reputation of being the first novelist to give a protagonist's role to male

3. Marguerite Radclyffe-Hall, *The Well of Loneliness* (Paris: Privately printed, 1928; reprint, New York: Pocket Books, 1950).

4. Alfonso Hernández Catá, *Cuentos pasionales* (Passional stories) (Madrid: M. Pérez de Villavicencio, 1907).

5. See Uva A. Clavijo, "Modernismo y modernidad en la narrativa de Alfonso Hernández Catá" (Ph.D. diss., University of Miami, 1991), especially pages 1–20.

homosexuality in the Hispanic world. Strictly speaking, this distinction is not correct, since eight years before this novel was published the Chilean Augusto D'Halmar had written *La pasión y muerte del cura Deusto* (The passion and death of Father Deusto), which was published in 1924.[6] In Cuba even before the 1920s, narratives such as *Las impuras* (The impure ones) (1919) by Miguel de Carrión and *Lujuria: Cuentos nefandos* (Lust: abominable stories) (1914) by Miguel de Marcos addressed same-sex sexuality. In reality, primacy is of little importance in studying the work of Hernández Catá, but since the point has been debated among the critics for several years, it may be worthwhile to clarify this detail here.

Hernández Catá's texts, contrary to Martí's, for example, do not imply a harmonious world that would overcome modern fragmentation through poetry; instead his narratives chronicle this fragmentation, focusing on precisely the changes that modernity and modernization have supposedly brought about. His novels and short stories seem to encourage his readers to take delight, with surprise and a little fear, in what is happening in the world. Although they contain moralizing and homophobia, it is a moralizing and a homophobia that seems to take pleasure in alarming yet enchanting or seducing their bourgeois audience, showing what is taking place in society. I also believe that some of his narrative texts are obviously influenced by certain positivist ideas on homosexuality and other areas of human behavior. This, as we shall see, is the case with *El ángel de Sodoma*.

The first noteworthy aspect of this novel's best-known second edition is that despite being a short work (188 pages), it is framed by a 30-page prologue written by Dr. Gregorio Marañón, and a 16-page epilogue by the lawyer and criminologist Luis Jiménez de Asúa.[7] With these "appendices" to the narration, the text is saying from the start that Hernández Catá's novel needs the justification and authority of a physician (a specialist in endocrinology, the branch of medicine that at the time claimed with greatest insistence to know the truth about homosexuality) and of a lawyer (who determined the new direction that society ought to take in terms of the legal aspects of homosexuality).

Dr. Marañón was a highly important figure in the Hispanic world of the period (and even well into the 1950s). In Latin America as well as in Spain, he wielded great influence, especially in relation to

6. Augusto D'Halmar, *La pasión y muerte del Cura Deusto* (The passion and death of Father Deusto) (Madrid: Editora Internacional, 1924; 3d ed., Santiago: Nascimento, 1969).

7. Hernández Catá, *El ángel de Sodoma*, prologue by Gregorio Marañón and epilogue by Luis Jiménez Azúa.

(homo)sexual matters. His ideas were especially prominent in Cuba starting in the 1920s. As I mentioned in chapter 3, in 1928 Mariblanca Sabas Alomá, one of Cuba's most visible and controversial feminists, brought Marañón's ideas into public debate, arguing that the Spanish doctor placed too much emphasis on the biological determinants of sexual orientation.[8]

Marañón's first concern in the prologue to *El ángel de Sodoma* is the dissemination of information related to the "sexual instinct"; he asks himself which moral problems a scientist should address when publishing his research in this field. Marañón claims to be so thoughtful and careful in this regard that he must be convinced that he "is doing the right thing" before publishing anything about homosexuality or intersexuality (he occasionally uses these terms synonymously). Nevertheless, he worries that the "almost autonomous character" of such studies might produce an uncontrollable problem when published, since once in the hands of the readers the text and the author's intentions part company.

With this conception of the writer's responsibility, Marañón tries to defend himself against the criticism of some of his earlier works on the same topic. His objective here is twofold: to try to contain conceptual dissemination, and to try to maintain, assure, and augment the authority of the positivist-medical discourse in matters concerning sexuality. He implies that this objective is achieved by asserting the truth value of his discourse's content, and by responding in the best possible way to traditional moral sensibilities when distributing information on sexual matters. Not surprisingly, for Marañón as well as for many intellectuals of the period, the contents of such writings are dangerous in that they can be misinterpreted by some readers, while others can take them to be pornographic. Despite this risk, scientific studies make for profitable reading, owing to the truth value attributed to them by society. What is more, this positivist-medical discourse denies that "the sexual problem" is "without solution."[9] For Marañón, "religion and moral solutions" have not brought, in so many centuries of rule over societies, the best answer to the problem, because they are not based on empirical science. In contrast, science liberates society from its mistaken traditional positions regarding sexual "aberrations," although this deliverance may come at a price: the risk of dissemination and misinterpretation of these studies by the unprepared reader.

8. Mariblanca Sabas Alomá, *Feminismo: cuestiones sociales—crítica literaria*. Havana: Editorial Hermes, 1930.

9. Marañón, prologue to Hernández Catá, *El ángel de Sodoma*, 20, 40.

According to Marañón, the contents of Hernández Catá's *El ángel de Sodoma* agree with those of scientific books on homosexuality, and this is as it should be, since "art and science nourish themselves from the same substance, which is life and its mysteries" (22).[10] In other words, once he discredits the religious and traditionally moralistic discourse, he works to assimilate or hinder the artistic or literary discourse, which had established itself at that time as possessing considerable authority. He proposes that scientistic discourse eliminate, at least partially, the autonomy of art. By assimilating two of the dominant discourses of the period (the religious and the literary), Marañón's scientistic discourse acquires great credence, which, of course, coincides with the authority that positivist discourse had acquired in Western countries since the nineteenth century.

For Marañón there is no clear division between art and science, for everything is science. Even so-called literary works appear now as scientific documents. Marañón contradicts himself a bit here, since on the one hand he declares that *El ángel de Sodoma* is the first novel on homosexuality to appear in Hispanic culture (overlooking *La pasión y muerte del cura Deusto*, *La juventud de Aurelio Zaldívar*, and other works), and on the other he assures his readers that these matters of sexual psychology "have been until very recently exclusively literary themes, and for that reason, all of modern sexual science feeds from, in part, inevitably, literature" (24–25).[11] It is clear that Marañón is thinking of Freud here, and of the inspiration that some of his ideas found in literature. But Marañón also says that, in addition to the Viennese psychoanalyst, two other sexologists have had a great influence upon him: Havelock Ellis and Iwan Block.[12]

Marañón views homosexuality as an error or incompleteness in human evolution, thereby reflecting the social Darwinism of his thought. He naturalizes the idea that evolution is a process of ascension to human perfection, which reaches its zenith in heterosexuality, specifically the heterosexuality of the virile male. But, contrary to the writings of Enrique José Varona and Dr. Benjamín de Céspedes, which I studied in section 1, Marañón insists that society be tolerant and understanding

10. Spanish original: "arte y ciencia se nutren de la misma substancia, que es la vida y sus misterios."

11. Spanish original: "han sido temas exclusivamente literarios hasta hace poco tiempo, y por ello toda la ciencia sexual moderna se nutre, en parte inevitablemente, de literatura."

12. For an account of Havelock Ellis's role in the spread of the term *homosexual*, see Jeffrey Weeks, *Coming Out: Homosexual Politics in Britain from the Turn of the Nineteenth Century to the Present*, rev. ed. (London: Quartet Books Limited, 1983), 3.

of homosexuals, treating them "as one treats a diabetic."[13] Homosexuality is a sort of deficiency in human evolution, but it is not a crime or a vice. All human beings possess certain bisexual traits as an "obligatory and fleeting phase,"[14] although when development is abnormal, intersexuality or homosexuality is the result. (It seems that Marañón occasionally differentiates between these two terms and proposes that homosexuality is "an intersexuality of the instinct" (33),[15] implying that intersexuality includes physical sexual abnormalities, whereas homosexuality is an error in the object of desire.)

For Marañón, the homosexual is the "offspring of strayed development" (30)[16] though not ill in the individual sense; nor is he a monster, nor a delinquent. *"Sexual abnormalities are not to be fought by uprooting them with force, but rather by blinding the source of their origin"* (32–33; emphasis in the text).[17] The remedy that "blinds the source" of the "abnormalities" is a "strengthening of the differentiation of the sexes, exalting the masculinity of men and the femininity of women" (ibid.).[18] To that end, Marañón proposes a pedagogy of obligatory heteronormativity to keep the "sexes" from contaminating each other. Marañón's statements clearly indicate that his ideology contains a (con)fusion and naturalization, very well established in his positivist discourse, between sex and gender, between chromosomal differences and gender roles. In this way the genders are naturalized and essentialist norms are established.

Marañón concludes his prologue by revisiting the theme of the danger of disseminating scientific information about sexuality, specifically that readers will misinterpret it or regard it as pornography. The solution to this practical and moral problem is to avoid details on sexual questions; in the "book of literature," the writer can and should deal with the problems of sexual psychology but without entering into details that could foster prurient readings. Hernández Catá's novel, asserts Marañón, belongs to that class of "sublime works" (36)[19] because

13. Spanish original: "como pudiera serlo el diabético." Jiménez de Asúa, epilogue to Hernández Catá, *El ángel de Sodoma*, 244.

14. Spanish original: "fase obligada y pasajera." Marañón, prologue to Hernández Catá, *El ángel de Sodoma*, 29.

15. Spanish original: "una intersexualidad del instinto."

16. Spanish original: "hijo de un extravío evolutivo."

17. Spanish original: *"Las anomalías del sexo no se combaten extirpándolas por la violencia, sino cegando la fuente que las origina"* (emphasis in the original).

18. Spanish original: "fortificar la diferenciación de los sexos, exaltar la varonía de los hombres y la feminidad de las mujeres."

19. Spanish original: "obras excelsas."

he treats so dangerous a matter as homosexuality, which ought only to be dealt with in a "book of science" and read by those trained for such reading, with great "delicacy"(a lack of details on sexual activity), by avoiding "sinful information" (sexual details). In spite of everything, Marañón does not completely cast aside religious rhetoric, thereby reinforcing the social power of his own discourse. Thus, the *modernista* style of Hernández Catá, with its elegant prose that sidesteps sexual explicitness, serves to ideologically contain the "dangerous" aspects or descriptions of homosexuality. Therein lies the book's value, according to Marañón.

But he also gives the following warning: "If anyone is unaware that, by the law of nature, there is a class of love bereft of the indescribable happiness of finding its complement in someone of the opposite sex, and if that person ought not to know such facts, this book should not fall into his hands" (37–38).[20] In this statement I should emphasize not only Marañón's desire to contain the misinterpretation of his writings, but also his affirmation of traditional heterosexual marriage as the only coupling that can bring about an "indescribable happiness." He assures the reader that *El ángel de Sodoma* is exemplary and useful, and that the text has moral virtue because "no man, upon turning the last page of this brief and impassioned book, will have before his eyes any image other than that of a noble, normal and fervent exaltation of Woman" (41).[21] It is also revealing that the doctor refers to homosexuality as "a love bereft, by the law of nature . . . of finding its complement" (38). As is customary in this type of discourse, the argument of the natural is brandished to defend the cultural, to allow ideological concepts to be naturalized but without defining exactly what "natural" means.

Before beginning our reading of Hernández Catá's novel, I believe it would be profitable to discuss Jiménez de Asúa's epilogue. This famous Spanish criminologist, besides reaffirming some of the ideas of the prologue, asserts that the novel is in agreement with "the most modern biological concepts."[22] He reports that Hernández Catá studied these matters thoroughly before writing his story, and that the

20. Spanish original: "Si alguien ignora que hay una clase de amor privado, por la ley de la naturaleza, de la inefable dicha de encontrar su complemento en un ser de sexo diferente, y si a ese alguien no le conviene conocer tal verdad, este libro no deberá caer en sus manos."

21. Spanish original: "Tengo por cierto que ningún hombre, al volver la última página del breve y apasionado libro, tendrá delante de sus ojos otra imagen que una noble, normal y fervorosa exaltación de la mujer."

22. Jiménez de Asúa, epilogue to Hernández Catá, *El ángel de Sodoma*, 242.

author "demonstrates to us the congenital nature of homosexualism" (243)—although it is actually unclear how the novel "demonstrates" this "nature" or cause, or in what sense Jiménez de Asúa can ensure this "demonstration." With even more insistence than Marañón, he declares that modern science has demonstrated the "organic origin" of homosexuality. As an international activist favoring legal reforms, he also uses the epilogue to attack the legal codes of Germany, Switzerland, Italy, Spain, and Chile for including homosexual practices among their crimes, demonstrating his familiarity with the works of Magnus Hirschfeld and other German legal reformers of the period. In the process he mentions his participation in the Second Congress on Sexual Reform, which was held in Copenhagen in July 1928; there the German penal code of 1927 was condemned.

Jiménez de Asúa also complains about maltreatment on account of his "progressive" position: "I have been the victim of clumsy attacks from the reactionary press, and even Government persecution, for having stated clearly, and in a clearly scientific fashion, problems of eugenics and sexology" (247).[23] But although he has openly protested the criminalization of homosexuality, he maintains that those who believe that *invertidos* (homosexuals) are defective don't realize "that they are truly ill" (ibid.).[24] All these statements lead me to conclude that Jiménez de Asúa was an exponent and propagator not only of legal reform but also of that which today is called the medical model of homosexuality: a representation of the homosexual in terms labeling him physically and mentally ill, replacing the traditional religious terms used in earlier representations.

Jiménez de Asúa's references in the epilogue to the ongoing public debates on homosexuality in Spain are illuminating for my study of Hernández Catá's work while revealing the struggle at the time among power discourses about homosexuality. According to the criminologist, the most important of these debates was the one occurring between him and Father Francisco Sureda Blanco, a Catholic priest who adopted what could be called the moralist-religious position of the time. In this view, positivists such as Marañón and Jiménez de Asúa were extremists who corrupted morality. As Jiménez de Asúa says,

23. Spanish original: "Yo he sufrido arremetidas torpes de los periódicos reaccionarios, y hasta persecución del Gobierno, por exponer serenamente, con designio científico, problemas de eugenesia y sexuología."

24. Spanish original: "sin percatarse de que son verdaderamente enfermos." *Invertido*, along with *homosexual* and *intersexual*, is the term preferred by scientists and lawyers of the period, as well as by Hernández Catá in this novel.

La novela de Hernández Catá que ahora epilogo y la obra magnífica de Gregorio Marañón tampoco se libran de la atolondrada revista de Sureda. Con su dogmatismo típico sentencia: "Si Hernández Catá divulga la miserable figura del martirio del anormal en *El ángel de Sodoma*, nos dirá al mismo tiempo el Dr. Marañón en *Los estados intersexuales de la especie humana*, que las aberraciones morales son estados morbosos. . . ." Para Sureda, sin disputa el homosexualismo no es un estado patológico de preferente orgía congénita, sino un vicio, una "aberración moral." . . . Esperemos confiadamente en que semejantes prejuicios serán barridos del orbe y que llegará un día en que los homosexuales estarán mirados como enfermos y no como delincuentes. (251–53)

[Neither Hernández Catá's novel, to which I now write the epilogue, nor the magnificent work by Gregorio Marañón can escape Sureda's reckless review. With his typical dogmatism he declares: "If Hernández Catá puts into circulation the wretched figure of the martyrdom of the abnormal in *El ángel de Sodoma*, Dr. Marañón tells us at the same time in *Los estados intersexuales de la especie humana* that moral aberrations are unhealthy states. . . ." For Sureda, homosexuality is undoubtedly not a pathological state of preferential congenital orgy but rather a vice, a "moral aberration." . . . Let us confidently hope that such prejudices will be swept from the face of the earth and that there will come a day when homosexuals will be seen as ill and not as delinquents.]

The epilogue ends with the same idea put forth in Marañón's prologue: the good example of the protagonist, José-María, who prefers death to "surrender." Marañón adds something more along these lines near the end of his article: that "the very force of his vitality" (read "the force of 'nature' ") "pushes [José-María] step by step towards death."[25] Once again scientistic discourse fights traditional religious arguments while at the same time creating a repressive discourse in the name of the natural (which, of course, is the dominion of science). What is hidden or at least contained in all these assertions is that José-María's suicide was caused by the social values of his culture, not "the natural."

Let us now examine how the novel tries to adapt itself to Marañón and Jiménez de Asúa's ideas and in the process produces some very revealing paradoxes. *El ángel de Sodoma* was Hernández Catá's most controversial narrative. The predominant theme in the story is the

---

25. Spanish original: "la fuerza de la vitalidad . . . empuja [a José-María] paso a paso hacia la muerte." Marañón, prologue to Hernández Catá, *El ángel de Sodoma*, 39.

unpracticed homosexuality of José-María Vélez-Gomara, who to his Spanish village seems to be the ideal youth: he is a wholesome person who takes good care of his two sisters and brother, and he carries his family name with honor. The plot is quite straightforward: While at the circus, José-María is dazzled by the physical beauty of a male trapeze artist. This reaction tortures him exceedingly, and he tries in vain to avoid or alleviate this attraction and to keep his "secret." After trying everything he can think of to keep from falling into homosexual practices, he resorts to traditional courtship, but after several months of banal relations with a young village woman named Cecilia, he is convinced that he cannot channel his desires in that direction. José-María's last chance is to go to Paris: there, in the anonymity of the great modern city, he would be able to express his homosexual desires unfettered. Paris is, after all, "the capital of sin," and its large size would allow him to forget the family name. Once there he meets a man, and they make a date for the next day. But just before he is to make his rendezvous, he receives a letter from someone in his village that reminds him of the honor associated with his name. The renewed guilt that ensues causes José-María to commit suicide by throwing himself on train tracks: "A long wail of steel and cries passed over his flesh, virgin and impure."[26]

The symbol that in José-María's mind represents the family honor is the Vélez-Gomara crest. The uncontrollable feelings of guilt that lead him to suicide revolve around the Name of the Father, which manifests itself in the memory of Santiago, José-María's biological father. This internalization of the Oedipal formation is highly contradictory. In fact, it could be said that the text deconstructs itself here, since we are told that Santiago, far from being an ideal father or paternal role model, was in reality an alcoholic wife abuser with many other personal defects. What is more, the story reveals that the gender roles of José-María's parents were switched. Here, following a Freudian orientation in the most superficial sense, Hernández Catá adds to the possible "genetic causes" of homosexuality that of an inverted Oedipal upbringing: José-María's father was a "dreamer of dreams not of multiplication but of subtraction," while his mother was "active, industrious, vulgar and practical" (ibid.).[27] Both parents die while their children are still young; in his only "heroic" paternal act, the father has killed himself so that

26. Spanish original: "Un largo estrépito de hierro y de gritos pasó sobre su carne virgen e impura." Hernández Catá, El ángel de Sodoma, 235.

27. Spanish original: "soñador de sueños no multiplicadores, sino de resta," "activa, hacendosa, vulgar y práctica." Ibid.

his children can collect on his life insurance policy. José-María, being the eldest, takes on the responsibility of raising his brother and sisters; he also takes on, or should take on, the Name of the Father. If the causes of José-María's homosexuality are physiological, as Marañón and Jiménez de Asúa maintain, the novel seems to contradict itself by adding psychoanalytic Freudian elements to the ideology implicit in the text.

Another element of José-María's conflict is the *gossip* factor, in other words the social pressure against homosexual practices, represented by the gossip in his village. Consequently, he is obliged to travel to Paris in order to experiment with homosexuality. But the novel does not completely abandon the physiological factor, nor that of the naturalization of gender roles; rather, it proceeds by the accumulation of all these ideas. First, the text implies that the protagonist's very name symbolizes his ambiguous sexuality: he is on the one hand *José* and on the other *María*, masculine and feminine together in one person. In addition, the good job he does in raising his brother and sisters earns him the title "a real mommy." José-María also has a certain contour in his hips and a lack of body hair, which are said to symbolize his hormonal problem in terms of his gender, his "hermaphroditism": "The pre-pubescent skin, the swelling forms, completed an image preceded by this thinking. An ambiguous halo of flesh and forms undecided between the genders distinguished his torso from Jaime's [his younger brother] hairier one. A mistaken neglect rounded off his features" (101).[28]

As is customary, scientistic positions, while trying to discredit religious discourse, do not completely abandon some of the latter rhetoric. In *El ángel de Sodoma* it is frequently mentioned that José-María wants to have sexual relations that are "sinful." I can note that from the diatribes of Varona and Céspedes to those of Marañón, Jiménez de Asúa, and Hernández Catá, scientistic-positivist discourse, in its desire to achieve power and authority, makes two contradictory but tactically effective moves: it discredits religious discourse (so powerful in that society), yet it uses that discourse in its rhetoric when convenient to affirm its power over its readers. Scientistic discourse also applies other types of arguments, such as psychoanalysis. Accordingly, in *El ángel de Sodoma*, Hernández Catá does not limit himself to presenting a case

28. Spanish original: "La piel impúber, las formas tárgidas, completaban la imagen ya anticipada por el pensamiento. Un halo ambiguo, de carne y de formas indecisas entre los dos sexos, diferenciaba su torso del velludo de Jaime [su hermano menor]. Equívoca dejadez afinaba las facciones . . ."

of "genetic homosexuality," but also adds the Freudian concept of the "abnormal" Oedipal formation, and makes use of the religious concept of moral condemnation.

Although the concept of sexual transgression (gender role inversion) dominates the novel, the text includes a series of other discourses of authority to assert that homosexuality is a monstrosity. To this end, Hernández Catá simultaneously uses genetic, evolutionary, psychoanalytic, and religious concepts. To all this I must add the national and class argument: it seems to be implied in this work that homosexuality is more closely related to corruption coming from other nations and races, in spite of Jiménez de Azúa's refusal of this argument. Tellingly, José-María had to go to Paris to try to practice his homosexuality. Paris, not Madrid or Havana, is the symbol of the corrupt city par excellence.

The reading of *El ángel de Sodoma* also reveals certain class implications. In several of his texts Hernández Catá obviously favors characters of certain social strata: the "heroes" of his novels are frequently from the bourgeoisie or the aristocracy, provided that they have certain values of traditional honor. This is why in *El ángel de Sodoma* there is so much emphasis on the question of José-María's class and that of the other "good" characters. José-María has remained in poverty and must work in a bank, but his honor is "irreproachable." Only his "deviation of instinct" betrays him, and, of course, since he has upper-class values and is so honest, the only solution to his problem is to abstain from homosexuality and ultimately die. In the name of the Name and of his class and gender, José-María must commit suicide.

The ideological web spun around homosexuality is complex, powerful, and effective. By the 1920s discursive changes had occurred and some modern discourses—specifically scientist positivism, in the case we are dealing with—proposed somewhat transformed interpretations of homosexuality that decriminalized it and expressed pity for those suffering from its "illness." Even so, what remains certain is that the discursive homophobic web is truly formidable.

★ FIVE ★
A Prison House of Womanless Men

During the 1920s and 1930s, in Hispanic literature in general and in Cuban literature in particular, new spaces were opened for representations of sexualities that had long been marginal. In Cuba the ideas of Gregorio Marañón, Luis Jiménez de Asúa, and other physicians, criminologists, and sociologists considered "progressive" (within the positivist positions of the time) became quite well known not only in books but also in widely circulated popular magazines. Feminist positions were also spread through newspapers, magazines, scholarly texts, and literary works such as those by Hernández Catá and Rodríguez Acosta. Carlos Montenegro's *Hombres sin mujer* (Womanless Men), serialized in a magazine in 1937 and appearing in book form in 1938, exemplifies this period of major social and discursive change.[1]

It is difficult to write about Montenegro's literary work without making some reference to his personal and political life, which was so filled with adventure and misfortune that his biography reads like a great novel of mishaps and extraordinary events, of extreme marginality and iconoclastic positions. In addition, his social and political marginality may be precisely what enabled his unusually bold treatment of the theme of homoeroticism between men. Montenegro was born in

---

1. Carlos Montenegro, *Hombres sin mujer* (Womanless men) (Mexico: Editorial Masas, 1938). In his recent book, *La maldición: una historia del placer como conquista* (Havana: Editorial Letras Cubanas, 1998), Víctor Fowler cites a Cuban edition of *Hombres sin mujer* published in Havana by Editorial Mamas in 1938. I have been unable to confirm this information.

Galicia, Spain, in 1900. After his family moved to Cuba in 1907, it experienced great economic hardship, so young Montenegro had to work as a sailor from the age of fourteen to eighteen. At nineteen, convicted of killing a man with a straight razor in a brawl, he received a fourteen-year sentence to be served in the Castillo del Príncipe de La Habana. According to Montenegro's version of events, he had killed in self-defense. He states in his personal accounts that his conviction was entirely unjust, underscoring his chief complaints against the penal system he denounced for a great part of his life: that those without funds or influential patrons receive severe and often unjust treatment in the courts.

His biography reveals that Montenegro spent practically his entire adolescence and youth in an almost exclusively homosocial atmosphere: on a boat during his adolescence and then in jail until the age of thirty one. In the prologue to *Hombres sin mujer*, Montenegro describes himself as a victim of the Cuban penal system, "a man who lost the best years of his youth in the reformatory which I now denounce";[2] he also implies that since his fellow inmates practiced homosexuality, he did so as well for several years. Moreover, it was during his incarceration that Montenegro's writing talents became known. He wrote numerous stories from jail that were published in some of the best-known Cuban magazines of the day, including *Social, Carteles, Bohemia,* and the literary page of the newspaper *Diario de la Marina*. Some notes on his work were also published in the renowned *Revista de Avance,* then the avant-garde Cuban literary publication. In 1944 Montenegro won the Premio Hernández Catá (Hernández Catá had died in 1940), the first of numerous prestigious literary honors he was to receive during his lifetime.[3]

Once Montenegro's work became known, various writers and intellectuals from Cuba, Spain, and elsewhere mobilized in an unsuccessful attempt to gain his release (Montenegro's sentence was later reduced by two years for good behavior). The efforts to free him included open letters to newspapers and written appeals to three Cuban presidents: Alfredo Zayas, José Miguel Gómez, and Gerardo Machado. One of the most notable Cuban intellectuals who lobbied for the commutation of Montenegro's sentence by writing to Machado was Enrique José Varona, considered the ideologue of what is known in Cuban cultural

2. Spanish original: "como un hombre que perdió los mejores años de su juventud en el reformatorio que ahora denuncio." Montenegro, *Hombres sin mujer,* 12.

3. See Enrique J. Pujals, "Carlos Montenegro: de la biografía a la narrativa" (Ph.D. diss., Rutgers University, 1978).

history as the "Generation of '23." (13). The Spanish criminologist Luis Jiménez de Asúa also joined the pardon movement by quoting legal principles in favor of Montenegro (43). In 1928 the *Revista de Avance* paid tribute to Montenegro for the literary award he had received from the magazine *Carteles* for his short story "El renuevo" (The sprout). The acclaim given him that year resulted in his recognition throughout the country as a writer.

From jail in 1927 Montenegro began corresponding with Emma Pérez, a female admirer of his stories. According to the literary critic Enrique J. Pujals, these are the first letters Montenegro had ever received from a woman. Montenegro later met her, and after a brief engagement they were married. Emma Pérez was a teacher of literature who later became a professor in the School of Philosophy and the School of Pedagogy at the University of Havana. She authored several books and served as editor of several social and political magazines (ibid.).

Once released from prison, Montenegro joined the Cuban Communist Party, and some years later became the editor of *Hoy*, the party newspaper. His affiliation led to his participation in the Spanish Civil War on the side of the Republic. But it was during those years, the late 1930s, that his political ideas began to change, causing him to become increasingly anticommunist. Starting in 1940, Montenegro joined Rolando Masferrer, who later would become a leading anticommunist and Fulgencio Batista's supporter in denouncing corruption in the Cuban Communist Party. His ideological shift and exile to Costa Rica (and later to Miami) once Fidel Castro's revolutionary government came to power in 1959 explains why socialist Cuba tried for some years to erase all trace of him from the world of literature. Montenegro's name does not even appear in the *Diccionario de la literatura cubana* (Dictionary of Cuban literature).[4] Also, while in Cuba and later in exile in Miami, his close friendship and political collaboration with Masferrer made him anathema in socialist Cuba. (Masferrer actively participated in the paramilitary activities carried out by Fulgencio Batista's government.) This series of events and political conflicts, coupled with the controversial themes and provocative questions of his writing, have hampered the dissemination and study of this iconoclastic writer's work.

In 1936, five years after Montenegro's release from prison, a congress on penal reform was held in Vienna that addressed, among other

4. *Diccionario de la literatura cubana* (Havana: Editorial Letras Cubanas, first volume, 1980; second volume, 1984).

topics, decriminalizing homosexuality. Among the participants was the Spanish criminologist Luis Jiménez de Asúa, who wrote the epilogue to Hernández Catá's *El ángel de Sodoma* (see chapter 4) and called for the commutation of Montenegro's sentence. On the basis of Jiménez de Asúa's position, Montenegro sent him a letter that was to have been accompanied by a story denouncing the abuses of prison life, particularly homosexuality among male prisoners in Cuba. In an interview granted to Pujals years later, Montenegro admitted that the story he was going to send to Jiménez de Asúa was delayed because his growing amount of material on the topic changed the story into a novel.[5] The work was eventually published in 1938 as *Hombres sin mujer*, and, according to Montenegro's own prologue, the text was intended to denounce the jailhouse abuse and frustration of the "womanless men" forced to have homosexual relations with each other.

As Montenegro's statements to Pujals seem to show, *Hombres sin mujer* caused a great commotion in the Cuban literary world at the time. But Montenegro, basically a rebellious iconoclast who did not allow himself to be easily intimidated, was frequently defiant in the face of what he called "skin-deep morality." He considered it his duty to be part of a moral imperative greater that the "superficial morality" of society, and it seems that it was this conviction that motivated the following statement in his prologue:

> No me interesa quien se sonroje o indigne por la lectura de estas páginas, mientras se considere ajeno a la realidad ominosa que divulgan: a su agitada moral de superficie opongo, en la medida de mi capacidad, el propósito auténticamente moral de desenmascarar la ignominia que supone arrojar al pudridero a seres que más tarde o más temprano han de regresar al medio común, aportando a este todas las taras adquiridas; opongo también la desesperación de esos seres, su dolor humano y su inevitable regresión a la bestia; opongo el interés mismo de la humanidad. (163)

> [I'm not concerned with anyone who might blush or become indignant upon reading these pages, while considering themselves apart from the ominous reality divulged therein: in place of their agitated superficial morality I offer, to the best of my ability, the truly moral proposal of unmasking the disgrace inherent in throwing onto the rubbish heap beings who sooner or later must return to the common order, bringing with them all their acquired defects; I offer the despair

5. Pujals, "Carlos Montenegro," 46–47.

of those beings, their human anguish, and their inevitable return to the belly of the beast; I offer the very interest of humanity.]

Hombres sin mujer was published in Mexico, but was negatively received in Cuba and Latin America mostly out of moral considerations. The response was more positive in Paris, where it was reprinted twice in the collection *La Terre Vivant* with a prologue by George Pillement.[6] In fact, it could be said that *Hombres sin mujer* caused a scandal in Cuba even before being published in book form, since the novel had already been serialized in national magazines. Montenegro himself related the following behind-the-scenes incident in an interview with Pujals:

> Venía disgustado porque acababa de saber que el jurado había renunciado. Yo concurría con *Hombres sin mujer*, y conociendo al jurado tenía esperanzas de ganar el premio. Un rumor que llegó hasta mí me informaba que la causa de la renuncia [de los miembros del jurado] se debía a la presentación de mi novela, que creyéndola hasta cierto punto aceptable, el lenguaje usado por mí la hacía impropia de un concurso oficial. Por puro accidente me encontré con tres de los cuatro miembros. Todos realmente capaces y aún adscriptos al llamado "Grupo de Avance." Antes de que yo aludiera al asunto de la renuncia, uno de ellos, al parecer hablando por los otros dos, me dijo: "—Pero por Dios Montenegro, no sabes aún que por algo se ha inventado el eufemismo." Yo no me caracterizo por la oportunidad de la réplica, pero en aquel momento mi mucho saber de lo que se trataba, me iluminó: —Sí, lo sé, y en presidio, aunque ustedes lo ignoren se usa mucho, por ejemplo: al pene se le llama "la paradoja."[7]

[I was disappointed because I had just learned that the jury had resigned. I had entered *Hombres sin mujer*, and knowing the jury I had hopes of winning the prize. I heard a rumor that the reason for their resignation was the entry of my novel, which, although acceptable up to a certain point, was unsuitable for an official contest due to the language used. By sheer coincidence I met up with three of the four members. All highly capable and even adherents of the "Grupo de Avance." Before I could mention the matter of the resignation, one of them, speaking on behalf of the other two it would seem, said to me "But my God, Montenegro, don't you know that euphemism was

---

6. Montenegro, *Hombres sin mujer*.
7. Pujals, "Carlos Montenegro," 160.

invented for a reason?" I'm not known for my quick replies, but at that moment my great knowledge of the matter enlightened me: "Yes, I know, and in prison, although you may not know it, it's used a lot; for example, they call the penis 'the paradox.'"]

The relation Montenegro establishes here between the words *penis* and *paradox* (and which he attributes to prison slang) serves as a point of departure for my reading of *Hombres sin mujer*. The greatest contribution of the text, in my opinion, is the discursive tension established by this paradox concerning the symbol of phallic power. However, the political-pedagogical objective stated by Montenegro in the prologue leaves gaps and contradictions that tear down his argument at its core. As I noted earlier, Montenegro says his novel denounces the Cuban prison system, which permits and fosters homosexuality among men, who engage in these practices only because there are no women. Montenegro also claims that his basic motive in writing it is to rectify a judicial and jailhouse wrong, but in reality the text does that and much more. *Hombres sin mujer* also offers insights on the formation of Cuban national subjectivity and its relationship to sexual orientation, gender, race, and class.

The plot of *Hombres sin mujer* is truly sordid, centering on the compulsive homosexual obsession of prisoners in a Cuban jail who are suffering extreme deprivation and frightful abuses of power. Homosexual practices are shown to be quite prevalent and frequent among the inmates, and are represented so explicitly that they could be said to be the moral nightmare denounced by Gregorio Marañón in his prologue to Hernández Catá's *El ángel de Sodoma*. As I noted in chapter 4, Marañón, in his desire to contain the dissemination of information from texts on sexual matters, stated in that prologue that "works of literature" should avoid sexual descriptions so as not to become pornographic. *Hombres sin mujer* was in this sense the most daring novel ever written on this theme in Cuba until the mid-1960s, when José Lezama Lima's *Paradiso* was published. Some would argue that, due to its "realism," *Hombres sin mujer* is racier than *Paradiso* owing to the explicit literary representation of homosexual acts.

The setting is a Cuban jail—supposedly the Castillo del Príncipe where Montenegro had been incarcerated. There a black rural Cuban named Pascasio Speek falls madly in love with a blond, white, eighteen-year-old new inmate named Andrés Pinel, ironically after earning the jailhouse reputation of being the only "incorruptible" man. From the day of his arrival, most of the prisoners desire Andrés with an uncontrollable lust. Pascasio tries everything to avoid falling in love with him. However, despite his supposedly cast-iron heterosexuality (his eight years in prison have been celibate, probably due to his scorn for homosexual practices), he is unable to contain his passion and love for the young inmate. After a series of incidents in which Montenegro emphasizes that the codes of behavior among inmates are very distinct from those of "free" society, Pascasio succumbs to his attraction for Andrés. He kisses him passionately on the lips, which Andrés accepts, and in fact seems to share the handsome black man's feelings.

As is customary in novels in which basic social norms are broken, the story ends in tragedy. Andrés, who now loves Pascasio, is in despair because Pascasio has been housed in the incorrigibles' cell and is being tortured terribly. Andrés then decides, after much doubt and hesitation, that the only way to save Pascasio from death is by making a pact—at great sacrifice—with Manuel Chiquito so that he will get Pascasio removed from the torture chamber. Manuel, who strongly desires Andrés and who always gets what he wants (thanks to his astuteness and contacts, he has lots of money and material resources), plans to obtain Pascasio's freedom in exchange for sexual relations with Andrés. This is the agreement, but what Andrés does not know is that Pascasio is going to be freed from the chamber for another reason: the intervention of Brai, the prison's *supermacho* kingpin, who is feared by all. When Pascasio leaves his confinement and goes seeking his lover, he finds him having sex with Manuel Chiquito. At the end of the novel, when Pascasio has killed Andrés out of jealousy and cut his own wrists with an electric saw, he falls into the arms of Brai, who seems very compassionate out of his admiration of Pascasio. He had even thought that the black countryman, due to his "manliness," would inherit his jailhouse power to become the *supermacho* who fears no one.

In the novel's prologue, Montenegro says the following about his literary intentions:

[N]o es mi objetivo el logro de un éxito literario más o menos resonante, ya que para ser leído con complacencia hubiera tenido que sacrificar demasiado la realidad, limitando con ella las posibilidades de alcanzar lo que me propongo, y que es la denuncia del régimen penitenciario a que me vi sometido—no por exepción, desde luego—durante doce años.[8]

[I]t is not my objective to achieve a more or less resounding literary success, since to make for pleasurable reading I would have had to

8. Montenegro, *Hombres sin mujer*, 11.

sacrifice reality too much, limiting the possibilities of achieving what I propose, which is the denouncement of the penal regime to which I have been subjected—and my case is not unique of course—for twelve years.]

With this statement Montenegro clearly implies that had he written the novel with literary intentions, this would have augmented the pleasure of the reader but diminished the reality of the work's point of reference. Nevertheless, *Hombres sin mujer* is far from being an innocent composition directly reflecting prison reality. In fact, the traits and narrative (literary?) strategies that this text shares with those of other naturalist authors (especially of the nineteenth century) are remarkable, especially works dealing with socially unacceptable relations, or with "fatal attractions" in which at least one of the lovers represents the stereotype of a racially and/or sexually marginal person. The similarities above all with *Bom-Crioulo* (1895) by the Brazilian Adolfo Caminha are many and fundamental.[9]

At first glance the novel seems to follow the postulates of the literary theory of naturalism by portraying the deterministic effects that a desolate atmosphere can have on a group of people. But if the atmosphere of this work reflects this theory, it can be said that some of the characters (above all Pascasio and Andrés) do not. As the critic Alfredo Villanueva-Collado states with wisdom and precision, the naturalistic atmosphere of this work is undermined by the tragic romanticism of the lead couple with its ingredients of frustrated love, betrayal, murder, madness, and suicide.[10] According to Emile Zola's naturalistic project in *Le roman experimental*, the author's objective should be to create an anthropological atmosphere dominated by the strictest parameters of scientific determinism. Therefore, the writer should concentrate his or her efforts on the use of experience, avoiding emotions and generalizations that lead to analyzing the why and not the how of the situation in question. The novel is, at least intentionally, a "scientific experiment." Environment and heredity should govern the behavior of the characters in the strictest fashion; individuals cannot escape from these omnipotent determinants. Nevertheless, Latin American naturalism—as embodied in *Hombres sin mujer*, for example—tends to emphasize environment over heredity, and its characters frequently

9. Adolfo Caminha, *Bom-Crioulo: The Black Man and the Cabin Boy* (San Francisco: Gay Sunshine Press, 1982).

10. Alfredo Villanueva-Collado, "Homoerotic, Heteroracial Relationship in the Latin American Naturalist Novel: *Bom-Crioulo* and *Hombres sin mujer*," *Romance Languages Annual* 7 (1995): 647–52.

suggest the possibility of overcoming determinism. These are the reasons that the naturalism of *Hombres sin mujer* is closer to social realism than to the naturalism espoused by Zola.[11]

The *machista* (male-oriented sexism) code dominates the atmosphere of *Hombres sin mujer*. This code supposedly works in a totalizing fashion, but in the final analysis its declared limits are not sustained in the narrative. Instead, the prisoners' sexual behavior is divided between the *machos* (butch males) and the *maricas* (effeminate faggots). The machos are strong, aggressive, and butch; have great tolerance for physical pain; never lose their cool; and never allow themselves to feel weakness or love (love is considered a weakness). In contrast, the *maricas* are expected to be exactly the opposite. Nevertheless, there seems to be no one in the novel (except, initially, Pascasio) who does not practice homosexuality. Therefore, rejection of homoeroticism per se is not always part of the *machista* code. At the beginning of the novel, Pascasio seems to have all the characteristics of a macho, but later in the text we find out he is in love with Andrés. Also, his blackness and rural origin are supposed to make him (at least initially) more "primitive," closer to "the wise harmony of nature."[12] Even so, according to the logic of the text, this "natural harmony" is destroyed by the pressure of his eight—year celibacy. But Pascasio's "primitive" trait has a paradoxical meaning, since on the one hand it implies his situation within the accepted sociosexual norms, and on the other his nearness to the "animalistic," the "bestial." These are the two sides of the concept of "natural" that are in conflict within Pascasio's character and are in fact one of the central paradoxes of the entire text.

The paradoxes that are found in this text are precisely what make me read *Hombres sin mujer* as an "inverted" metaphor for the formation of the national and homosexual Cuban subjectivities. In the novel an unusual living situation—prison—is represented, and in this space the mechanisms that construct the norms of legitimacy by which Cuban national homophobia is formed are simultaneously denied and reproduced. The text constantly implies that the formation of the codes of conduct and the definition of the prisoners' subjugation are artificial, and that things are radically different in the outside world. This means that the sexual definitions arising from the society beyond prison walls are naturalized. Nevertheless, what I propose in my reading of this novel is that, precisely because prison is a "special" circumstance,

11. Ibid., 647.
12. Montenegro, *Hombres sin mujer*, 135.

we can more easily deconstruct the postulates proposed by it and "discover" the construction of sexual roles and social abjection in Cuban society at large. In such a special situation, sexual codes are still insufficiently reiterated, and therefore they appear to be more contrived. But these constructs may very well be based on the same formative mechanisms of society at large, so that these mechanisms of subjectivity formation in the text are basically no different than those of Cuban society in general. Perhaps the injurious interpellations and mechanisms of violation that construct the "homosexual identity" in Cuban society are very much like those represented in this novel, and suffer from similar paradoxes.

Hombres sin mujer is a text that proposes the rejection of an abusive situation, yet reproduces several of the postulates and consequences of that situation. The logic of this novel proposes that in prison homosexuality is brought about by the abnormal situation of no women, and also implies that this sexuality is a deviation from nature (heterosexuality). The expected and oft-used logic that insists on presenting heterosexuality as natural, normal, and original permeates the entire work in spite of the actions depicted in the narrative implying the opposite. It is also implied (to the point of becoming explicit at times) that, since the oppressive situation of the prison system forms abusive subjectivities, Pascasio and Andrés are heroes for having overcome this formation (at least somewhat and in an iconoclastic way). What are the qualities of these two characters that make them "different"? A deconstructive reading actually leads me to question some of the implications of the novel's main characters. The logic of the work seems to insist that the characterization distinguishing these two men from the others is their capacity to love: they don't just desire each other physically but love each other, and their mutual sentiments are full of a sense of sacrifice and even of martyrdom. Such a love in a homosexual relationship contradicts the *machista* code prevalent in prison while also contradicting the *machista* code in society outside. Therefore, the narrative tries to tell us that jailed men have homosexual relations only because of the lack of women, but it also leads to a quite different conclusion: the possibility of erotic love between men is a way of overcoming machismo. And here we should ask ourselves: is Pascasio and Andrés's love affair a "deviation" of nature that produces imbalance in the just system of machismo, or is it what allows a resistance to the system and therefore leads to a possible escape from its evils? The logic of Montenegro's text seems to posit the first answer at times, and at others the second.

Like any code that tries to naturalize certain behaviors which have yet to be sufficiently reiterated, the seams of the constructs of this text are quite apparent. The novel proposes that there are good and bad behaviors, and therefore the story endeavors to classify and codify some of them (frequently based on injurious interpellations). At the beginning of the story Pascasio is spoken of as a "real man," since he alone abstains from homosexual activities; Manuel Chiquito is depicted as one of the most corrupt, perhaps since he achieves everything based on his economic power and doesn't seem to love anyone but merely desires them carnally. In fact, Manuel may be regarded as a representation of the abusive capitalist system that is ultimately responsible for the creation of the prison itself. Nevertheless, the homosexual activities in this novel are extremely prevalent and many characters engage in them for many reasons, so it isn't easy to maintain that all "deviant" sexual desire in this jail stems from the corruption of Manuel Chiquito's money, nor that such homosexual desire is exclusively the result of a lack of women.

Some characters in the novel seem to have a true sexual and/or love interest in each other. La Morita, for example, loves Pascasio, although his love is unrequited. Brai, the *supermacho* whom everyone fears because he could "eat the ears off" of anyone who opposes him, acknowledges that he "has boys" because he wants to have them and not because such behavior is imposed on him in any way. Besides, some of the prison guards also participate in homosexual activities, contradicting the logic that jailed men have homosexual relations only out of inaccessibility to women. And in classifying the sexual activities and different types of sexual "orientations" in jail, the text tells us that among the "womanless men" are those who are "effeminate by nature" and others who are "effeminate by convenience." It is never clear what these differences consist of, whether they are products of the prison situation, whether they come from outside, or whether they are something "natural." What is more, a long list of terms is repeatedly used in the text to describe the characters practicing homoeroticism (which is all the characters). This is why I believe the text can be read as an implicit questioning not only of the concept of the "Cuban man" but also of the very concept of homosexual in the sense that positivism, for example, uses the term.

The naturalization of the very concept of manhood and of homosexual identity is placed under scrutiny by the multiplicity of terms referring to homoeroticism and the (in)differences implicit in those classifications. Moreover, the overlapping of sexual and racial elements in the novel adds to this questioning and allows for reflection on the discursive crossroads implied in the formation of these subjectivities. In this sense, the first thing to be noted in the relation between race and sex in *Hombres sin mujer* is that heteroracial-homoerotic relations appear frequently, the most noteworthy of these being the principal couple of Pascasio and Andrés. Racial differences and sexual attraction are emphasized; that is, black men or mulattos frequently show a strong sexual preference for white men, and sometimes (as in the case of Andrés) this preference is requited. Also represented in the novel is the stereotype of the black man, since Pascasio is depicted as strong, handsome, coarse, and sexual. The encounter between Pascasio and Andrés is above all a representation of a persistent Cuban sexual fantasy. The fact that Pascasio is black situates him within a long history in which the black race is represented as the source or motivation of sexual "deviations" and "excesses." But in Montenegro's text the race is also associated with a closeness to nature, and so in the midst of this discursive complexity the question emerges: is Pascasio's race what brings him, at the beginning of the story, into "the harmony of nature," or, on the contrary, is it what leads him, in the end, to deviate from or break the *machista* code with his love for Andrés? The text leaves this question unanswered.

In my reading of *Hombres sin mujer* I should mention that Pascasio frequently imagines an idyllic vision of a woman in a very beautiful cane field. This fantasy is the utopian moment of the text and as such it permits, on the one hand, a deconstruction of the narrative's "reality," and, on the other, an envisioning of other possible solutions to the ideology implied by the text. In effect, Pascasio—who as a rural black is thought to be closer to nature—imagines himself loving and caressing a beautiful woman in a cane field. His dream represents freedom and the solution for the "womanless men." If this world were to come about, that is, if Pascasio were "free," he could be happy with his woman in a magnificent field of sugar cane. But this possibility is undermined when one pauses to reflect on this utopia and to ponder that "out there" life is neither free nor perfect. Instead of radically separating "outside" and "inside," it is worthwhile to relate them in several ways. It is precisely the "outside" Cuban society of the day (the 1930s) that creates the "inside" world, the prison that Montenegro criticizes so harshly. It seems that what the text of *Hombres sin mujer* can show us (unintentionally, of course) is precisely which mechanisms of subjugation function in the formation of Cuban subjectivity in general. The difference between "outside" and "inside" resides mainly in the *degree* of reiteration with which gender, race, class, and "sexual orientation" have been naturalized.

Here it should be added that at the end of *Hombres sin mujer* an event takes place that may be read as significant. After Pascasio has killed Andrés and slashed his own wrists, he falls into the arms of Brai, who expresses anguish because he feels that Pascasio could have been his successor, the inheritor of the position of *supermacho*, respected and feared by all. With this ending, Brai becomes the representative of the only remaining vestige of goodness, in a sort of heroic position. This ending could not be more paradoxical. The *supermacho* feared for his ability to "eat the ears off" of his opponents represents the possible ideological closure of the text. At this point I ask myself: how can the text close with this "solution" after showing the horrors machismo can produce and the abjection that results from this abuse? This is where "inside" and "outside" connect in such a dramatic way. The spaces dominated by machismo are both the "inside," with its behaviors still insufficiently reiterated so as to seem natural, and the "outside," with its mostly naturalized codes that impose a series of mechanisms of subjugation very similar to those "inside." Montenegro's novel, which at times represents a subversion of machismo and its consequences, at other times brings about an ideological closure in which machismo reaffirms itself in the center of power—this time in an exaggerated way, since it is Brai, "the ear eater," who personifies this closure. This is why *Hombres sin mujer* can be read as a metaphor of the nation at large, of the mechanisms and possible consequences of its contradictory *machista* code.

Within this ideological crossroads implicit in the text, other questions can be asked to further our reflection on this work: is Brai the ultimate representative of the *machista* code, or does he, with his obvious sympathy for Pascasio and even for the love relationship between Pascasio and Andrés, represent a rupture in the dominant system? Briefly put, homoeroticism itself is not the greatest subversion of this novel after all; rather, it offers the possibility of a reading that questions those mechanisms that produce an injurious subjectivity through the *machista* regime. As Michel Foucault proposes, all subversion is derived from the same conditions of violation, since there is nothing apart from the discourses of power. But in the midst of these logical paradoxes of violation a subversive reading may be proposed as a possibility permitted by the text.

I should clarify that the deconstruction of the logic of *Hombres sin mujer* is not done so as to invalidate the contributions of this novel, but rather to show the incoherence of its resistance and its paradoxical subversion. Starting from this realization, we can perhaps perceive more coherent possibilities of resistance toward a more effective social objective. Interpellation always creates more than it wants, and means much more than any implicit referent; this text implies much more than what it aspires to and means more than Montenegro explicitly proposes. It is worthwhile, then, to ask ourselves a final question implied in my reading of *Hombres sin mujer*: does Montenegro's text propose that the perversity of the penal system centers on the corruption produced by homoerotic practices, or on the contrary, does this perversity reside in the exaggerated replica of the *machista* code? As I have argued in this chapter, my reading of this text leads me to the idea of a prison house of womanless men that copies in an exaggerated and little-codified way the *machista* mechanisms of which the "great Cuban national family" is composed. The "womanless men" are not really any different from anyone else, and both the ideology of "inside" and the utopia of "outside" are shown to be full of gaps.

///

REVOLUTIONARY NORMATIVITIES AND THEIR EFFECTS

It is undeniable that the Cuban Revolution of 1959 was radically nationalistic from the very beginning and aspired to cleanse the country of everything its leaders and many of its people had seen as national ills: exclusive reliance on sugar cane as a cash crop, economic and cultural dependence on the United States, inequality of the social classes, and governmental as well as behavioral immorality. The revolution proposed to resolve these injustices, so social justice for certain excluded groups was central to its project. There was also at this time a real sense that it was necessary and urgent to recover the national dignity that had been lost during Fulgencio Batista's regime (1952–58), when all manner of corruption was fostered and supported.[1]

The revolutionaries adopted extreme postures in many arenas, not just with military and economic matters, but also in terms of behavior and even sexuality.[2] In order to protect the country from everything "corrupted," one had to be ever more nationalistic, and to become more nationalistic it was necessary to revive some of the country's best and worst traditions, including homophobia. Cuba's worst homophobic moments were not the first years of the revolution. In fact, this initial period was one of national euphoria, and the revolution seemed directed toward becoming a fairly tolerant system

1. See Marifeli Pérez-Stable, *The Cuban Revolution: Orgins, Course, and Legacy* (New York: Oxford University Press, 1993).

2. See Ian Lumsden, *Machos, Maricones, and Gays: Cuba and Homosexuality* (Philadelphia: Temple University Press, 1996), especially pages 55–80.

when it came to matters not strictly related to the survival of the new political and social order. But by the early to mid-1960s the revolutionaries had added an aggressive homophobia to their political and social agenda, leaving homosexuals in a very helpless position. It is only fair to insist that the homophobic construction of Cuban nationalism is an indisputable reality, and not all of the homophobic excesses of the revolution can be attributed to the personal prejudices of its leaders. It should therefore be said that what was truly extraordinary about the situation at that time was not the homophobic positions themselves, but their convergence, extremism, and institutionalization.[3]

The relationship between the representations of nationalism and homosexuality in Cuba reached its homophobic apex in the period from the mid-1960s to the mid-1970s. During this decade various social and discursive forces that had been present for many years, in addition to new ones, converged. Radical nationalism's homophobia, as well as that of international socialism, united with all sorts of positions inherited from religion, the Eurocentric Enlightenment project, and positivism, giving rise to a veritable persecution of gays and lesbians. In this introduction to the relationship between the representation of homosexuality and nationalism during the revolutionary years, I will start by dealing with two events of great importance in better understanding the period from the mid-1960s to the mid-1970s: the Unidades Militares de Ayuda a la Producción (Military units to aid production [UMAPs]) from 1965 to 1968, and the Primer Congreso Nacional de Educación y Cultura (First national congress of education and culture) of 1971.[4] The year 1961 was crucial as a precursor of these two events: after the Marxist-Leninist character of the revolution and its subsequent direct confrontation with the United States was established, certain homophobic tendencies emerged that, beginning in 1965, would become radicalized and institutionalized in the UMAPs and other forms of social repression.

3. See Ana María Simo, "Interview with Ana María Simo," interview by Ian Daniels, *Torch* (New York), 15 December 1984 and 14 January 1985. See also Lourdes Argüelles and Ruby Rich, "Homosexuality, Homophobia and Revolution: Notes toward an Understanding of the Cuban Lesbian and Gay experience," pts. 1 and 2, *Signs* 9, no. 4 (summer 1984): 683–99 and 11, no. 1 (1985): 120–36.

4. See Allen Young, "Commentary: 'The Cuban Gulag.' Homophobia and the American Left," *The Advocate* 388 (10 July 1984): 35; "Cuba: Gay as the Sun," in *Out of the Closet: Voices of Gay Liberation*, ed. Karla Young and Allen Young (New York: New York University Press, 1992), 206–50; and *Gays under the Cuban Revolution* (San Francisco: Grey Fox Press, 1981).

It was in 1961 that a massive raid was conducted in Havana's Colón neighborhood in search of "pederasts, prostitutes and pimps," earning it the name "Night of the Three P's."[5] Yet at the time some observers viewed this event as a temporary eradication of the corruption in the Cuban capital. It did not at all seem directly related to a systematic repression aimed specifically at homosexuals, nor did it appear to be an institutionalization of their abjection in the concept of the Cuban nation. Nevertheless, as Carlos Franqui (once editor of the newspaper *Revolución*) has noted, Night of the Three P's was the "first massive roundup" of the revolution.[6] According to Franqui, this sort of activity, coming in the midst of such a tense political situation, and under the threat of the most powerful country in the world a mere ninety miles away, lent itself perfectly to abuses of power by *machistas* obsessed with power and control.[7] This entire initial period of the revolution was characterized by a "purging of vices," and to this end the government started programs aimed at reforming prostitutes through job training, giving them instruction in such skills as tailoring. Prostitution, drug addiction, and homosexuality were strongly associated with one another in the Cuban cultural imagination, and several revolutionary leaders exploited this situation for their own political objectives.

Also in 1961, the gay writer Virgilio Piñera, then the country's most distinguished playwright,[8] was arrested.[9] His detention, which lasted around twenty-four hours, concerned many Cuban artists and writers, since by then they had begun to worry that their freedom of speech and artistic expression would be curtailed by the new regime. Piñera was a prestigious writer who had been a supporter of the revolution from the first days of its victory.[10] The true reasons for his arrest cannot be

5. See Carlos Franqui, *Family Portrait with Fidel* (New York: Random House, 1984), 138–41; and Guillermo Cabrera Infante, in Néstor Almendros and Orlando Jiménez-Leal, eds., *Conducta impropia* (Improper conduct) (Madrid: Editorial Playor, 1984), 134–35.

6. See Franqui, *Family Portrait with Fidel*, 139.

7. Ibid., 141.

8. For an account of Virgilio Piñera's troubles with the Cuban government in the 1960s, see Guillermo Cabrera Infante, *Mea Cuba* (New York: Farrar, Strauss and Giroux, 1992), 331–60. See also the insightful articles by José Quiroga, "Fleshing Out Virgilio Piñera from the Cuban Closet," in *¿Entiendes? Queer Readings, Hispanic Writings*, ed. Emilie L. Bergmann and Paul Julian Smith (Durham, N.C.: Duke University Press, 1995), 168–80; and "Virgilio Piñera: On the Weight of the Insular Flesh," in *Hispanisms and Homosexualities*, ed. Sylvia Molloy and Robert McKee Irwin (Durham, N.C.: Duke University Press, 1998), 269–85.

9. See Lumsden, *Machos, Maricones, and Gays*, 59–60.

10. For a detailed account, year by year, of Piñera's life and work, see Teresa Cristófani Barreto, *A Libélula, a pitonisa. Revolucão, homosexualismo e literatura em Virgilio Piñera* (São Paulo: Editora Iluminuras, 1996), especially pages 109–71.

known with absolute certainty; we have only theories ranging from the personal prejudices of police officers to complex political motivations. In his book *Mea Cuba*, Guillermo Cabrera Infante alleges that on the particular day Piñera was arrested, he left his house on Guanabo Beach dressed "scandalously" in shorts, a multicolored shirt, and sandals— very unusual public attire for a Cuban male at the time. It has also been argued that the president of the local Committee for the Defense of the Revolution wanted to take personal possession of Piñera's house by implicating him in a public and moral scandal.[11]

In reality, Piñera had produced very few works with an obvious homosexual theme, but his physical appearance alone betrayed him as an "effeminate man"; that was enough to place him in a very disadvantageous position.[12] As he dramatically states in his brief, posthumous autobiographical account, "La vida tal cual" (Life as such): "Having only just achieved the age at which thought becomes something more than spitting out your drool and waving your little arms, I realized three things so filthy that I was never able to wash myself clean of them. I learned that I was poor, that I was a homosexual, and that I liked art."[13] In this account, Piñera considers poverty, homosexuality, and artistic vocation "divine misfortunes."[14]

As might be expected, Piñera's life changed greatly on 1 January 1959 with the triumph of Fidel Castro's revolution. By then Piñera was well known, above all as a playwright, since his most important play, *Electra Garrigó*, had been staged on more than one occasion.[15] (Piñera actually had never been an ideologically committed writer, and his ideas varied quite a bit from those of the leftist writers of the period.) Also, by the beginning of the revolutionary period in Cuba, his gayness had become known. But once the revolution arrived, he integrated himself with enthusiasm, one could even say with frenzy, into the political process then under way. During the first days of the revolution Piñera published and participated in the well-known magazine *Lunes de Revolución*, the semiofficial government organ, and he joined in political activities with intensity and apparent optimism

11. Cabrera Infante, *Mea Cuba*, 317–48.
12. Ibid.
13. Virgilio Piñera, "La vida tal cual," *Unión* 3, no. 10 (April–June 1990): 23. Spanish original: "No bien tuve la edad exigida para que el pensameinto se traduzca en algo más que soltar la baba y agitar los bracitos, me enteré de tres cosas lo bastante sucias como para no poderme lavar de las mismas. Aprendí que era pobre, que era homosexual y que me gustaba el Arte."
14. Ibid.
15. See Cristófani Barreto, A *Libélula, a pitonisa*, 110–71.

toward what he perceived as the dawn of a wonderful new era for Cuban society and culture.[16] His enthusiasm was abruptly brought down to earth with his arrest in 1961. He never completely recovered from this incident, and although he continued publishing and participating in the country's cultural and political activities for a few more years, his alienation from the revolutionary process continued to increase. By the beginning of the 1970s he had become almost completely cut off from Cuban cultural life.[17] Only recently, many years after his death, has the figure of Virgilio Piñera begun to experience a sort of rehabilitation in socialist Cuba, a sort of mea culpa—always from the position of power, from the position of a system that attempts to control even its own remorse—for the abuses he suffered.[18]

Piñera was victimized by the "virilization" of the "new man" of the Cuban Revolution. During this early stage of the revolution, the idea of forming a new subjectivity and a "new man" in this "new" society began to take shape.[19] It was thought that this revolutionary Cuban subject ought to be free of the impurities of the bourgeois past, willing to sacrifice for his country, ready to renounce utilitarian values, and eager to possess a great disposition and aptitude for the struggle (a physical struggle, if need be) for nationalist and socialist ideals. The "new man" also ought to be virile and highly macho. A representation of the homosexual had only a negative place in this construct, and was therefore targeted in the attack on the "bad habits" of the past that the new regime undertook throughout the entire country.

It seems that the key year in studying the beginning of institution-alized homophobia is 1965 (according to Carlos Franqui, it began in 1964).[20] All the negative ideas Cubans had about homosexuals con-verged in that year, and some of communism's prejudices were added to them, resulting in a truly systematic homophobic repression of gays. The idea that homosexuality was closely related to crime, drug addic-tion, venereal disease, and gender inversion became widespread (the genders were considered, of course, to be a natural phenomenon, not socially constructed roles). Some of international socialism's negative

16. Ibid.

17. Cabrera Infante, *Mea Cuba*, 317–48.

18. For a thoughtful opinion about the Cuban state's attempts to control even its own "rectification" about homosexuality, see José Quiroga, "Homosexualities in the Tropic of Revolution," in *Sex and Sexuality in Latin America*, ed. Daniel Balderston and Donna J. Guy (New York: New York University Press, 1997), 133–51.

19. See Juan Goytisolo, *En los reinos de Taifa* (Barcelona: Editorial Sex-Barral, 1986), 175.

20. See Franqui, *Family Portrait with Fidel*.

concepts stemmed from the Soviet Union, which had declared homosexuality illegal in 1934 despite the fact that the Bolshevik Revolution initially instituted radical reforms in favor of homosexual rights.[21]

How could the "new man" (and also the "new woman," as was implied) be freed from the scars of capitalism? That was the key question for the revolutionary leaders of the day, principal among them Che Guevara, an insistent proponent of the theory of the "new man" and one of the staunchest homophobic leaders of the revolutionary period.[22] But Che Guevara was not the only leader to openly flaunt his homophobia in the Cuba of the mid-1960s. Other officials and even Cuban intellectuals of the day launched pointed attacks against homosexuality. The leftist writer Samuel Feijóo led a campaign against homosexuals from the pages of the newspaper *El Mundo* and, after an extended trip to the Soviet Union, proclaimed that homosexuality no longer existed there, since socialism was able to cure social ills and deviant behavior of that sort.[23]

It was in the midst of this charged atmosphere that the forced labor camps called UMAPs were formed in 1965. These camps were designed primarily to "rehabilitate" those persons (almost all of them young men who had reached the age of military service) thought to be "antisocial." Among the detainees were those who refused to study or work, Jehovah's Witnesses who resisted military service for religious reasons, young delinquents, and finally the "immoral," among whom were included homosexuals. The UMAP camps were centered around Camagüey Province and aided in the production and harvest of fruits and other crops. Although precise documentation is not easy to obtain, it is known that initially some recruits were treated so inhumanely that some of the officials responsible were later executed. Indeed, the working environment in these camps was very harsh, even cruel and at times criminal. The idea was that in this environment the "antisocial" would be forced to perform agricultural labor alongside the local rural inhabitants and would thereby be cured of their bad habits and customs. Within this ideology the countryside was thought to possess certain redeeming qualities that cleansed the evils of the city.[24]

21. See Brad Epps, "Proper Conduct: Reinaldo Arenas, Fidel Castro and the Politics of Homosexuality," *Journal of the History of Sexuality* 6, no. 2 (1995): 231–83, especially pages 237–39.

22. For an article on Che Guevara's homophobia directed against Virgilio Piñera, see Quiroga, "Fleshing Out Virgilio Piñera from the Cuban Closet," 168–80.

23. See Samuel Feijóo, *El mundo*, 15 April 1965.

24. See José Yglesias, *In the Fist of the Revolution: Life in a Cuban Country Town* (New York: Pantheon Books, 1968), 275.

However, the UMAPs became the focus of outrage and protest, both nationally and internationally. In Cuba, the Unión de Escritores y Artistas de Cuba (Cuban writers and artists union [UNEAC]) rallied against the internment and harsh treatment of intellectuals in the UMAPs. It is also said that Raquel Revuelta, a Cuban artist affiliated with the Communist Party since before the revolution, mounted an energetic protest, since several dancers and artists from her Teatro Estudio had been interned. European leftist intellectuals such as Graham Greene, Gian Giacomo Getrinelli, and Jean-Paul Sartre also voiced their objections. And it was in 1965 that American writer and gay activist Allen Ginsberg visited Cuba. In spite of his sympathy for socialism and the Cuban Revolution, Ginsberg had several disagreeable encounters with officials and expressed his rejection of the authoritarianism that was dominating Cuban politics at the cultural level. In his characteristically iconoclastic manner, Ginsberg broached the gay topic with some of the leaders, and the reply he received was often quite negative. He was finally expelled from Cuba.[25]

In the face of these protests from home and abroad, the Cuban government finally decided to close the UMAPs. The exact date of their closure is not easy to pinpoint, but it seems to have been in 1967 or 1968, a little more than two years after their establishment. Once the government had decided to close them, it was determined that the local economy in Camagüey Province would be temporarily affected by the sudden drop in the workforce. Due to this consideration the final closing of the camps was postponed by several months.

But the institutionalization of Cuban homophobia during the second half of the 1960s was not based solely on rationalizations of social hygiene or even just on revolutionary fervor, anti-Americanism, or the typical positions of Stalinist communism. As is often the case when social groups are discriminated against, attacks were articulated so that several discourses were joined and juxtaposed to increase the effectiveness of the rejection and condemnation. Thus a complex discursive network was formed based on the combination of a variety of social prejudices difficult to separate from one another. The Cuban situation was not exceptional in this regard. Among the arguments that served as the foundation for the homophobia of the UMAPs, I have noted the following: homosexuality is a corrupt and immoral practice; homosexuals must be forced to do hard agricultural labor so

---

25. See Allen Ginsberg, "Interview with Allen Ginsberg," interview by Allen Young, *Gay Sunshine Interview* (1974): 25–27. Reprinted in Young, *Gays under the Cuban Revolution*, 20.

that the redeeming qualities of the rural atmosphere could cure their ills; homosexuals, being weak and therefore different from the base of macho Cuban culture, are perfect targets for recruitment by the enemy (American capitalism mainly); homosexuals are a threat to the nation because they corrupt children and young men and thus impede the formation of the "new man"; homosexuality constitutes an inversion of the "natural" gender roles and therefore breaks the basic laws of nature; and finally, homosexuality is the result of the distortions of capitalism, from which it may be concluded that socialism could now eradicate this social problem just as it could eradicate prostitution, drug addiction, and other ills and vices.

In addition to these conceptions, by the mid-1960s ideas on homosexuality were being articulated in Cuba by doctors and educators that added layers of reasoning on top of the previous ones. Among these were Freudian explanations insisting that the sexual formation of children began at a very young age, so they needed a strong male presence in their lives. Among certain cultural groups at that time, citing Freud was a way of calling on written authority to resolve any issue on a sexual matter. The psychoanalytic theory expounded by Cuban educators and doctors emphasized Freud's stages of sexual development and his belief that homosexuality arises from a boy's early identification with his mother and alienation from his father; they rarely if ever refer to the lesbian girl. Nevertheless, this programmatically adopted Freudianism, despite its contradictions with the ideology of a purely Cuban-socialist nationalism, fell very well within the objectives and inclinations of the Cuban Revolution and its project of forming "new men." In 1965 a report by the Ministry of Health concluded that as there were no known biological causes for homosexuality, there was, therefore, no convincing proof of hormonal, genetic, or somatic causes, and no biological treatment could be effective in curing homosexuality. This conclusion clearly implied that the "causes" were social; it was a matter of the family environment where the mother spoiled the boy excessively and had too much contact with him from birth until late in his youth, and the father was either absent or weak. Thus the son lacked a role model or identified with an insufficiently masculine father figure. Were all this true, the conclusion would be that strict measures could and should be taken in the sexual education of boys from a very young age.[26]

---

26. See Marvin Leiner, *Sexual Politics in Cuba: Machismo, Homosexuality, and AIDS* (Boulder, Colo.: Westview Press, 1994), 38–42.

In this project of "virilization," "effeminate boys" ought to go to special schools for "problem children," where psychiatrists, psychologists, and educators would give them proper and intense guidance. These boys were indoctrinated and even made to play rough games with toy pistols and swords regularly. They were also constantly pressured to practice baseball, the "ideal sport" for the "virilization" of boys and young men. Among the many objectives of this educational project was that if the causes of homosexuality were now seen as more social than biological (although, in spite of everything, Cuban doctors and educators never completely abandoned their biological theories), the method of arriving at a determination of homosexuality was frequently centered on external factors: the boy's mannerisms. As one of American researcher Marvin Leiner's gay informants explains, "My parents would not believe it if I told them that those macho-looking friends of mine are all gay!"[27]

Besides these "virilization treatments," in the mid-1960s the Cuban regime undertook a systematic campaign at all levels (including the legal) to expel homosexuals from the armed forces, the universities, the Communist Party, and highly influential government posts, as well as from positions charged with the education of boys and young men. The Consejo de Cultura's (Council of culture) "Resolution Number Three" was implemented to systematically eliminate homosexuals from any position in which they could conceivably "corrupt minors" or have a negative influence on the formation of the "new man."[28] Homosexuals had traditionally been constructed in Cuban society as persons excluded and rejected, and now the revolution institutionalized this exclusion and rejection at every level. But precisely because of this institutionalized rejection of the homosexual in relation to the dominant national discourse, the category of homosexuality became a more obviously constitutive part of the very concept of the Cuban nation. In spite of so many efforts to expel homosexuality from the concept of the revolutionary "new man," this time of great homophobic furor in Cuba brought signs of the homosexual specter never before seen: works and personal postures by writers and artists in which homosexuality occupied a central role. In fact, the attention given the "homosexual problem" in the discussions and resolutions of the First National Congress of Education and Culture in 1971 are a very

27. Quoted by Leiner, *Sexual Politics in Cuba*, 34. Leiner does not give the Spanish original of this quotation.

28. For an extensive account of the relationship between homosexuality and education in Cuba during the revolutionary period of the 1960s and 1970s, see ibid., 21–59.

telling indication of the discursive need that homosexuality met, by opposition, in the concept of the Cuban nation.[29]

During this extremely repressive atmosphere from the mid-1960s to the mid-1970s, those persons who seemed to promote homosexuality were endlessly persecuted and censored. But rather than experiencing a decline in the homosexual discourse in the face of this systematic opposition, Cuba underwent a considerable emergence of gay-themed works and gay and lesbian people rebelling against the system, both publicly and semipublicly. One of the most widely discussed cases, nationally and internationally, was the "scandal" caused by the publication of the novel *Paradiso* (1966) by José Lezama Lima (studied in chapter 6). In this work are not only several very daring scenes of homosexual encounters between young men, but also in-depth discussions of some theories regarding the nature, causes, and meanings of homosexuality that are at times very different from the direction given to such discussions by the Cuban Revolution. For a brief time the novel was removed from circulation, but due to Lezama Lima's fame and the influence of several revolutionary intellectuals who favored its publication—along with the narrative's highly baroque style, which made it less accessible to the general public and therefore less politically dangerous to the Cuban state—it returned to bookstores. Moreover, very early in the 1960s Severo Sarduy, a writer who later distinguished himself with a work that could well be called queer in the meaning given to that term today in U.S. academia, left Cuba en route to Paris. He never returned from this trip, taken in connection with an official program. (I discuss Sarduy's political and literary positions in chapter 7.) Then in 1969, the Cuban gay writer Calvert Casey committed suicide, leaving some unpublished texts revealing his homosexuality and his tremendous fear of being discovered as a gay man in Cuban society.[30]

I have already referred to the ostracism suffered by Virgilio Piñera that began in 1961. Stories and novels by Reinaldo Arenas began to appear toward the end of the 1960s and the early 1970s; they soon formed the center of his political conflict with Cuban authorities because of, among other things, the homosexual scenes represented in some of his texts. (I study Arenas's autobiography in chapter 8.) With

29. See "Declaración del Primer Congreso Nacional de Educación y Cultura," *La Gaceta de Cuba* 90–91 (March–April 1971): 2–13. See also *Memorias del primer congreso de educación y cultura* (Havana: Instituto Cubano del Libro, 1971).

30. For an account of Casey's life and work, see Víctor Fowler, *La maldición: una historia del placer como conquista* (Havana: Editorial Letras Cubanas, 1998), 128–40.

few exceptions, most of his works were published outside Cuba, since he sent his manuscripts abroad to be published—something Cuban officialdom considered an act of treason at the time. Arenas distinguished himself early in his career as a rebel who showed no respect for Cuban laws and guidelines, defying everything he considered restrictive of and oppressive to his activities, and personal life style, and the publication of his work.[31]

In addition to the UMAPs, one of the most institutionally homophobic events that took place in Cuba on the national level was the First National Congress of Education and Culture in 1971. This congress officially designated homosexuality as an intrinsically "antisocial" and "socio-pathological" behavior; accordingly, it decided that all signs of homosexual deviation should be strictly rebuffed and prevented in order to contain any spreading of homosexual practices. It was established that homosexuals should be denied employment in institutions where they might have an influence over young people. It was also established that homosexuals could not be permitted to represent Cuba through cultural activities abroad. In conclusion, the congress recommended severe legal sanctions against any homosexual responsible for the corruption of minors as well as for those who displayed incorrigible antisocial behavior.[32] All these resolutions were not simply the opinions of an assembly of prominent educators and politicians, for in a system such as that in socialist Cuba, where little or no separation existed between the state and civilian society, they quickly became national policy adhered to by all governmental agencies.

Finally, by the mid-1970s homosexual persecution in Cuba had begun to diminish. Gone were the massive purges of writers and

31. The bibliography on Reinaldo Arenas's political stance and his relationship with the Cuban government is copious. See, among others, Juan Abreu, "Presencia de Arenas," in *Reinaldo Arenas. Recuerdo y presencia,* ed. Reinaldo Sánchez (Miami: Ediciones Universal, 1994), 13–20; Armando Álvarez Bravo, "Reinaldo Arenas: 'Escribir es un acto de irreverencia,'" *El Nuevo Herald,* 21 April 1990), 1D, 5D; Ottmar Ette, editor, *La escritura de la memoria. Reinaldo Arenas: textos, estudios y documentación* (Frankfurt am Main: Vervuert Verlag, 1992); Vincent Canby, " 'Improper Conduct': Exiles Indict Castro Regime," *The New York Times,* 11 April 1984, C19; Edwin Ellis, "Reinaldo Arenas and His 'Act of Fury': A Writer in Exile Documents Repression in 'El Central,' " *The Advocate* 388 (10 July 1984): 38, 40; Robert Richmond Ellis, "The Gay Lifewriting of Reinaldo Arenas: *Antes que anochezca,*" *A/B: Auto/Biographies Studies* 10, no. 1 (spring 1995): 126–44; Epps, "Proper Conduct"; and Emilio Bejel, "Arenas's *Antes que anochezca:* Autobiography of a Gay Cuban Dissident," in *Reading and Writing the Ambiente: Queer Sexualities in Latino, Latin American, and Spanish Culture,* ed. Susana Chávez Silverman and Librada Hernández (Madison: University of Wisconsin Press, 2000), 299–315.

32. See comments by Lumsden, *Machos, Maricones, and Gays,* 73–75.

intellectuals, and Resolution Number Three, which played a major role in the legalization of homophobia, was abolished by order of the Supreme Court in 1975. In 1976 the Ministry of Culture was created and Armando Hart was named its minister. He had distinguished himself among the revolutionaries for his more "liberal" position on homosexuality and other cultural questions. The creation of the National Work Group on Sexual Education in 1977 served as a conduit for somewhat more flexible and actualized positions on human sexuality. As gay activist and scholar Ian Lumsden has noted, from that point onward "conditions began to improve for homosexuals in the arts." He adds, "Oppression of homosexuals would become more and more similar to what had occurred informally in most other Latin American countries, including liberal democratic ones such as Costa Rica."[33] Regulations against homosexuals became somewhat more informal and less systematic and official.

Legally speaking, by that time in Cuba homosexuality per se was not a crime, but the decrease in homophobia beginning in the mid-1970s should be qualified. The Penal Code of 1979 did not eliminate certain discriminations against homosexuals. Public displays of homosexual behavior remained illegal, although private homosexual behavior was not. Of course, any homosexual act with a minor (someone under the age of sixteen) was still penalized severely, much more so, in fact, that an equivalent heterosexual relationship. Also, this Penal Code included the Ley de peligrosidad (Law of dangerousness), a vague statute that left much to the discretion of the often homophobic judges. Under this law almost any behavior considered antisocial that expressed "socially disapproved vices" could carry a penalty of one to four years of "therapy" or "reeducation."[34]

One of the most important aspects of this slow, difficult, and uneven social change was that by the end of the 1970s the Cuban Communist Party no longer considered homosexual behavior to be in fundamental contradiction with the revolutionary process. Homosexuality went from being a crime even in private to being principally a psychological or medical problem. As Marvin Leiner points out, "Although this change in itself did not end the suffering of gay people who were victims of prejudice, it was a significant move toward more liberal attitudes that allowed a challenge to homophobia to take root."[35] By

33. Ibid., 80.
34. For an account of the relationship between homosexuality and the law in Cuba, see ibid., 81–95.
35. Leiner, *Sexual Politics in Cuba*, 43–44.

the mid-1970s a national discussion had begun on what was called the Family Code, which gave a certain legitimacy to the voices calling for change in the roles of men and women and in society in general. This dialogue allowed for a certain degree of questioning of homophobia.

Even the influence of the Soviet Bloc was not as extremely homophobic as it had been. In 1979 the Cuban National Work Group on Sexual Education published the Spanish translation of *El hombre y la mujer en la intimidad* (Man and woman in their intimacy) by East German sexologist Siegfried Schnabl.[36] His opinions on male and female sexuality were novel compared with prevailing views in East Germany and Cuba, and the book caused a sensation. The greatest surprise was the book's final chapter, "Homosexuality in Men and Women." In spite of its brevity (only ten pages in length), it caused true commotion in Cuban educational and intellectual circles of the day. It proposes a very different vision of homosexuality than that which had been previously imposed by the revolution. Schnabl condemns East German society for practicing a homophobia that was emotionally destructive to homosexuals and increased their suffering and even their suicide rate. He states that homosexuality is not a disease, but simply a variant of human sexuality. Homosexuals, he explains, do not suffer from homosexuality but rather from society's discrimination and abuse. Apart from their sexual orientation, homosexuals are no different from people considered normal. These ideas caused a veritable explosion of interest in Cuban society. Although printed in an edition of only fifteen thousand copies (which in Cuba was quite small for a work of this kind), Schnabl's book became a best-seller, being passed from one reader to the next. Everyone wanted to read this famous treatise, and since it came from another socialist country, it was seen as less dangerous and less suspect of "foreign influence," a term that frequently meant direct interference from the United States.[37]

All these changes took place in the second half of the 1970s, but in the summer of 1980 an event occurred that halted this social progress: the exodus of some 125,000 Cubans from the port of Mariel. As it is well known, among the "undesirable," the "antisocial," and the "scum" expelled by the Cuban government through Mariel were a large number of homosexuals.[38] One of the "antisocials" who had managed

36. Siegfried Schnabl, *El hombre y la mujer en la intimidad* (Havana: Editorial Científico-Técnica, 1979).

37. See Leiner, *Sexual Politics in Cuba*, 44.

38. Lumsden, *Machos, Maricones, and Gays*, 78–80. See also Henk van de Boogaard and Kathelijne van Kammen, "Cuba: We Cannot Jump over Our Own Shadow," in *IGA Pink*

to find his way through Mariel was Reinaldo Arenas, who had become internationally famous as a gay dissident writer. Homophobia returned with a vengeance to Cuba, and homosexuals were once again labeled as *escoria* (scum), since the Cuban government was trying to portray those who were leaving as undesirable persons, as the dregs of society who wished to leave because they couldn't abide a "healthy" country like Cuba. The official Cuban government newspaper *Granma* stated that "[e]ven though in our country homosexuals are not persecuted or harassed . . . there were quite a few of them in the Peruvian embassy, in addition to all those involved in gambling and drugs who find it difficult to satisfy their vices here."[39] In spite of the statement that "in our country homosexuals are not persecuted or harassed," it is undeniable that the discourse of Cuban officialdom at that time tried to associate gays and other "undesirable" groups with the corruption and negative attitudes that the Cuban people supposedly rejected. The Cuban government even published a documentary on the events of Mariel and the Peruvian embassy titled *Escoria*, the principal slogan of which was "get rid of them."[40] Within Cuba the government organized acts of repudiation against those who were leaving or who showed signs of wanting to leave. These acts were essentially acts of public rejection committed by Cubans who favored the government; they verbally and at times physically abused those hoping to take part in the exodus. The point was to show the existence of two very distinct groups: those who were leaving because they were antisocial, and those who were staying because they were good citizens.

With these events, Cuba's image abroad worsened considerably. This damage to Cuba's reputation was exacerbated by the documentary *Conducta impropia* (Improper conduct), produced outside Cuba by Néstor Almendros and Orlando Jiménez Leal. These two directors were avowedly opposed to the ruling system on the island, which they attacked by various means, including the disclosure of the Cuban government's homophobia.[41] *Conducta impropia* revisits the UMAPs, based on the statements of people who had been interned there at the end of the 1960s; the homophobic policies of the First

Book, 1985: A Global View of Lesbian and Gay Oppression and Liberation (Amsterdam: COC, 1985); and the editorials of *Granma*, 7 April 1980, 10 April 1980, and 2 May 1980.

39. *Granma*, 7 April 1980.

40. Spanish original: "que se vayan."

41. Néstor Almendros and Orlando Jiménez-Leal, *Improper Conduct*. The script of this documentary is found in Almendros and Jiménez-Leal, *Conducta impropia* (Madrid: Editorial Playor, 1984).

National Congress on Education and Culture of 1971; and circumstances related to the Mariel boat lift. Several people interviewed in the documentary voice their highly negative opinions of the Cuban regime in general, and some of them were already world renowned, such as Reinaldo Arenas, Heberto Padilla, Guillermo Cabrera Infante, and Carlos Franqui, among others. But the rest of those interviewed were everyday Cubans whose stories were included in the documentary in order to emphasize a very negative vision of Cuba. The documentary leaves the viewer with the opinion that Cuban homophobia had not lessened at all from the time of the UMAPs.

Conducta impropia ends with the words of René Ariza, a Cuban writer and playwright then in exile in southern Florida, who had served a five-year jail term in Cuba. The reasons for his incarcerations are not exactly clear from his statements, but he implies that it was due to his being "different" and displaying improper conduct:

> The most untrue thing about it isn't exactly what happens but why it happens. Being different, being queer, engaging in inappropriate conduct, is something not only prohibited [in Cuba] but also completely repressed, which can even land you in prison. I think that's something that's been in the Cuban character for a long time, that isn't exclusive to Castro; there are many Castros and everyone has to watch out for the Castro they have inside. It's an attitude we carry around. For a long time we've borne a series of designs, of molds, and we're very conditioned by it all. It's a vicious circle, and we've fallen completely into paranoia, a paranoia we all maintain, both the persecutors as well as the persecuted, since the persecuted seem to be the persecutors. Everyone suspects everyone.[42]

The documentary was filmed at the beginning of the 1980s, but since then there have been obvious improvements in the treatment of homosexuals by Cuban officials. As Ian Lumsden says, "although Cuba and its government remain homophobic, there is little evidence

42. Spanish original: "Lo más infundioso de la cosa no está exactamente en qué sucede sino en por qué sucede. Ser distinto, ser extraño, tener una conducta impropia, es algo no sólo prohibido [en Cuba] sino completamente reprimido y puede costarte la prisión. Eso yo creo que está dentro del carácter del cubano de [desde?] hace mucho tiempo, que no es privativo de Castro, y que hay muchos Castros, y que hay que vigilarse el Castro que cada uno tiene dentro. Es una actitud que arrastramos. Arrastramos una serie de diseños, de moldes de hace mucho tiempo, y estamos muy condicionados por todo. Es un círculo vicioso, y se ha caído completamente en una paranoia, una paranoia que la sustentan todos, la sustentan tanto los que persiguen como los perseguidos, puesto que los perseguidos parecen ser los que persiguen. Todo el mundo sospecha de todos." Ibid.

to support the contention that the *persecution* of homosexuals remains a matter of state policy. On the contrary, there is considerable evidence to suggest that the government is now seeking to devise a much less repressive way of regulating homosexuality."[43] In fact, it would not be an exaggeration to say that beginning in the 1980s the situation of homosexuals in relation to government policy was improving progressively. By the end of that decade, not only had official persecution of homosexuals decreased substantially, but works having very daring homoerotic themes were allowed to be published, sometimes with encouragement and even with prizes awarded in local and national literary contests. This change, especially from 1988 onward, has brought about a wave of writing in which new and open representations of homosexuality in Cuba play a central role. What is even more important is that these representations are made in terms that could be called positive, at least in the sense that this would be true in the gay literature of western European countries or the present-day United States. Several of these texts are written from the perspective of "friendly participants" in contrast to "hostile nonparticipants," as previous texts had been.

I should make the proviso that the Gay and Lesbian Association of Cuba (GLAC), which tried to organize on 28 July 1994, has not been able to do so successfully. Some members of this association attempted to regroup on 24 January 1995 under the name Acción por la Libertad de Expresión de la Elección Sexual (Action for the freedom of expression of sexual choice [GALEES]), but were unable to receive any form of official recognition. According to Ian Lumsden, "Members of GLAC were not subject to any specific repression, although they, like many other Cubans, lived tense moments that include more street *redadas* [raids] in the weeks that followed the refugee exodus in the late summer of 1994."[44] It is instructive to read Lumsden's interview on 7 March 1995 with Andrix Gudin Williams, the principal organizer of the Cuban Gay and Lesbian Association. Here Williams, in answer to a report in the 24 January 1995 issue of *The Advocate*, says that it was not true that the "[Cuban] government security forces launched a crackdown so brutal that leaders of the group [GLAC] [had] to shut it down."[45] Of course, we don't know how free Williams was to express this opinion.

43. Lumsden, *Machos, Maricones, and Gays*, 80. See also the informative and perceptive article by Paul Julian Smith, "Cuban Homosexualities: On the Beach with Néstor Almendros and Reinaldo Arenas," in *Hispanisms and Homosexualities*, ed. Molloy and McKee Irwin, 248–68.

44. Lumsden, *Machos, Maricones, and Gays*, 80.

45. Ibid.

At least it may be stated that the previous representations of homosexuality in Cuba are being radically questioned, including their relationship with the concept of citizenship. Among the most notable examples in this regard, the critical and popular acclaim of the Cuban film *Fresa y chocolate* (Strawberry and chocolate) stands out.[46] This film deals explicitly with the discrimination against homosexuality that has existed in Cuba as well as the need to integrate homosexuality into the very concept of nationhood. (I analyze this film in detail in chapter 9.) Other examples include the documentary *Mariposas en el andamio* (Butterflies on the scaffold), which, although virtually unknown in Cuba, is at least proof that a documentary dealing with and defending transvestites in a town near Havana called La Güinera was allowed to be made.[47] (I study this documentary in chapter 11.) There are also popular songs such as "Pecado original" (Original sin) by Pablo Milanés and "El tiene delirio de amar varones" (He's boy crazy) by Pedro Luis Ferrer, which defend the right to same-sex loving relations. In addition, numerous contemporary poems, short stories, and a few novels deal more openly with gay and lesbian relations in comparison to what had been permitted in Cuba earlier (I expand on this issue in chapter 10).

Among the authors who have now written and/or published essays or literary texts of this sort are Abilio Estévez, Miguel Mejides (the theme of whose story has been essentially re-created by Francisco López Sacha), Pedro de Jesús López Acosta, Marilyn Boves, Leonardo Padura Fuentes, Roberto Urías, Norge Espinosa, Ena Lucía Portela Alzola, Jacqueline Herrand Brooks, Alberto Acosta Pérez, Mirta Yáñez, Fátima Paterson, Manelic R. Ferret, Mercedes Santos Moray, Alejandro Aragón L'Oria, Senel Paz, Alexis Pimienta, Juan Carlos Valls, Francisco Morán Lull, Salvador Redonet, Odette Alonso, Damaris Calderón, and Francisco García González. At present, many of these writers live in Cuba, while some live abroad. Several of their works began to appear in 1988, and one can frequently see in them the expression of a *machista* world that has discriminated against and abused homosexuals while attempting to suppress everything that could be interpreted as homosexual.[48] Nevertheless, I believe that the simple

46. The film *Fresa y chocolate* (Strawberry and chocolate) (1993) was directed by Tomás Gutiérrez Alea and Juan Carlos Tabío, and based on Senel Paz's short story *El lobo, el bosque y el hombre nuevo*.

47. The documentary *Mariposas en el andamio* (Butterflies on the scaffold) was directed by Margaret Gilpin and Luis Felipe Bernaza, and produced by Kangaroo Productions (1996).

48. See Alfredo Alonso Estenoz, "Tema homosexual en la literatura cubana de los 80 y los 90: ¿renovación o retroceso?" and Jesús Jambrina, "Sujetos *queer* en la literatura cubana:

fact that this issue is being so openly dealt with from a homosexual, gay, lesbian, or queer perspective, coupled with the great abundance of these texts produced in a little over a decade, clearly indicates some sort of transformation in the Cuban culture regarding homosexuality.

To all this must be added the 1997 Premio de Literatura Hispana en los Estados Unidos (Prize for Hispanic literature in the United States) of the distinguished Cuban cultural organization Casa de las Américas, which was awarded to Sonia Rivera-Valdés for her 1998 collection of short stories, *Las historias prohibidas de Marta Veneranda* (The forbidden stories of Marta Veneranda).[49] The majority of Rivera-Valdés's "forbidden stories" make references to lesbian women and, on two occasions, to gay men. The feminist and queer positions implicit in these stories are perhaps the most noteworthy characteristic of the collection. The success of *Las historias prohibidas* within Cuba has been remarkable. On a similar note, I should add here that Cuban researcher and critic Víctor Fowler has dedicated himself in recent years to the study and publication of works on the representation of homosexuality in his country. His writings have been published by several Cuban magazines and his book on the topic was published in Havana in 1998.[50] Thus, if we take into consideration all the information available to us today, we can say that despite its recent history of institutionalized homophobia, Cuba has become a country in which the representation of homosexuality is more open, permitted, and public than ever before.[51]

hacia una (posible) genealogía homoerótica." Both Estenoz and Jambrina read their papers at the 2000 Latin American Studies Association Annual Conference, Miami, Fla., 15–18 March 2000. I have obtained a copy of their presentations through the generosity of these two critics.

49. Sonia Rivera-Valdés, *Las historias prohibidas de Marta Veneranda* (The forbidden stories of Marta Veneranda) (Havana: Ministerio de Cultura, Colombia/Casa de Las Américas, Cuba, 1997).

50. Fowler, *La maldición*. Recently, other Cuban critics who have dedicated most of their recent research efforts to the study of the representation of homosexuality in Cuban literature include Alfredo Alonso Estenoz and Jesús Jambrina.

51. I have not included in this introduction the extremely important issue of AIDS and how Cuban AIDS patients are treated, because this would mean a new research that I prefer to leave for another occasion. For an extensive discussion of AIDS in Cuba, see Lumsden, *Machos, Maricones, and Gays*, 160–77.

SIX

Creative Redemption in
a Providential Teleology

By the time Fidel Castro's nationalist revolution was spreading over the entire island at the close of the 1950s, the neobaroque writing of José Lezama Lima (1910–76) had become one of the most remarkable achievements of Cuban culture of the period. Both the political revolution and the neobaroque art, each in its own way, articulated a profound discontent with the national situation; both thought, from very different perspectives, that something was deeply wrong in Cuban society and that a radical cure was needed. Lezama Lima's work initiated a radical questioning of the Eurocentric Enlightenment project and brought about a serious reconsideration of the question of homoeroticism. Lezama Lima's aesthetic defined itself as the "art of Counter-Reformation" and therefore of Counter-Reason, Counter-Science, and at times Counter-Homophobia. My reading of Lezama Lima's texts centers on the idea that they are anti-Enlightenment and antipositivist responses to the national situation at the time that trigger a radical, complex discussion on many of the postulates of the modern world, including the modern construct of homosexuality.

Lezama Lima believed that everything began with poetry. In one sense his cosmology is a reaction to an era of profound political and social crisis, a time best defined from his perspective as "prosaic" in every sense of the term. Lezama Lima was scarcely twenty when he took part in the student demonstration of 30 September 1930 against the government of Gerardo Machado (1925–33). The two decades preceding the poet's involvement with Cuba's revolutionary history were times of worldwide instability. Cuba was greatly affected by American neocolonialism, and in Lezama's texts we can easily identify the tenor of a poet shaped by an era that had exiled artists within their own society. Lezama Lima's poetics can be viewed as a response to the alienation of the 1920s and 1930s, including the revolution against Machado, the interventionist policy of the United States, the Spanish Civil War, and the depression. Latin America saw the European political and social crisis as a series of fragmentations that seemed to confirm the dehumanization and decadence of Western civilization. Lezama Lima reacted by creating a poetic universe as a counterpoint to these momentous circumstances. Seen in this light, Lezama's work is directly related to that of José Martí, since both sought to reestablish poetry as a basis for culture and as a response to modern fragmentation.

Among the paths open to a poet growing up amidst great adversity is the option of retreating from the immediate in order to explore other possibilities and engage the contradictions of his/her time. In art, this "distancing" is often voiced as a utopian image, a symbolic substitute for the absence of hope. Like the seventeenth-century Spanish baroque poet Luis de Góngora, Lezama Lima chose to write for an elite audience able to grasp his labyrinthine textual strategies. Although his work can be seen as an alienated discourse, Lezama Lima strove not only to give aesthetic legitimacy to the neobaroque but also to provide it with historical meaning. One of his greatest cultural contributions is his theory of "Latin American expression," with which he develops a complex and anti-Enlightenment vision of Latin American culture.[1]

Lezama Lima, along with other Cuban intellectuals and artists of his time, founded *Orígenes* (Origins), a magazine he directed from 1944 until 1956 and through which he began to establish an international reputation. The magazine frequently published German writers such as Georg Hegel and Oswald Spengler in translation, and their writings acquired new meaning when interpreted by Cuban intellectuals. The French were represented by Arthur Rimbaud, Stéphane Mallarmé, Paul Valéry, and Paul Claudel, and Saint-John Perse was a particular favorite of Lezama Lima's. English writers who often contributed were G. K. Chesterton, Virginia Woolf, Dylan Thomas, and especially T. S. Eliot.

1. I have studied this issue in my *José Lezama Lima, Poet of the Image* (Gainesville: University of Florida Press, 1990), 123–47.

The United States was well represented by George Santayana, William Carlos Williams, and Wallace Stevens.[2]

Lezama Lima's life and work existed against the specific backdrop of not only the Machado and Batista regimes during his formative years, but also the Cuban Revolution of 1959. There are those who consider him the victim of a socialist system that isolated him and prevented his participation in Cuban cultural life. On the other hand are those who maintain that he was not at all opposed to the revolution and enjoyed wide publication and increasing fame during that period. Clearly, Lezama Lima was enthusiastic toward the revolution during 1959 and the early 1960s. His essays throughout that decade heralded the revolution as the triumph of Cuba's finest aspirations. Still, his enthusiasm was tempered early on by attacks from *Lunes de Revolución* (Mondays of revolution), a literary supplement to the newspaper *Revolución* (Revolution). In 1961 political circumstances in the Cuban cultural world led to the cessation of *Lunes de Revolución*, and some of Lezama Lima's detractors either went into exile or remained silent for several years. In 1962 Lezama Lima was named one of six vice-presidents of the newly created Union of Writers and Artists of Cuba, whose president was the poet Nicolás Guillén, a Communist Party member and poet laureate of the Castro regime.

When Lezama Lima published *Paradiso* in 1966, it sparked a controversy that prompted government officials to temporarily block its distribution (ostensibly because of the book's explicit homosexual scenes). Yet the novel soon reappeared in bookstores. *Paradiso*, and the controversy surrounding it, greatly enhanced Lezama Lima's reputation. However, a serious clash eventually occurred between Lezama Lima and officialdom that originated with the Padilla Affair of 1968–71.[3] The account of this controversy has been given many times over. As far as Lezama Lima was concerned, its most important element was Heberto Padilla's retraction of his antigovernment stance in which he named Lezama as a fellow counterrevolutionary. This accusation had been denied by Lezama and his friends, but he was never again asked to contribute to Cuba's state-controlled national journals and was denied travel permits to participate in international congresses—acts of repudiation and censorship against his political and literary stance.

Nevertheless, despite the negative cast of the controversy over *Paradiso* and the Padilla Affair, Lezama Lima never publicly opposed the

2. Ibid., 2–13.
3. See Lourdes Casal, *El caso Padilla* (Miami: Ediciones Universal, 1971).

government, though he often complained about it in his correspondence with his sister.[4] Whatever his true opinion was of the revolution, he definitely experienced de facto censorship during his later years. Then, with the posthumous growth of his international literary fame in the late 1970s, the Cuban government began to promote the study of his work, and new editions of his texts were published. Although it is undeniable that purely political motives were behind this new policy, the government's promotion of his writings can also be explained by the great importance Lezama Lima gave to the construction of *cubanidad* (Cubanness), an abiding interest of the Revolution.

Of the Latin American writers claiming the baroque as a valid means of rereading and criticizing modernity from their part of the world, perhaps the most all-encompassing was Lezama Lima. His recycling of the baroque attempts to discredit the modern master narratives of Science, History, and the Subject.[5] Lezama Lima's systematic deconstruction of these principles constitutes an attempt to position Latin America's marginality and its imperfect modernity in a positive light. That is why his texts often direct their attacks against several of the fundamental values of the Enlightenment version of modernity. The assumption by critics is that Latin Americans, having never completely assumed their modernity, and being only partially modernized, are predisposed to recycle the baroque as a critical and paradoxical form of dialogue with contemporary culture. Lezama Lima's neobaroque confronts the imperfection of the Latin American modern experience by cannibalizing cultural constructs produced in the modern hegemonic centers.[6] Octavio Paz has said that the waning of modernity gives rise to a "resurrection of buried realities, the reappearance of the forgotten and the repressed which, like at other times in history, can lead to a regeneration. A returning to the origin is almost always an upturning: renovations, rebirths."[7]

To study Lezama Lima's position on the relationship between the constructs of Latin American nationalism and homosexuality, I must

4. José Lezama Lima, *Cartas (1939–1976),* ed. Eloísa Lezama Lima (Madrid: Editorial Orígenes, 1979).

5. For an interesting study of the relationship between the neobaroque and the Eurocentric Enlightenment project, see Irlemar Chiampi, *Barroco e modernidade* (São Paulo: Editora Perspectiva, 1998).

6. Ibid.

7. Spanish original: "resurrección de realidades enterradas, reaparición de lo olvidado y lo reprimido que, como otras veces en la historia, puede desembocar en una regeneración. Las vueltas al origen son casi siempre revueltas: renovaciones, renacimientos." Octavio Paz, *La otra voz. Poesía y fin de siglo* (Barcelona: Seix Barral, 1990).

first explain some of his fundamental ideas. This will allow me to contextualize the meaning of the homosexual subject within what Lezama Lima called his "poetic system of the world." His texts are so dense and difficult to read—so baroque—that their very complexity becomes an element worthy of study. For those familiar with Latin American literature, Lezama Lima is a true giant of letters and culture, but the nature of his texts has perhaps impeded a greater diffusion of his work. His detractors accuse him of being hermetic and unintelligible, while his supporters revere his texts as the most extraordinary intellectual and artistic adventure ever carried out by a Latin American writer.

The great difficulty in accessing Lezama Lima's texts is a fundamental and deliberate aim of his poetic project. He insists that the obscure, the mysterious, and the difficult can awaken our interest through the attraction of the unknown. To penetrate what we do not understand, he is convinced, is to contribute to the progressive history of knowledge itself. This is why his writing praises baroque art and delights in the strange, the exceptional, and the dense. Metaphor, far from limiting itself to a cosmetic role, is for Lezama Lima the foundation of all reality. He considers the metaphor's "excessive" qualities as reflecting the characteristics of the Image, which in his poetic system is the potential power of the possible, the power of what has not yet been created. For Lezama Lima, the Image is like a magnet influenced by everything that has not yet been, but which could be created. This possibility invites discovery and is the power that attracts our creative capacity. This also implies that he conceives of the Image as the creative power that arises from the lack of a natural order. According to Lezama Lima, there is no stable, constant Nature, but rather a standing invitation to create something new. This is his basis for a providential history that progresses toward some sort of redemption, although he thinks of this history as a providential religious progression very distant from the Enlightenment historical philosophy. Unlike Hegel, Lezama Lima's historical progression does not proceed toward a dialectic of self-awareness of the Idea, but toward a constant mystery, which in turn is geared toward some form of religious salvation. Despite its heterodoxy, his work is profoundly Catholic.

The Lezamian metaphor intends to make visible and finite that which is invisible and infinite through the realm of the Image. For Lezama Lima, metaphors are not discoveries of what already exists but are a human means employed to seize the infinite. He holds no faith in a language that simply reproduces the intelligible world or the natural world, as the neoclassicists try to do. For him the so-called laws of the world and of nature are unstable and not necessarily the same as the laws of the intellect in the rational sense. His metaphors imply instability, dynamism, and progressive change. In his "poetic system of the world" the Image is the attraction that the world of the uncreated exerts on the created, and the metaphor is the human means to relate or erase world differences and thus contribute to the constant creation of the universe. This isn't the reproduction of a world, but rather the creation of one, hence the radical rejection of all representative or mimetic art. Thus for Lezama Lima a text's difficulty, far from being an obstacle, is a necessary invitation to create: as he remarked, "only the difficult is stimulating."[8] Poetry, the center of all knowledge, is an invitation to the still unfelt and unknown. "Actually," said Lezama, "the problem of understanding or lack of understanding, is an irrelevancy when evaluating artistic expression."[9]

In this extremely complex poetic system, Lezama Lima radically re-elaborates Dante's theory of the Image from the last part of the third book of the *Divine Comedy*.[10] For Dante, "high fantasy" is the most elevated and sublime function of the imagination, as is shown when the poet, after the dreams, has visions of earthly paradise without the help of Virgil, who symbolizes human reason. Dante also understood that in addition to poetic vision, the imagination is related to expression, and expression is in turn associated with memory and language. So at the end of Dante's *Paradiso*, the artist wins a noble victory by privileging imagination over reason. Yet on the other hand the artist also achieves victory over mysticism, since the poet approaches poetic vision in human terms and with the mediation of expression. At the end of *Paradiso* Dante loses hope while seeking an adequate means of expression; he is aware of the abyss between his vision and the universe of language. One of Dante's greatest literary contributions, which Lezama Lima integrates into his poetics, is the placement of the imagination above reason. As with Dante, poetic activity in Lezama Lima attempts to

8. Spanish original: "sólo lo dificíl es estimulante." José Lezama Lima, "Mitos y cansancio clásico," in *Obras completas*, (Mexico City: Aguilar, 1977), 2:279.

9. Spanish original: "En realidad, entender o no entender carecen de vivencia en la valoración de la expresión artística." José Lezama Lima, "Respuesta y nuevas interrogaciones. Carta abierta a Jorge Mañach," *Bohemia* 40 (2 October 1949): 77.

10. For a general study of the historical evolution of these ideas, see Karl D. Uitti, *Linguistics and Literary Theory* (Englewood Cliffs, N.J.: Prentice-Hall, 1969), especially pages 38–62. For an insightful analysis of the relationship between history and rhetoric in Dante, see Guiseppe Mazzotta, *Dante, Poet of the Desert* (Princeton: Princeton University Press, 1979), especially pages 227–74. For a study of Dante's concept of language, see André Pézard, "La langue italianne dans la pensée de Dante," *Cahiers du Sud* 34 (1951): 25–38.

restore the Edenic purity lost from human tongues by original sin. In Christian mythology, the original language, derived from Adam's first words to God, bore a natural and necessary relationship between signifier and signified as well as between speaker and listener. This harmony was broken by original sin. Following Lezama Lima, we can say that the act of imagination is an artifice made possible by the fragmentation of true nature by time and sin. Thus conceived, poetic imagination is the expression of a second nature or "supranature," which becomes a subversion of the rational order. This substitution tries to recover a mythical meaning to substitute for Western rationalism.

From a certain point of view (and only from a certain point of view), Lezama Lima's theory of the Image can be associated with some postmodern concepts, especially in the sense that Friedrich Nietzsche, Martin Heidegger, and Jacques Derrida can be called postmodern. Their project is at the margin of metaphysical reality, and it privileges poetic discourse over scientific or logical discourse. Within this way of thinking, rationalist metaphysics has never had the metaphysical plenitude it has claimed, but rather has hidden that lack of presence within a rational system that avoids dealing with the Image. In Lezama Lima's discussion of Nietzsche, he believes that he and Nietzsche both arrive at a meaning of the human being as a creative subject that constantly transcends itself. Also, Lezama Lima bases his concept of history on a metaphorical construct. He conceives of history as a narrative process integrating myth as well as history. This "fictionalized history" is not too different from that of Nietzsche, although for Lezama Lima, unlike for the German philosopher, history does have a sense of progression toward a fundamental improvement in the religious sense. This providential philosophy is what distances Lezama Lima's theory from postmodern conceptions. It is also one of the factors that separates his vision from that of Severo Sarduy, as I explain in the next chapter.

Regarding the difference between Lezama Lima's theory of the Image and positivism, it is important to recall Heidegger's distinction between the methodology of scientistic positivism and the intellectual process of the "essential thinker," by which he means Nietzsche. This characterization might just as easily refer to Lezama Lima. The positivist scientist, though recognizing the limits of knowledge, never considers that the unknown cannot be known, for the unknown is simply what we do not yet know. However, the "essential thinker" accepts that there is an unknown region that can never be known, either rationally or scientifically. If the scientist inquires in order to obtain utilitarian answers, the thinker inquires to find the basis from which he or she can presume to ask the question. Yet for Lezama Lima, to question at this profound level is to have already been given an answer. Lezama Lima's interest in Nietzsche, Heidegger, Mallarmé, Joyce, Proust, and other writers who share his poetic orientation is based on the idea that, within their distinct epochs and perspectives, they signal important manifestations of a radical subversion of rationalist metaphysics. This subversion undermines the ideology grounded in rationalist abstraction, realistic representation, and subjective individualism.

For Lezama Lima, poetic creativity is situated outside the accepted limits, but this "breaking of the boundaries" can carry with it a deep and irrecoverable fragmentation of the subject as well as a constant alienation of the creative subject with language and with the world. Lezama Lima's solution to this paradox is to assimilate all its contradictions with his theory of the Image. His Image assimilates the subject, language, and the world within the creative potential found in the absence of limits, in the void left by the lack of a natural order. Lezama also relates the breaking of the boundary and being outside the law with a configuration of erotic desire essential for poetic creativity. Hence the importance of illicit sexual situations (homosexuality, for example) in his texts: the poem is like an illicit erotic act of penetration into the creative power, which stems from a fundamental absence of a stable nature in the human subject.

Lezama Lima fictionalizes his "poetic system of the world" principally in his novel *Paradiso*, which depicts the life of José Cemí, a pseudo-autobiographical poet. The subject represented in this text is fragmented by crisis because of the alienation between himself and the world and between himself and language. Nevertheless, as the narrative unfolds it reveals meaning in the search for unity in the fragmented protagonist. The first seven chapters of *Paradiso* deal with the family history and the intellectual, emotional, and sexual formation of José Cemí. Chapters 8 and 9 (especially the latter) narrate the beginning of his participation in the world of both friendship and history; the theme of Cuban history appears in several of the chapters. The fourth chapter tells of the Olaya family (the family of José Cemí's mother) and their return from Jacksonville, Florida, to Havana in 1902, the same year the Cuban Republic began. In the fifth chapter, Rialta Olaya and José Eugenio Cemí, the future parents of José Cemí, meet and begin to fall in love at a dance attended by Tomás Estrada Palma, the first president of the republic. Thus the novel relates, in a fictional manner, not only a self-referential narrative of the author but also one of Cuban history.

In *Paradiso* a relationship is formed between philogeny and on-togeny, between the protagonist's biography and Cuba's political life during the first decades of the twentieth century. The story jumps back in time in the sixth chapter to tell of events that supposedly took place during Cuba's War of Independence (1895–98). All of these historical references are related to the theory of Latin American and Cuban history that Lezama develops in his book *La expresión americana* (Latin American expression) as well as in some of his other essays.[11] He perceives history as a series of "imaginary eras" that mark humanity's progression. He even states that the Cuban Revolution of 1959 belongs to a sort of new "era" of fulfillment. Of course, Lezama Lima developed this concept in the midst of the great enthusiasm brought about by the triumph of the revolution in the early 1960s.

Chapter 6 also relates the death of Colonel José Eugenio Cemí and the great void this causes in young José, who must now fill that void with poetry. The colonel is emblematic of the Father, of Nature, and his absence marks the lack of a stable natural order that would permit the unity of the subject. José Cemí is now an orphan and must find a substitute for his natural father. The vocation of his poetic creativity must fill the void left by the essential lack of the natural. Also, Cemí is asthmatic (he lacks "natural" air and must learn to breathe "artificially") and explores eccentric or illicit sexuality, in most cases homosexuality.

In the second section of the novel (chapters 7 through 12) the story becomes increasingly imaginative, and it is difficult to find a thread of realism. It is precisely in this section, especially in chapters 8 and 9, that Lezama Lima wrote some of the most daring scenes of homosexual encounters published in Cuba up to that time (with the possible exception of Carlos Montenegro's *Hombres sin mujer* of 1938). These chapters contain highly complex dialogues in which different interpretations of homosexuality are discussed. In chapter 8 the episodes are related to Cemí's life at school, where, as a passive observer, he makes a series of sexual discoveries. The prodigious sexuality of the characters Farraluque and Leregas is described here. This sexuality is very meaningful for two reasons: it occurs shortly after the chapters telling of the death of Cemí's father, and the sexual activity is almost entirely homosexual. In the absence of his father, young Cemí must form his own sexual code.

---

11. Spanish original: "eras imaginarias." For a study of the "imaginary eras" in Lezama Lima, see Bejel, *José Lezama Lima*, 123–47.

Time and again, *Paradiso* proposes that lacking an absolute nature, a supranatural substitute must be sought, free of temporality and human reproduction. Within this context, homosexuality becomes an emblem of poetry: it is a search for the similar that transcends time and reproduction. It aspires to a creativity that goes beyond the "natural," toward a state Lezama Lima defines as "beyond the limits." It is then a metaphor that is inscribed into the center of the vacuum created by the absence of the natural. Homosexuality in *Paradiso* is also presented as an excess that, precisely because it goes beyond the permitted limits, announces the possibility of a creative surplus. It is in this sense that the erotic and the aesthetic in Lezama Lima find their greatest creative potential, suggesting that only what goes beyond the limits can lead to a penetration into the new and the unknown.

The final section of chapter 9 is dedicated almost completely to the theme of homosexuality. Fellow athletes of Baena Albornoz, the captain of the rowing crew, catch him in the act of homosexual relations with a freshman named Leregas. We are told that both men are expelled from the campus through "the vulgar science of condemnation," but Cemí distances himself from all the gossip. Later, Cemí is at the university with his friends Fronesis and Foción, the three conversing extensively about the possible meaning of homosexuality. Fronesis propounds a series of opinions on homosexuality, which Foción sees as a "surrealist" (read "psychoanalytic" or "Freudian") interpretation of the theme. For Fronesis, all sexual deviation is a manifestation of ancestral memory, but he considers sex, like poetry, "convincing stuff, not problematical."[12] Fronesis comes close to a psychoanalytic viewpoint when he notes, "The seasons of man cannot be successive, that is, there are men in whom this state of innocence, this living in childhood, persists through life" (264).[13] This opinion approaches the Freudian idea that sexual deviation results from a fixation at some stage of childhood. Fronesis says, "A child who . . . remains forever fixed in childhood, always has a tendency toward this kind of sexuality, that is, locating sex in otherness, the other one similar to himself" (ibid.).[14]

12. Spanish original: "materia concluyente, no problemática." José Lezama Lima, *Paradiso*, 3d ed. (Mexico City: Ediciones Era, 1973), 263.

13. Spanish original: "Las estaciones en el hombre no pueden ser sucesivas, es decir, hay hombres en los cuales este estado de inocencia, ese vivir en niñez, pervive toda la vida."

14. Spanish original: "El niño . . . que se fija para siempre en la niñez, tiene siempre tendencia a la sexualidad semejante, es decir, a situar en el sexo la otredad, el otro semejante a sí mismo."

Foción argues that Fronesis's psychoanalytic interpretation attempts to explain the inexplicable and suffers from a "mechanicism" and "causalism" that cannot be justified (265–66). For Foción—a homosexual character who shows sexual interest in Fronesis—homosexuality is not a deviation, a vice, or a voluntary decision; it is something more profound than any justification. One of the most dramatic passages during Foción's exposition on homosexuality is his paraphrasing of Ecclesiastes: "There is a way that to a man seems straight; yet its end is the way of death,"[15] finally adding that "on Judgment Day pregnant women and nursing mothers will be put to the sword" (ibid.).[16] In this manner the text reaffirms the idea of homosexuality as a search for the supranatural, liberated from the constraints of reproduction and time.

Foción's concludes his remarks about sexual deviation as follows: "Everything that we consider sexual deviation today rises up in a reminiscence, or in something that with no fear of being pedantic I call a hypertely [that which goes beyond every limit] of immortality, a search for creation, for a succession of the creature beyond all causality of blood and even spirit, the creation of something made by man as yet completely unknown to the species. The new species would be the justification for the hypertely of immortality" (268).[17] Next he gives a series of commentaries on the varied attitudes of some of the most renowned homosexuals in history: the two Barba Jacobs (one from the sixteenth century and the Colombian from the twentieth, who took the previous Jacob's name), Leonardo da Vinci, Julius Caesar, Cesar Borgia, Oscar Wilde, and so on. He also mentions scientific studies such as those by the English sexologist Havelock Ellis. After this conversation, Foción and Cemí speak of Platonic dialogues, surmising that these have always served as the models for this type of inquiry.

In the eleventh chapter a heated discussion ensues between Foción and Fronesis's father in a cafe in the city of Santa Clara. Foción has gone there to see his friend, only to find Fronesis's father waiting to

15. Spanish original: "hay caminos derechos, que esos caminos tienen una finalidad, y no obstante, son caminos para la muerte."

16. Spanish original: "en el día del Juicio Final las mujeres embarazadas y las que están lactando serán pasadas a cuchillo."

17. Spanish original: "Todo lo que hoy nos parece desvío sexual, surge en una reminiscencia, o en algo que yo me atrevería a llamar, sin temor a ninguna pedantería, una hipertelia de la inmortalidad, o sea una busca de la creación, de la sucesión de la criatura, más allá de toda causalidad de la sangre y aún del espíritu, la creación de algo hecho por el hombre, totalmente desconocido aún por la especie. La nueva especie justificaría toda hipertelia de la inmortalidad."

confront him about his homosexuality and his attraction to Fronesis. These events give rise to Foción's madness and his hospitalization in an insane asylum. By the end of the chapter, however, he has overcome this madness.

The relationship between Foción and Fronesis's father takes an unexpected turn in the ninth chapter of *Oppiano Licario*, Lezama Lima's last, unfinished novel and a sequel to *Paradiso*.[18] Here Fronesis's father reconciles with Foción and asks him to help his son, who is very ill in Paris. Although Lezama Lima died before finishing this novel, remaining documents (especially a draft of the work and an interview with Reynaldo González about it) give some clue as to the author's plans for the text.

In the interview Lezama Lima says, "[At the end of *Oppiano Licario*] I try another coupling between Cemí's daughter, the daughter of the image, who would rather marry the son of madness, of Foción; that is to say, the union of the image with madness."[19] From this we learn what Lezama Lima projected for *Oppiano Licario*'s conclusion: a "solution" that favored a synthesis between Foción's descendant and that of Cemí. As critic Arnaldo Cruz-Malavé has brilliantly explained, for Lezama Lima "homosexuality is not only the obstacle that must be overcome to restore the family and national succession. It is not only the substance of evil or the queer body that must be purged from the family and national organism. Homosexuality is also the very ontological condition of the adolescent poet, the family and the nation."[20] Cruz-Malavé adds that "*Paradiso* is not so much about conquering that void [of sterility and want] as about filling it up: founding the paternal image of the nation on it . . . constituting the subject, the family and the nation on the unproductive homosexual eros."[21]

18. José Lezama Lima, *Oppiano Licario*, 2d ed. (Mexico City: Ediciones Era, 1978).

19. Spanish original: "Procuro entonces [al final de *Oppiano Licario*] otro emparejamiento entre la hija de Cemí, la hija de la imagen, que prefiere casarse con el hijo del loco, de Foción; es decir, la unión de la imagen con la locura." Reynaldo González, "Entre la magia y la infinitud," in *Lezama Lima: el ingenuo culpable* (Havana: Letras Cubanas, 1988), 140–42.

20. Spanish original: "la homosexualidad no sólo es el obstáculo que hay que vencer para restaurar la sucesión familiar y nacional. No sólo es la sustancia del mal o el cuerpo extraño de que hay que depurar el organismo familiar y nacional. La homosexualidad también es la condición ontológica misma del poeta adolescente, la familia y la nación." Arnaldo Cruz-Malavé, *El primitivo implorante. El "sistema poético del mundo" de José Lezama Lima* (Atlanta: Rodopi, 1994), 89–90.

21. Spanish original: "*Paradiso* no es tanto vencer este vacío [el de la esterilidad y la falta] como colmarlo: fundar sobre él la imagen paterna de la nación . . . constituir al sujeto, la familia y la nación sobre el improductivo eros homosexual." Ibid., 90.

For Lezama Lima, history is the reflection of the Image projecting itself through the historical process and through time. According to his viewpoint, history is an ascending spiral, the continuity of which is guaranteed by the rebellious human subject. His world vision includes a mythic teleology of the Cuban nation that has a discursive connection with nineteenth-century Cuban nationalist discourse.[22] Within Lezama's poetic system, Cuban history includes a "baroque gentleman of Independence" exemplified by Carlos Manuel de Céspedes, whom nationalists consider the hero of the initial moment of Cuba's Ten Years' War in 1868.[23] But it is the figure of José Martí that plays the central role in Lezama Lima's Cuban mythology. For him, Martí voices a literary revolution whose ends will be realized in the course of history: with Martí, "poetry becomes a choral song." Lezama refers to Martí as "a fertile god, an engenderer of the Cuban image. He arrived by means of the image to create a reality, and at our very foundations lies this image as the support that sustains the counterpoint of our people."[24] In this national mythology, the death of Martí becomes a fundamental part of what might be called the myth of the hero entering the city.[25] This type of hero always enters the city dead: "We see how he has been dragged through the rain after his death, how fainting from his steed he prompted the few who saw it to remark that perhaps he had groaned, how he has been buried and unburied . . . his head separated from his trunk, as in those shrieking displays of the Mongolian cavalry, staged before the gates of the city."[26] The city is Santiago de Cuba, a metaphor that supports the image of the rebel hero, who, as long as he remains in the forest or mountains, cannot shape the history of his people. From this point of view, the city is the metaphor within which the image of the hero is contained and expanded at the same time, and

22. See Rafael Rojas, *Isla sin fin: contribución a la crítica del nacionalismo cubano* (Miami: Ediciones Universal, 1998), especially pages 30–45.

23. José Lezama Lima, "Céspedes: el señorío fundador," in *Imagen y posibilidad*, ed. Ciro Bianchi Ross (Havana: Editorial Letras Cubanas, 1981), 25.

24. Spanish original: "siendo un dios fecundante, un preñador de la imagen de lo cubano. Llegó la imagen a crear una realidad, en nuestra fundamentación está esa imagen como sustentáculo del contrapunto de nuestro pueblo." Lezama Lima, "El 26 de julio: imagen y posibilidad," in *Imagen y posibilidad*, 21.

25. In 1979, I attended a lecture by Cintio Vitier in which he presented the idea of "the myth of the hero entering the city" in Lezama Lima's work.

26. Spanish original: "Vemos cómo ha sido arrastrado después de muerto bajo la lluvia, cómo ha sido enterrado y desenterrado . . . cómo su cabeza separada del tronco, como en los alardes chillantes de una caballería mongólica, ha sido mostrada a la entrada de la ciudad." Lezama Lima, "La posibilidad en el espacio gnóstico americano," in *Imagen y posibilidad*, 104.

thus it is within the city that the aspirations of the hero can be fulfilled. Otherwise, history would remain only as a possibility, since the image of the hero in the forest has to be realized in the urban metaphor.

It is also interesting to note that although Havana is the space within which Cemí realizes himself as poet in *Paradiso*, it is Santiago that appears as the promised city in Lezama Lima's myth of the rebellious hero. Since urban space is the historical metaphor of the possibilities of the Image in this specific mythology, it is of utmost importance whether the hero enters the city dead or alive. It is within this context that Lezama Lima associates the figure of Martí with the Cuban Revolution of 1959: "But Martí touched the earth and kissed it and created a new causality, as all the great poets do. This was the prelude to a poetic era among us; so that we can now begin to live in an era that is infinitely affirmative, central, creative. It is the discovery of the ring, of the absolute circle. The hero enters the city."[27]

José Lezama Lima represents himself as a subject in crisis through José Cemí of *Paradiso* and *Oppiano Licario*. He portrays this protagonist as seeking his salvation in a society that has undermined the health of the psychological subject. The only solution Cemí can pursue for his personal, sexual, and historical crises is to become a poet in a world lacking a stable nature. Both novels tell the story of his vocation as writer and poet, since only in this way can a fragmented being in crisis aspire to reinvent itself and begin anew. Although the subject remains fragmented, his only cure is self-invention; this self-invention is an exorcism that is not only personal, aesthetic, literary, and psychological, but also historical. The historical sense of salvation throughout Lezama Lima's work must be understood in the sense of an "imaginary history" that provides a "redeeming" thread to a subject lacking a stable nature. This is where the representation of homosexuality and Cuban national teleology connect within his poetic system of the world. His work not only attempts to achieve an "imaginary and redeemed" story of José Lezama Lima—it also aspires to establish the possibility of redemption for the Latin American and Cuban subject seeking a new history or a new story that can resolve his earlier crisis and failure. Although we could read Lezama Lima's opinions on homosexuality as evidence that he still felt a high degree of guilt and internalized

27. Spanish original: "Pero Martí tocó la tierra, la besó, creó una nueva causalidad, como todos los grandes poetas. Y fue el preludio de la era poética entre nosotros, que ahora nuestro pueblo comienza a vivir, era inmensamente afirmativa, cenital, creadora. Encuentro del anillo, del círculo absoluto. El héroe entra en la ciudad." Ibid., 103–4.

homophobia in his final days, his work undeniably opens new possibilities for discussions on this social taboo. And it does so based on a system
of anti-Enlightenment and antipositivist thought that allows for new
perspectives on human sexuality as well as on nearly every element
of the foundation of modern culture from the start of the eighteenth
century. But there was another gay Cuban thinker who questioned the
principles of progress, history, subjectivity, and representation even
more radically than did Lezama Lima. This was Severo Sarduy, whom
I will study in the next chapter.

★ SEVEN ★

A Queer Response to
Postmodern Simulation

In the 1960s José Lezama Lima was the Cuban thinker and writer who best articulated the relationship between the rediscovery of the baroque and the questioning of traditional ideas on homoeroticism in his country. In many ways, Severo Sarduy (1937–93) was the successor to the neobaroque position initiated by Lezama Lima. Yet Sarduy, far from faithfully following in the footsteps of the master, modified his aesthetic and world vision, at times quite radically. Even so, Sarduy never strayed from a recycling of the baroque, which in his work was initially influenced by structuralist theories, and later by poststructuralism.

A comparison of Sarduy and Lezama yields similarities and differences, both personal and political. Neither publicly expressed opposition to the Cuban socialist government, yet while Lezama Lima remained in Cuba his entire life, Sarduy left for Paris in 1960, very early in the revolution, and never returned. There are also class differences between the two writers: Lezama was an aristocratic *criollo* (Cuban of Spanish ancestry born on the island) from Havana, while Sarduy was a proletarian from the former province of Camagüey. Moreover, their experiences in "coming out of the closet" were also quite different. In spite of the *Paradiso* "scandal," Lezama Lima and his family always denied or at least avoided any mention of his homosexuality, while Sarduy was openly gay very early in life, after taking up permanent residence in Paris. From that time onward, he apparently never denied that aspect of his life. At the time of their deaths—Lezama's in

Cuba in 1976, of a lung ailment, and Sarduy's in Paris in 1993, of complications from AIDS—both were viewed as true giants in Latin American literature.

As with Lezama Lima, in order to contextualize Sarduy's conceptions of homosexuality, homoeroticism, queerness, and "Cubanness," we must examine the basis of his work. The connection between Lezama Lima's baroque literary style and that of Sarduy is that both recycle the historical baroque, employing the ornamental metaphor along with verbal and rhetorical complexity so as to give aesthetic and historical legitimacy to anti-Enlightenment art and literature. But Lezama Lima uses religious and providential arguments that are undermined by Sarduy, who radicalizes some of Lezama's postulates, thereby arriving at a very different position. For example, although Lezama's representation is neobaroque and based on a form of destruction of the referent, which disappears to emerge acculturated, his writings ultimately imply a metaphorical subject capable of absorbing differences and constructing a providential world and a mythical national history. His writing contains a subject and a teleological progression as well as a form of Catholic divinity, although it is very heterodox. All of these elements are missing in Sarduy. For him the logic of temporal progression is replaced with a spatial logic where the subject of the writing is only a mark or posture implied by his textual strategies, which propose a radical simulation as their only meaning(lessness). Representation in Sarduy, then, is a simulation that unfolds on a corporeal surface. For Lezama Lima the force behind writing, life, and knowledge is a form of void that serves as religious creativity and as an Image based on the lack of a stable nature. Sarduy radicalizes that Lezamian void, making of it a "black hole" that swallows up rational meaning, religious ideas, and providential progression. His texts propose that subject, author, and the representation of history should be consumed by a form of senselessness. In this context Sarduy is clearly much closer to postmodernism than is Lezama.

Sarduy's first novel, *Gestos* (Gestures) (1963),[1] is somewhat realistic in its representation, but his subsequent novels have no discernable chronology or chain of events. His stories are frequently a series of complex and compulsive metamorphoses that constantly accentuate the falseness of codes that demand some type of closure or arrest. The constant simulations or role games in his texts make them a radical affront to literary genres and personal genders. Thus the figure of the

1. Severo Sarduy, *Gestos* (Gestures) (Barcelona: Seix Barral, 1963).

queer transvestite is much more important than those of the homosexual, the gay, or the lesbian, since the latter presuppose somewhat
stable identities and identifications, whereas the former symbolizes
transformation and excess. For example, Sarduy's novel *Cobra* (Cobra)
(1972) tells of a series of metamorphoses experienced by a transvestite
living in Paris during the 1960s.[2] This transvestite appears at times as
a dwarf, at others as a member of a group of Tibetan lamas or as an
Indian tourist, and so on. For Sarduy, as with postmodern theory, the
tension lies between the original and its copy, and not between the
world and transcendence as it does for Lezama. There is no original
for Sarduy; rather, everything is a copy of a copy of a copy. There also
is no real referent, but only a perennial caricature of a referent that
never really existed. The transvestite, then, does not imitate women,
but rather implies excess and extravagance in the luxury of detail.
Since Woman as such does not exist either in postmodern theory or
in Sarduy's neobaroque art, the original of the transvestite cannot
exist either. In reality, in Sarduy's way of thinking, women also imitate
something that does not exist; therefore, the transvestite truly lacks a
real, fixed model.

Sarduy's first clearly experimental novel is *De donde son los cantantes*
(Where the singers come from) (1967). In it he challenges, among
other discourses, linear history and "national identity,"[3] and critiques
the bases of modern bourgeois hegemony. In the third section of this
novel, "La entrada de Cristo en La Habana" (Christ enters Havana),
he describes the procession of a wooden Christ figure from Oriente,
Cuba's easternmost province, to the city of Havana, on the western
part of the island. As the figure travels westward it slowly rots, finally
falling to pieces. This disintegration occurs as the characters Auxilio
and Socorro, who can be taken to represent black culture in Cuba,
are killed from government helicopters. As the procession approaches
the capital, Cuban consumerist society is evinced by elegant buildings,
self-service shops, and the like. Finally, when the figure of Christ arrives
in Havana, snow blankets the city. The narrative seems to imply that
as the procession gets closer to the capital, the origin of nationality
disintegrates, becoming progressively more foreign, more consumer
oriented, and more dominated by the white culture, which pushes
out other cultures; moreover, a precursor of postmodern culture is

2. Severo Sarduy, *Cobra* (Cobra) (Buenos Aires: Editorial Sudamericana, 1972).
3. Severo Sarduy, *De donde son los cantantes* (Where the singers come from) (Mexico:
Editorial Joaquín Mortiz, 1967).

evident. So Sarduy is parodying, among other things, the discourses of nationalism and of origin, as well as those of bourgeois culture. Another possible reading of "La entrada de Cristo en Habana" is as an ironic image of Fidel Castro, who led, Christlike, a caravan of revolutionaries from Oriente to Havana during January 1959, a few days after the triumph of the revolution, which followed President Fulgencio Batista's removal at the beginning of the New Year.[4] The theoretical base of this political reading is the simulation that undermines every historical process. In Sarduy's texts, there is no history in the linear or ontological sense, only constructs based on contradictory and precarious discourses.

But Sarduy's theory of simulation presents some theoretical and political problems. A reading of *Colibrí* (Hummingbird) (1985), one of his last novels, is useful for studying this issue.[5] This work contains the following passage: "God is simulation. He who pretends the most is the chosen one."[6] This quotation points to the problem of representation, one of the main topics of the novel and a persistent preoccupation in most of Sarduy's texts. In this sense the story line of *Colibrí* typifies the extreme experimentalism of Sarduy's works. The novel's events take place with no apparent relation of cause and effect, and the names as well as the "identities" of the characters frequently change and transform themselves with no apparent motivation.

To provide a very brief and rather forced summary of the story, we can say that it deals with a good-looking young blond man with very dark eyebrows. The reader learns absolutely nothing about where he comes from, for lack of origin and genealogy is a constant in Sarduy's characters. Despite being quite muscular, he is called Colibrí (along with other synonyms) for the agile way he leapt from a boat taking him to La Casona, a homosexual sadomasochistic bordello. There Colibrí participates in a wrestling match with a hairless, obese Japanese man. Several older, wealthy homosexuals observe the struggle, which arouses them. They offer money to the victor, who turns out to be Colibrí. In spite of the rich men's desire for Colibrí and the money they offer him, he is unavailable to them, since the Bordello's owner, La Regente, is in love with Colibrí and wants him for herself. (She may also be regarded as a representation of a transvestite or transgendered person.) Colibrí,

4. For an insightful and original study of this novel, see Roberto González Echevarría, *La ruta de Severo Sarduy* (Hanover, N.H.: Ediciones del Norte, 1987).

5. Severo Sarduy, *Colibrí* (Bogota: Editorial La Oveja Negra, 1985; 1st ed., Barcelona: Editorial Argos Vergara, 1984). All quotations will come from the 1985 edition.

6. Spanish original: "Dios es simulación. El que más finja es el elegido." Ibid., 69.

who seems interested in homosexual relations only, rejects her and flees into the forest, pursued by hunters hired by La Regente. Colibrí escapes from La Casona several times in the story when La Regente's henchmen are on the verge of capturing him. We also learn that while in the forest, Colibrí has sex with the Japanese man. At the end of the work, Colibrí overthrows La Regente and rules La Casona, becoming as much a tyrant as was his predecessor.

All of these adventures are told in such an unrealistic manner that there can be no doubt that the text as a whole proposes a radically experimental effect. *Colibrí* is a novel that tries at all costs to prevent readers from interpreting it as a mimetic or realistic representation, even if they were to follow the parameters demanded by the new Latin American novel of the 1960s. A text of this nature brings up two questions: what are the nature and goals of this experiment, and is this experiment successful?

Although there are various ways of reading this novel, *Colibrí* can be seen as an experiment that continues Sarduy's project of radically altering practices of representation. The personal relationship among Severo Sarduy, Roland Barthes, François Wahl, and Philippe Sollers is well known, and there was also a close ideological relationship between Sarduy and these members of Tel Quel (a group of intellectuals who once published a highly influential journal by the same name), especially during his "structuralist phase."[7] Like the other writers and artists who were related at some point with the leftist structuralism of Tel Quel, Sarduy aspired to a revolution of hegemonic ideology at the most basic level: that of the signifier. Sarduy himself referred to his neobaroque aesthetic as a *"Revolutionary baroque machine* that keeps repressive society from its (barely) hidden goal: to capitalize bodies and goods" (emphasis in the original).[8] Also important to note is that Sarduy stated the following on more than one occasion: "What does a practice of the baroque mean today? Is it a desire for obscurity, for exquisiteness? I would dare to state the contrary: to be baroque today is to threaten, judge and parody at its very core the bourgeois economy, based on the thrifty administration of goods: the

7. Both Roberto González Echevarría and Adriana Méndez Rodenas believe that *Colibrí* represents a substantial change in Sarduy's stylistic and ideological direction. See González Echevarría, *La ruta de Severo Sarduy*, 211–42; and Adriana Méndez Rodenas, Review of *Colibrí*, by Severo Sarduy, *Revista Iberoamericana* 51 (1985): 399–401.

8. Spanish original: *"Máquina barroca revolucionaria* que impide a la sociedad represiva su propósito (apenas) oculto: capitalizar bienes y cuerpos." This is said by Sarduy in an interview by Jean Michel Fossey, "Severo Sarduy: Máquina barroca revolucionaria," in *Severo Sarduy*, by Jorge Aguilar Mora et al. (Caracas: Fundamentos, 1976), 19.

space of signs, language, symbolic support of society, guarantee of its functioning and of its communication."[9]

One of the corollaries of Sarduy's project implies that this revolution of the signifier is achieved by denying the reader every sort of security related to the unity of the human subject. This subject always appears in these texts as decentered and as simply an effect of textual practice. The author, the narrator, and the implied reader in these texts lack the unity and continuity that traditional ideology grants them. It is a stripping away of masks so unbelievable that every rational process is shown to be nothing more than a simulation. Our supposed unity as subjects is only an effect of textuality and of the symbolic system we have been brought up in, which is the social order that has constructed our subjectivity. From this we may deduce that if textual practices are altered at their base, the formation of a new subjectivity will be achieved. Sarduy's project is radical and ambitious, yet fraught with risks.

Let us take a closer look at the techniques Sarduy uses in *Colibrí* to dismantle subjectivity (and realistic representation along with it). I have already mentioned the experimentalism of the story line. We should not overlook the innumerable examples of unusual transformations of characters, the illogical jumps in the chain of events, unbelievable metaphors, and narrators struggling to control the story. Also, not only is nature described very strangely, but, stranger still, some actions take place in the midst of a still life. On one occasion, for example, Colibrí escapes among the trees of a winter landscape that is actually a painted backdrop. It is as if the text were saying that if the landscape had been described conventionally, readers might fall for the mimetic illusion that they were reading the representation of a real countryside, of a referent outside of the text. Thus the narration supports the Derridian idea that nothing exists apart from textuality, as attested to by this quotation from *Colibrí* : "There isn't . . . the slightest door in the wall . . . nor anything that would allow us to go behind representation."[10]

9. Spanish original: "¿Qué significa hoy en día una práctica del barroco? Se trata de un deseo de oscuridad, de exquisitez? Me arriesgo a sostener lo contrario: ser barroco hoy significa amenazar, juzgar y parodiar la economía burguesa, basada en la administración tacaña de los bienes, en su centro y fundamento mismo: el espacio de los signos, el lenguaje, soporte simbólico de la sociedad, garantía de su funcionamiento, de su comunicación." See Severo Sarduy, *Barroco* (Buenos Aires: Sudamericana, 1974), 99–100. Sarduy repeats this same idea, almost word for word, on page 6 of his interview with Fossey, ibid., 1. See also the excellent discussion of this issue in Adriana Méndez Rodenas, *Severo Sarduy: el neobarroco de la transgresión* (Mexico: Universidad Nacional Autonóma de México, 1983), 137–148.

10. Spanish original: "No hay . . . la menor puerta en el muro . . . ni nada que nos permita pasar detrás de la representación." Sarduy, *Colibrí*, 21.

Another deconstructionist technique used frequently in this novel is the continual changing of the characters' names. La Regente also appears as La Gerente, La Mandona, La Dueña de los Caballitos, and so on; Colibrí is also called Zun-Zún, Pájaro Mosca, El Perseguido, and El Torturado, among other names, according to the situation. The instability of names, so common in Sarduy's work, is highly important in achieving the dismantling of the realist notion of subjectivity. As psychoanalyst Jacques Lacan notes, a person's name is among the elements contributing most to the illusion of unity and continuity of the subject. By dismantling the stability of the name (the stability of the Name of the Father, as Lacan puts it), the text of *Colibrí* is undermining not only one of the fundamentals of univocal and continuous subjectivity, but also the bases of realistic representation that depend so much on the unity of the subject who is assumed to be narrating. The crisis in the symbol system of accepted values, understood as a crisis of that which constitutes the limits of intelligibility, appears as a crisis of the name and of the morphological stability that the name seems to confer.

Besides the instability of their names, the figurations of the characters themselves lack a stable identity. They transform themselves to such an extreme that at times the character who is initially called El Gigantito (The little giant) becomes confused with La Enanota (The big dwarf), who transforms herself into a nun with certain characteristics associated with Sor Juana Inés de la Cruz, who at times seems like La Regente, and so on. This technique of metamorphosis was begun by Sarduy in his novel *De donde son los cantantes* with the characters Auxilio and Socorro, and its purpose is to lay bare the fictitious and unstable status of the characters, exposing them as a crisis of referentiality. All these techniques (and many others) have the same objective: the radical rupture of the traditional concept of mimetic representation, and the creation of a text as production or process of the formation of subjectivity. The result is a representation that aspires to completely change the way the reader perceives the world at the level of the signifier. This implies that the reader, as a subject supposedly produced by textuality, becomes another type of person upon reading a text so radically different from a realist representation, and changes the bases of his or her subjectivity.

As stated in Sarduy's novel, all these techniques demonstrate "the influence that all simulation implies on the real."[11] But where is the

11. Spanish original: "el influjo sobre lo real que implica toda simulación." Ibid., 16.

agent of this radical critique in his theory? If the human subject of this conception of representation is nothing more than a textual effect, how can we articulate the possibility of an effective resistance to the oppressive symbolic order that Sarduy denounces? Also, does Sarduy's text imply a certain type of queer resistance to traditional subjectivity? It could be argued that, given Sarduy's stated revolutionary objectives, even the theoretical negation of a traditional subjectivity ought to come from somewhere, from some locus, and that his theory ought to be based on and have consequences for the policy of daily life.[12] This is why it is necessary to determine whether Sarduy's discourse can articulate an effective resistance in the struggle against the dominant social order. Even if human subjectivity is constituted by and for the symbolic system from which it arises, it also can be argued that the multiplicity of interpellations and contradictions that form the subject allow for the possibility of a contesting subjectivity, which requires some form of active agent to articulate this resistance. In *Colibrí*, La Regente is undeniably an interpellation that tries to impose itself on Colibrí, and that he, from his queer position, sets up a possible rupture in that system of oppression. Colibrí rejects La Regente's come-ons precisely because he is queer, and this rejection is one of the fundamental cracks in the dominant system s/he represents.

Some critics have pointed out that Colibrí's name functions as a mark of the queer characteristics that this work proposes as a possible resistance to dominant discourse. (*Colibrí* means "hummingbird," and *pájaro* [bird] is a slang term for homosexual in Cuba.)[13] The basis for this interpretation becomes clear when we read how the narrator (supposedly a representative of the "real author" in this instance), in one of the few moments of somewhat realistic discourse, tells of how his father said to him, "My God, boy! I'm going to tell it to you straight. You're a man now, and no Sarduy has been a *pájaro* up till now. And I don't want people pointing at me in the street."[14] This implies that Sarduy uses his own "queer condition" in his works as a means of resistance to the established order, which gives me a foothold to discuss the specific issue of the queer as a resistance discourse in this text.

12. For a brilliant discussion of this issue, see Paul Smith, *Discerning the Subject* (Minneapolis: University of Minnesota Press, 1988).

13. See González Echevarría, *La ruta de Severo Sarduy*, 232; and Méndez Rodenas, *Severo Sarduy*.

14. Spanish original: "Chico, qué barbaridad! . . . voy a hablarte sonante y cantante. Ya tú eres un hombre y de los Sarduy, hasta ahora, no ha habido ningún pájaro. Y yo no quiero que nadie me señale en la calle." Sarduy, *Colibrí*, 113.

Colibrí's "queer condition" gives rise to fluidity and constant change in La Regente's system, since the body that rejects submission to the law, or situates itself against the dictates of the law's power, is supposed to free itself to some degree from the symbolic system.[15] This queer body challenges the norms that govern the intelligibility of sex and text.

According to Sarduy's theory, such fluidity and resistance come from the generating void that produces what he calls the impulse of simulation.[16] Nevertheless, what his theory does not seem to imply is the existence of an active agent who could organize political resistance in the midst of the textual cracks and tensions. Who resists, and from where? Maybe a theory of resistance is only possible when the specific history of the subject in question is taken into account. *Colibrí* is a text that aspires to radically dismantle the traditional subjectivity of modernity. However, it seems to me that Sarduy's project might fall beyond the possibility of an effective resistance to the established world. Also, since all readers already possesses many subjective identifications by the time they read a text, perhaps Sarduy's text mistakenly aspires to transform its readers through the textual processes of reading. In other words, the text of *Colibrí* implies that every subject who reads a text that radically dismantles the signifier reconstitutes itself into a new subject. But this process does not seem to take into account the fact that every reader already comes made up of such a variety of subjective positions that the aspiration of a text that tries to carry out a revolution exclusively by these means and with these techniques is perhaps illusory. Maybe a text like *Colibrí* can only show ambiguity, ambivalence, and the fluidity of subjectivity in general in a theoretical manner. It can, therefore, point theoretically to the possible dismantling of the traditional systems of meaning. Nevertheless, it is doubtful that this project could produce a revolution in the lives of its readers and in contesting political struggles.

The text of *Colibrí* also invites me to reflect on the relationship between desire and power. We know from Michel Foucault that the oppressor not only controls and represses the oppressed, but also plays an integral part in the formation of the oppressed subject and vice versa. The formation of Colibrí's subjectivity is based on authority, persecution, and violation on the part of La Regente, so Colibrí *is* partly the master of the La Casona bordello. La Regente's desire for

15. This obviously is a Lacanian idea that seems quite applicable to the sexual "deviation" in *Colibrí*.

16. For the concept of *impulse of simulation* (*pulsación de simulación*), see Severo Sarduy, *La simulación* (Caracas: Monte Ávila Editores, 1982).

Colibrí, to possess him and control him, eventually forms the behavior and desire of Colibrí himself, which is clearly evident at the end of the novel when he emerges as a dictator like La Regente. Sarduy's text privileges this reading, but in an ambivalent and contradictory way. On the one hand it aspires to produce a radical rupture at the level of signifier with a text that tears down the realistic and *machista* discourse at its heart. Yet on the other hand the end of the novel implies that power can condition the subject's desire so as to only permit an inversion of power, not a resignification.

Here I must bring out the idea of *failed reading* that Lacan proposes as a possibility for rejecting the laws of symbolic power, a reading that interprets the laws of the symbolic order in a "deviate" or mistaken way. This interpretation stems from interference or interruptions from the imaginary order, and from this position Lacan articulates a contesting discourse of disobedience to the law.[17] This notion allows me to propose another reading of *Colibrí* as a text in which the possibility of escape exists for the reader. It is a text that never completely possesses the reader, and its failure in this sense is as great as that of La Regente in her/his relationship with Colibrí. So we must ask again (and from another perspective): how can the power of the offense be mobilized and overcome by means of the terms that articulate that same power? Violation becomes a trauma when it leads to a compulsive repetition of destruction. But this repetition can at the same time be the condition for affirmation in the face of the offense. By defectively repeating hegemonic forms of power, the possibilities of resignification of the oppressive terms are opened. One key means of resistance consists of stirring around in the sites of ambivalence produced at the discursive limits of power, such as occurs with marginal sexuality, for example. There are ideological and personal crossroads that allow for dissidence; the power structure is never absolute, never totally closed. However, it can be argued that subjectivity must possess an active agent with the capacity to organize the demands that have formed it. Such an agent would be situated precisely at the crossroads of the interpellations, where the ambivalence is most pronounced.[18]

It is true that some forms of resistance end up being replications of the dominant system. That is why parody of the forms of power is alone insufficient to establish effective resistance. Denaturalizing

17. See Judith Butler's interpretation of Lacan in *Bodies That Matter: On the Discursive Limits of "Sex"* (New York: Routledge, 1993), 139.
18. Ibid.

the sexual genders (as well as the literary genres) may not be enough to unleash an effective attack on the established order. This order frequently rehearses its own denaturalization on the discursive limits of its system, not with the objective of undermining itself, but rather to affirm its symbolic boundaries.[19] *Machista* systems at times allow gays and lesbians a space, not so as to rupture the system, but rather to mark the limits of legal and acceptable sexuality. The practice of a queer discourse is not always synonymous with effective subversion. And this is where some of Sarduy's queer posturing is worth reflecting upon.

Sarduy's essay *La simulación* (The simulation) (1982) is one of the most lucid critiques of a queer aesthetic or credo.[20] It shows identity to be an expression and not a destiny; language, an unending series of simulations; and genders, one of the moments articulated by the patterns constructed by the dominant discourses. In Sarduy's texts not only the national identity is undermined at its core, but also homosexual identity is radically questioned, along with any difference based on categories of identity.[21] In *Colibrí* specifically, we must remember that homoeroticism arises in the midst of an all-encompassing and powerful system, and perhaps this is why the accumulated forces of prevailing power inundate and annihilate the fragile resistance that the character Colibrí's "queer condition" could potentially bring with it. But here I must make the exception that, in a certain sense, Sarduy's theory implies that in reality Colibrí doesn't completely imitate La Regente, but rather tries to incorporate the fixedness of the model she represents in order to disappear, to die. This is the highest ideal of Sarduy's "neobaroque of simulation," of a world in which all representation is a simulation that lacks external referent, and so behind the impulse of simulation there is emptiness and death. But for Sarduy, this emptiness is "a germinating void whose metaphor and simulation are visible reality."[22] All these reflections lead me to conclude that *Colibrí* is neither an effective resistance nor a complete subordination, but rather the coexistence and tension of both possibilities.

As I have indicated throughout this chapter, one of Sarduy's constant themes is the death of the subject, of historicity, and of realist

19. Ibid.

20. Sarduy, *La simulación* (Caracas: Monte Ávila Editores, 1982).

21. See Oscar Montero, "The Queer Theories of Severo Sarduy," in *Between the Self and the Void: Essays in Honor of Severo Sarduy*, ed. Alicia Rivero-Potter (Boulder, Colo.: Society of Spanish and Spanish American Studies, 1998), 65–78.

22. Spanish original: "una vacuidad germinadora cuya metáfora y simulación es la realidad visible." Sarduy, *La simulación*, 20.

representation, all concepts stressed by poststructuralist and postmodern theories. But this does not imply that for Sarduy the effort of writing is a useless game or a completely evasive posture with no possibility for some type of resonance in the political or cultural world. There can be no doubt that Sarduy's work constitutes a rejection of the modern ideas of Progress, Truth, Authenticity, mimetic Representation, and History. But although his texts can be read from a postmodern perspective, they can also be read to imply some form of political and cultural activism on his part. If the postmodern discrediting of the historic conceptions of modernity is part of his vision, his way of viewing the world can also favor an affirmation of a marginal Latin American position and of a marginal queer condition. Although there is no History in the traditional sense for Sarduy, there may be petite new histories previously crushed by hegemonic historic teleology. Within his queer position, Cuban national history is seen as a form of myth. With the discrediting of the modern master narratives of Progress, Humanism, Science, and Technology—"transcendent" categories perceived by Sarduy and poststructuralists as hegemonic forms serving to subjugate and normalize all reality—there arise new possibilities of interpretation of everything previously excluded. Sarduy's response can be read as a reply from the Latin American, Cuban, and queer peripheries. His texts gather up the pieces of modernity in order to criticize them and dismantle the historicist and patriarchal canons. Sarduy's style attempts to position itself as a form of resistance from the cultural limits of the centers of power. His texts aspire to lay bare the crisis of hegemonic modernity.

★ EIGHT ★

The (Auto)Biography
of a Furious Dissident

O bsession with homosexuality is never simply an obsession with sexual orientation alone. This is very obvious upon a critical reading of _Before Night Falls_ (1992) by Reinaldo Arenas (1943–90),[1] an autobiography in which gay desire and political power are furiously interwoven. As a text that draws its creativity from its very paradoxes as well as from an absence of authority, Arenas's work emerges as a struggle among a wide range of conflicting and contradictory forces. This struggle goes far beyond the rebelliousness of a gay man who dedicated his literary output to the indignant seeking of vengeance for the harassment he suffered at the hands of the Cuban political system. To view Arenas's work exclusively in this light would be to reduce it to just another example of the discourse produced by a soldier of the Cold War. I am convinced that this autobiography is more than that—much more. A critical reading of _Before Night Falls_ reveals its complexity and leads to a questioning of how autobiographical writing relates to the struggle between desire and power, as well as between dissidence and transgression.

In December 1990 Reinaldo Arenas committed suicide in New York City, ending his suffering from AIDS. Although only forty-seven years

---

1. Reinaldo Arenas, *Antes que anochezca (Autobiografía)* (Barcelona: Tusquets Editores, 1992); trans. Dolores M. Koch under the title *Before Night Falls (A Memoir)* (New York: Penguin Books, 1993).

old at the time of this death, Arenas left a truly impressive body of work: eleven novels, several collections of short stories, a poetic trilogy, six plays, various essays, and his autobiography.[2] It is no exaggeration to say that, in a sense, all his works are autobiographical and his life was a continuous attempt to write its own story—as is perhaps the case in the life of all writers, or, indeed, of everyone.

The protagonist of *Before Night Falls* first emerges while relating the story of his unfortunate life to come: his mother was "tricked" by a man promising marriage only to abandon her and their child. This picaresque narrator-protagonist next tells of his childhood in his grandparents' dilapidated house, and of his family—all poor peasants from an isolated region in eastern Cuba. These people instilled in the child a deep hatred for his father, even to the point of teaching him a song with obvious Oedipal overtones in which a child kills his father to avenge his mother's suffering. This absence of the father, coupled with the violence with which its symbolism is established, is the first and most fundamental crisis of authority in the text. The family itself, including the mother, seems to despise this "child of sin." But this same scorn, neglect, and occasional verbal abuse open up a space for creative escape, according to the protagonist: "My existence was not even justified, nobody cared. This gave me an incredible opportunity to escape."[3] Based on his description, we may ask ourselves, is Arenas's work, especially his autobiography, a means of self-justification in the midst of these feelings of abandonment? Is this self-justification unique to Arenas, or is it simply a variation on an unchanging theme, particularly when a writer narrates his/her own story?

It is evident that throughout the text Arenas develops an implicit theory of creativity and sexuality; this theory is tied in with a creative paradox (creative in the sense that it becomes a dramatic means of supplementing the text). Also evident is a continuous denunciation of the abuses of power brought on by institutionalized machismo along with other forms of political and social control, all of which

2. For an article that gives an overview of Arenas's entire literary output, see Ottmar Ette, "La obra de Reinaldo Arenas," in *La escritura de la memoria. Reinaldo Arenas: Textos, estudios y documentación*, ed. Ette (Frankfurt am Main: Vervuert Verlag, 1992), 95–138. Eduardo Béjar, in his excellent book *La textualidad de Reinaldo Arenas. Juegos de la escritura posmoderna* (Madrid: Editorial Playor, 1987), explains the philosophical importance of Arenas's works.

3. Spanish original: "Mi existencia ni siquiera estaba justificada y a nadie le interesaba; eso me ofrecía un enorme margen para escaparme." Arenas, *Antes que anochezca*, 5.

limit and attempt to annihilate creativity and sexuality.[4] Arenas also points out that the limitations imposed by this power have had terrible consequences for all societies, not only the Cuban. Yet, as the narrator-protagonist confesses, it was precisely because of this denigration and familial oppression that he was able to obtain "an incredible opportunity to escape." This "escape" is not limited to a simple withdrawal from society, but rather gives rise to an uncontrollable desire to create: the boy is compelled to compose the "gaudy operatic songs" that form part of his first "shows" and that he belts out at the top of his lungs in the open countryside, alone and far from his family.

If we take into account the narrator-protagonist's creative delirium in *Before Night Falls*, as well as his obsession with producing "shows" (which is due, at least in part, to the lack of attention and the frequent abuse received at home), we can tentatively conclude that the theory of desire and power implicit in Arenas's work is similar to that of Freud.[5] Seen in this light, power is a force apart from yet interdependent with desire, thereby producing a hydraulic effect: the "brute force" of desire (the libido), upon being sublimated, emerges as the creative force of civilization. Nevertheless, I believe that the theory of desire and power implicit in Arenas's work is more Utopian than Freudian, since time and again it insists that desire is a polymorphous force, instinctive and natural, that can only express itself freely in a universe where power has disappeared. Thus, in Arenas, power is not only separate from desire, but also completely pernicious to it. What the protagonist seeks is the total absence of rules, a utopia where desire can express itself in a limitless world. This fiercely utopian ideology, implicit in *Before Night Falls*, appears to disregard the interdependence of power and desire. As Michel Foucault has observed, desire is conditioned by power; without it, desire would lack meaning and expression. In opposition to this idea, Arenas's text presents us with a narrator-protagonist who constantly describes himself as an individual in crisis, a crisis that is almost exclusively the result of external limitations produced by three interwoven forces: the *machista* tradition, the family as a representative of tradition, and the state. The union of these forces creates a castrating limitation of the individual, who demands "only" that "they let him

4. Almost the entire autobiography points to the struggle between power (family, society, and state) and desire, which, according to Arenas, is a presocial force associated with sexuality and creativity.

5. For a study of the Freudian concept of desire and its Lacanian version, see Ellie Ragland-Sullivan, *Jacques Lacan and the Philosophy of Psychoanalysis* (Urbana: University of Illinois Press, 1986), especially chaps. 2 and 5.

live." According to the logic of the text, this implies that he must be liberated from all rules and restrictions, since for him all truly authentic life "opposes all dogma and political hypocrisy."[6]

In a number of ways, the implications of desire in *Before Night Falls* are related to another dilemma: the opposition between the rural and the urban. Just as Arenas implies that desire is an instinctive and presocial force leading to a utopia unregulated by power, he often perceives the countryside as something natural, where the forces of nature are conducive to a polymorphic sexuality without rules or dogmas. And yet it is precisely in this opposition between city and country that I find one of the most complex paradoxes of the text. On the one hand, the narration constantly dwells upon the unfortunate isolation of the countryside and the oppression experienced by the protagonist-narrator as a child in his grandparents' rural home. Yet the countryside also is emphatically proposed as a place of promiscuous "natural" freedom, where everything (or almost everything) is permitted, including bestiality, incest, homosexuality, and bisexuality. In other words, the country is a polymorphic sexual space: "There is no truth to the theory, held by some, about the sexual innocence of peasants. In the country, sexual energy generally overcomes all prejudice, repression, and punishment. That force, the force of nature, dominates" (40).[7] Arenas continues, "In the country, I think, it is a rare man who has not had sexual relations with another man. Physical desire overpowers whatever feelings of machismo our fathers take upon themselves to instill in us" (ibid.).[8] All these statements can be seen as the confessions of a gay peasant who becomes a writer, a profession that allows him to give voice to his "sexual identity," and to tell the "truth" about his life, condition, and social milieu.

Nevertheless, these statements exhibit a conceptual complexity rife with paradox. First of all, although these affirmations may have a high degree of validity in terms of actual practice in the Cuban countryside, the text confuses the concept of nature with that of brute force, equating desire with a kind of "naked pleasure" (naked in the sense

6. Spanish original: "es enemiga de todo dogma e hipocresía política." Arenas, *Antes que anochezca*, 15.

7. Spanish original: "Es falsa esa teoría sostenida por algunos acerca de la inocencia sexual de los campesinos; en los medios campesinos hay una fuerza erótica que, generalmente, supera todos los prejuicios, represiones y castigos. Esa fuerza, la fuerza de la naturaleza, se impone."

8. Spanish original: "Creo que en el campo son pocos los hombres que no han tenido relaciones con otros hombres; en ellos los deseos del cuerpo están por encima de todos los sentimientos machistas que nuestros padres se encargaron de inculcarnos."

of being stripped of all socializing processes). Within this frame of logic, to live in the countryside is to be "close to nature," which is considered a pure erotic force conducive to a polymorphic sexuality. This vision of "the natural" does not recognize that so-called nature is already an interpretation—always ideologically charged—of a certain environment. It refuses to acknowledge it as a phenomenon filtered by acculturated human consciousness, radically different from brute force or naked pleasure.

Yet the paradoxes inherent in the opposition between the rural and the urban do not stop there. The protagonist-narrator of *Before Night Falls* relates how, after his first sexual experiences, and especially after his first gay experience, he was filled with feelings of guilt. The free and polymorphic eroticism that he sees in the countryside (as a product of being close to nature) appears to contradict the boy's feelings of guilt, since guilt is always the product of an intense process of socialization. This concept of eroticism also contradicts the abusive oppression to which he is subjected by his entire family. If it is true that the Cuban peasant is sexually voluptuous, this is not necessarily due to a "closeness to nature" or to "the natural" being an inherently nonproblematic phenomenon. Intense homoerotic activity and guilt seem to go hand in hand in these accounts of the countryside.

In rural men, we are told, "[p]hysical desire overpowers whatever feelings of machismo our fathers take upon themselves to instill in us" (40).[9] However, if these parents (I think that Arenas meant "parents" and not "fathers," as Koch translates the word) are also peasants, is it not paradoxical to say on the one hand that "the force of nature" overcomes the socialization of the peasants, and to insist on the other that the parents, who are also peasants, inculcate "*machista sentiments*" in their children? It is unlikely that a community of puritans will, simply by virtue of living in the middle of the country, stop being puritanical. If we accept the accounts offered in Arenas's text, the concept of nature is a complex process of socialization that simultaneously produces homoerotic activity and guilt in the Cuban situation. Furthermore, the idea of the countryside as a happy place, harmonious and free of prejudice, is clearly a pastoral idealization. The calamities suffered by the boy during his childhood there can hardly be described as happy, free, or harmonious. Indeed, his need to

---

9. See Koch's translation in Arenas, *Before Night Falls*, 19. Spanish original: "los deseos del cuerpo están por encima de todos los sentimientos machistas que nuestros padres se encargaron de inculcarnos."

escape in order to produce his creative experiments arises from these
repressive conditions. The paradox of the countryside in this text can
be summarized as follows: on the one hand, it is a place of freedom and
natural, uncomplicated sexual activity; on the other, it is a repressive
and terrible place of intolerable scarcity.

The other pole of the city/country binomial poses a similar paradox
in *Before Night Falls*. Various tensions plague the narrative's conceptualization of the city. The protagonist-narrator experiences his
first change in environment as a teenager, when economic difficulties
force his grandfather to sell his land. Then entire family moves to the
provincial town of Holguín, which the protagonist-narrator regards in
an entirely negative light. According to the text, the uprooting of the
family was necessitated by the worsening economic conditions experienced by peasants under the Batista regime. In reality, this was not a
situation exclusive to Cuba, but rather a socioeconomic phenomenon
of global proportions, in which a massive migration from country to
city occurred, with the corresponding transformation of peasants into
urban workers.

Next the protagonist-narrator reflects nostalgically on the country
house he left behind: "In that hut with its thatched roof, where we had
suffered so much hunger, we had no doubt also lived the best moments
of our lives. This was perhaps the end of our period of absolute
poverty and isolation, but also the end of a kind of enchantment,
exultation, mystery, and freedom that we would never find again"
(55).[10] So, despite his calamitous childhood there, once distanced from
that environment he idealizes (at least partially) his early years in the
countryside through the nostalgic filter of the past.

Interestingly, Arenas names three principal factors as the possible
source of his creativity in the countryside: the abuse and lack of
affection from his family, the indiscriminate eroticism of "nature," and
the peasant mythology (generally represented by the grandmother).
In the provincial town of Holguín during the 1950s, however, the
thirteen-year-old future writer identifies much more urban creative
influences: radio soap operas and movies (almost all from the Unites
States or Mexico). Also while in Holguín, the protagonist's sexuality
was ambiguous. Although he had discovered and recognized his gay
inclinations at the age of six while watching some naked boys bathing

---

10. Spanish original: "Sin duda, en aquella casa de yagua y guano, donde tanta hambre
habíamos pasado, también habíamos vivido los mejores momentos de nuestra vida; ter-
minaba tal vez una época de absoluta miseria y aislamiento, pero también de un encanto,
una expansión, un misterio y una libertad, que ya no íbamos a encontrar en ninguna parte."

in a river, his erotic experiences were almost all heterosexual: he had girlfriends and once went to a brothel, where he had his first heterosexual relations with a prostitute. In terms of creativity and sexuality, he gives an almost entirely negative interpretation of his life there: the move to the city did not bring with it more sexual freedom, and although he was writing novels, they were, in his opinion, very bad and tacky. For these reasons Holguín symbolizes an intermediate step of sorts between country and city. The protagonist's great urban (re)velation will occur in Havana.

Most of *Before Night Falls* concentrates on the protagonist's life in the capital city of Havana as well as his life after the Cuban Revolution of 1959. (Naturally, as significant events, all revolutions invite self-analysis in terms of "before" and "after.") Arenas portrays Havana paradoxically: on the one hand it represents liberation from the limitations of the countryside and the provincial town, while on the other it is the very place where the protagonist encounters his worst enemy, the Cuban state, in all its proximity and ferocity. Thus every stage in the narrator-protagonist's life has been a move from one oppression to another. Rather than a story of progressive liberation, the text narrates a process of increasing, ever-worsening oppression, including the protagonist's life in New York, where he suffers the physical horrors and social alienation of AIDS.[11] According to this account, the city (specifically Havana) is in some respects more permissive than the country, allowing the protagonist to engage in entirely anonymous homosexual activity; yet in another sense it is the setting for the great battle between desire and power. This battle, as the narrative tells us, results from the encounter between the marginal sexuality of a creative and rebellious gay man and the coercive power of the state, which ultimately persecutes and incarcerates him. This power is symbolized in the text by the figure of Fidel Castro, the supreme macho Father who ought to be eliminated, but toward whom the protagonist simultaneously demonstrates obsessive feelings of hatred and concealed attraction.[12]

---

11. For a theory of coming out of the closet, see Eve Kosofsky Sedgwick, *Epistemology of the Closet* (Berkeley and Los Angeles: University of California Press, 1990). In her insightful and influential work, Sedgwick explains how and why each "coming out" is often a new form of entering another closet. My own view regarding Arenas's coming out follows some of Sedgwick's suggestions.

12. For a magnificent discussion of this issue, see Brad Epps, "Proper Conduct: Reinaldo Arenas, Fidel Castro and the Politics of Homosexuality," *Journal of the History of Sexuality* 6, no. 2 (1995): 231–83.

As previously stated, the sublimation of desire, according to the Freud's psychoanalytical model, is the foundation for creative output in a civilization. In *Before Night Falls*, however, creativity is the ally of sexuality, not its sublimation. It is a utopian universe wherein creativity is almost synonymous with a limitless sexuality. Yet there is something else at play here: this "place without limits" is often found in a world in which life and death nearly converge. The forces of sexuality seek to attain life with such extreme delirium that they overflow and end up pouring into death. Moreover, it is the phantom of death that incites and hastens creativity. Arenas always lived as if a merciless clock were constantly reminding him that he must furiously create before death arrived, before night fell. For Arenas, writing is a matter of obsessive creativity always situated between Eros and Thanatos.

This living in the "in-between" zone characterizes all the works of Arenas, not just his autobiography. Through them he lives not only between life and death, but also between light and darkness, country and city, sanity and insanity, the search for truth and the absolute disdain for all reality, realistic detail and fantastic hyperbole, and the struggle for liberation and suicide (or suicide as liberation). As with all autobiography, *Before Night Falls* is an obsession to remain alive, to give semblance to that which is no more, dramatically accentuated by Arenas. This is why Paul De Man says that the predominant rhetorical figure of all autobiography is prosopopoeia, the figure of speech that gives voice and face to the dead or the voiceless.[13] (It is pertinent to note that *Webster's Dictionary* defines *prosopopoeia* as "a figure in rhetoric by which things are represented as persons, or by which things inanimate are spoken of as animated beings, or by which an absent person is introduced as speaking, or a deceased person is represented as alive and present.")[14]

The text of *Before Night Falls* informs us of a double meaning to its title: at first, when the autobiography was begun (after the protagonist's escape to Lenin Park in Havana), it meant writing before nightfall, when darkness no longer permitted him to see; now, in the present enunciation of the text, it signifies the hurried need to finish writing before his imminent AIDS-related death. Although the figure of death in Arenas's text is more dramatic than in many autobiographies, the genre always addresses a life that disfigures itself

13. See Paul De Man's classic essay "Autobiography as Disfigurement," in *Modern Language Notes* 94 (1979): 919–30.
14. *Webster's New Universal Dictionary*, 2d ed., s.v. "prosopopoeia."

through the process of writing: writing as the death of life, yet at the same time the uncontrollable desire to preserve it.[15] To write about something alive implies a substitution of the life being described by the "life" that is being written; therefore, the moment of writing only acquires its reality when the life described is no longer present. For this reason the title of Arenas's work could apply to all autobiographies, because all are obsessed with the moment "before night falls," before death arrives. Or perhaps the contrary is true: perhaps this and all other autobiographies ought to be titled "after night fell," since from the reader's point of view, the life that becomes writing (the *bio* that becomes *graphia*) is read when only the latter prevails.

More than anything else, the autobiography of Reinaldo Arenas is concerned with the conflict between homoerotic desire and political power, and with all the complexities and interdependencies implied in these terms. As stated earlier, this struggle is charged with a complex paradoxical tension. Confronted with this problematic struggle, we may ask: Why is there such a detailed confession of sexual experiences? To whom is the text directed? Is there an authority figure in this text despite its strong refusal to respond to any authority? All autobiography seems to be a kind of confession aspiring to self-reparation and self-justification, as if to say, "You failed to acknowledge me and I will tell you who I am, so that you will recognize my value as a unique individual."[16] If we continue with this line of thought, Arenas's confession in his autobiography is clearly self-reparation in the face of his marginalized sexuality, viewed by Cuban society (and many others, for that matter) as a serious breach of socially acceptable behavior. *Before Night Falls*, like most of Arenas's works, is in a sense a monumental "coming out of the closet," but a coming out that always ends up in another terrible situation. It is also an endless and frustrated demand for recognition from either an ideal reader or an ideal Father.

The narrative describes innumerable sexual experiences of every kind: besides those relating to incest and bestiality, so numerous and prodigious are the homosexual encounters that the protagonist himself says that by the beginning of the 1970s, he estimates having had sexual relations with some five thousand men. In addition to questioning the truth of this hyperbole, I would also underscore here the degree of rupture that such spectacular marginal sexual activity

---

15. Besides De Man's article, for a study of these ideas see Alberto Moreiras, "Autobiografía: pensador firmado (Nietzsche y Derrida)," *Anthropos* 29 (December 1991): 129–36.
16. Ibid.

signifies, as well as the obsession with recounting it in such detail. In effect, these revelations can be interpreted in many ways: as a way of enlightening the reader, an insult to the establishment, a cunning bid for recognition, a declaration of the "naturalness" of this kind of sexuality, an expression of disdain and aggressiveness toward potential readers, and an expression of self-hatred.

It is interesting to note that in *Before Night Falls* the narrator-protagonist dedicates his life to rebelling against the *machista* power structure with the goal, explicit or implicit, of liberating himself from that power. One could actually say that this is the central theme of the text. Nevertheless, and in spite of the centrality of this insistence, the protagonist declares his uncontrollable attraction toward, his tremendous desire to have sexual relations with, a "real man"—a "macho." In fact, the narration speaks disparagingly of gay men who have sexual relations with other gay men, referring to them as *locas* (fags), a highly insulting and denigrating term in Cuban and Latin American culture. For the narrator-protagonist, attraction between two gay men is simply incomprehensible. This expression of desire is key to understanding the complexity of the desire/power relationship, since, while fighting against machismo as public enemy number one, there also exists the desire to have sexual relations with "a macho," the prototypical representative of the oppressive system—something akin to the paradoxical love/hate relationship with the figure of Fidel Castro.[17] This is an obvious example of the internalization of power in desire, of the interdependence of the power that oppresses desire and that is at the same time an integral part of the object of desire. Certainly, Arenas's internalization of power responds to the specific social conditions under which he grew up. In Cuban society, homoerotic relationships are often based on the masculine/feminine binary, and Arenas was unable to free himself from this mold.

Another thought-provoking aspect of the text is the prodigious description, great detail, and voluminous number of examples of Arenas's sexual encounters with both known and unknown partners. All these descriptions give the impression that he was compensating for and perhaps also avenging a guilt of monumental proportions by means of a compulsive confession, which in turn attempts to fill an apparently bottomless void. This is the void upon which the textuality of *Before Night Falls* is founded, and in which homosexuality can be seen as a breach of the rules of the establishment, but which can also

17. See Epps, "Proper Conduct."

be interpreted in Lacanian psychoanalytical terms. Since the search for the total object of desire is an impossible goal and in this text there is such a tremendous vacuum of authority, the human subject, in order to enter into some form of sociability or accepted language, must somehow abandon his aspiration of absolute grandeur—that is, the all-encompassing object of desire. This renunciation of absolute grandeur is strongly resisted by the protagonist of *Before Night Falls*. In other words, he shows great difficulty in renouncing his narcissistic fantasy, the aspiration of the imaginary absolute object of desire.

In Arenas's text we encounter a human subject that refuses to accept that desire is only partial and imperfect; as a subject he has difficulty participating in the symbolic social exchange. Therefore, in order to attempt to "solve" this dilemma and somehow participate in the symbolic social order, the subject must seek a tradition that inscribes him into a type of language or socialization.[18] This is why Arenas's autobiography (and, in the end, all autobiography) is a retrospective construction of an absolute idealization that never existed, but without which the human subject cannot continue to live, let alone write. Moreover, this writing or living can only be achieved through the metonymic pursuit of partial objects of desire. In *Before Night Falls* there is an extreme dramatization of a crisis of authority, but it is this very crisis that makes the text not only possible but particularly fascinating. However, if we are to have a text at all, this crisis of authority cannot be absolute. All discourse must have at least some form of ideological sender—a representative of an authority that permits entry into language.

The visible sender of *Before Night Falls* is the image of gay Cuban writer Virgilio Piñera, whom Arenas elevates as his symbolic hero, the symbol of some form of Law, or a substitute for the "original" absent Father. Yet, the figure of Piñera as sender or bearer of (literary) tradition is rather problematic, because he is elevated to this role precisely for having been perceived by Arenas as the dissident writer par excellence, the maximum representative of transgression. Therefore, the figure of Piñera leads to what is called a composition in abyss. This symbolic figure can send only two messages to Arenas: to write, and to transgress (or to write transgressing). The message of transgression conveys another form of void, or crisis, whose meaning can be interpreted as the very limit of modernity: Arenas idealized the figure of Piñera because he imagined him to embody literary rebellion, the art of constant rupture

18. See Ragland-Sullivan, *Jacques Lacan*.

and tireless artistic dissidence. This is the limit of the art of modernity: an art based on the constant breaking of tradition, or on a tradition of constant breaking and rupture.[19] It is for this reason that the art implied in *Before Night Falls* points to the typical crisis of modernity, and accordingly, to the possibility of the postmodern.

All this explains the obsession in this text with literary work, with the compulsion to write and to write about the process of writing. In a way, this is the only message that can be viewed as affirmative. There is no doubt that in Arenas's text, as in the autobiographies of so many other writers, much self-justification stems from the prestige of being a writer. It is the equivalent of saying, "Since the readers of this autobiography may not be aware of who I am and why I did what I did, I will tell them who I am: I am a gay man of peasant origin who possesses the courage (the boldness, the authenticity, the sincerity) to tell them all the details I can remember of my sexual and political adventures; but furthermore, I am a writer, extremely dedicated to my literary production, even in the most terrible and sublime moments." Literary work is the center of self-justification in the difficult life of this persecuted gay man. In this sense, it is interesting that writing justifies the life of the protagonist, just as the life of the protagonist justifies the writing (in the sense of "real" facts that can be proven). It is as though his work and life were interwoven and interdependent: the literary work is both inside and outside the protagonist's life, just as the protagonist's life is inside and outside the literary work. Thus we return to the same basic paradox: life, in order to justify itself, must write itself; yet to write about something alive is in a certain sense to kill it, since it is written about when life is already absent.

Before Night Falls frequently concerns itself with the narrator-protagonist's literary production, and with how his manuscripts were written, then lost or confiscated by the Cuban authorities, only to be recovered and lost yet again. The autobiography, too, was written on more than one occasion, as we are told by the text. In fact, the "final version"—the one we read today—wasn't *written* in the literal sense, but rather was tape-recorded by Arenas so that some friends could then posthumously transcribe and publish it.[20] According to the narration, the narrator-protagonist began to write his autobiography as a fugitive from justice. It is perhaps in this section that the most

19. This idea is often associated with Octavio Paz's *Los hijos del limo* (Barcelona: Seix-Barral, 1974).

20. See Liliane Hasson, "*Antes que anochezca (Autobiografía)*: una lectura distinta de la obra de Reinaldo Arenas," in *La escritura de la memoria*, ed. Ette, 165–73.

extraordinary events are related. The adventures and misadventures of the protagonist of *Before Night Falls* appear to take on special significance and dramatic effect in the sections that tell of his persecutions, arrests, escapes, re-arrests, and re-escapes in his struggle against Cuban political power. So prodigious are these adventures that at least the more outstanding of them deserve mention and some measure of interpretation.

As related in the text, Arenas's greatest persecution began in the summer of 1973 on the beach at Guanabo, where he and a friend named Coco Salá (who accompanied him on many of his homoerotic adventures) had sex with some teenagers. These teenagers robbed Reinaldo and Coco of their belongings, and Coco called the police. The teenagers were detained, but they accused Reinaldo and Coco of being *maricones* (fags) who tried to fondle them. As a result, the accusers became the accused and vice versa. Both men were arrested. Reinaldo was found guilty in court of "perverting minors," yet Coco was not even accused. Reinaldo, free on bail, began a series of attempts to leave the country and go anywhere, by any means possible. The text states that he asked his friends in Paris for a plastic life raft, a fake passport, and underwater gear. Then, despite being free on bail, Reinaldo was re-arrested. In prison again, he managed to escape by diving into the ocean while the guards were on a coffee break. He swam a number of kilometers to a beach far from the prison. The truth or falsehood of all these events cannot be completely proven or refuted, but this amazing story is only the beginning of an almost interminable series of extraordinary escape adventures. In the midst of so many calamities, Arenas decided in a moment of desperation to kill himself by slitting his wrists with shards of glass. After losing consciousness, he miraculously awoke some hours later, hungry and with the blood on his wrists clotted. After this he traveled to Oriente Province (several hundred kilometers from Havana), in order to try escaping via the U.S. naval base at Guantánamo. Unsuccessful in this endeavor, he went to Holguín, where his mother and other family members were living— and where everyone, or almost everyone, and especially his aunt Ofelia, as the text informs us, hated him and wanted to see him recaptured. From Holguín, Reinaldo took a train to Havana with his mother. Upon his arrival he was once again arrested, and once again managed to trick the authorities, showing them a false ID card.

Of all the adventures and escapes in this section of the autobiography, perhaps one of the most important (from various points of view, including that of the preeminently romantic adventure) occurred in

Lenin Park on the outskirts of Havana, where the protagonist took refuge during his never-ending escape. Although this section is titled simply "The Escape," it could just as well have been called "The Phantom of the Park" (or perhaps "The Phantom of Lenin," if taken in the political sense), because it recounts the fugitive life of the protagonist in an extremely marginal situation (he lived in hiding in the park for several days or weeks). From this hideout, or underworld, he sent signs of his presence to representatives of the establishment in order to confuse or surprise them with his abilities as a fugitive. In fact, the narration tells us that while Reinaldo was hiding in the park, he arranged for friends in Europe to send telegrams to important figures of the Cuban regime (inside Cuba), informing them that he was already out of the country. The symbolism of the Lenin Park adventures can be read romantically (in the Promethean sense of the term)[21] because of the intricate relation of frustrated and unattained love, a love mainly for the text he is writing, his autobiography, which he began to compose at that time. It is also romantic because the hero sends forth ambiguous signals from a hidden, marginal, and nocturnal world to the established world that persecutes him, which in psychoanalytic terms would be something like the return of the repressed. Furthermore, in Lenin Park Reinaldo compulsively reads the *Iliad*, a book brought by a friend during one of his clandestine visits. It would not be an exaggeration to see the fugitive's reading of this classic as symbolic of a self-justification of the "other life"; that is, the life that Arenas is narrating, one that has so many things in common with the hero of the *Iliad*.[22]

The implicit questioning of the validity of this self-reflexive writing coincides with the questioning of the national discourse, because throughout the entire text the concept of nationality as proposed by Cuban socialism is rejected, and a "new" nationalism is set forth based upon "rescuing" the lost history, or stories, of marginality—in this case,

21. See Harold Bloom, "The Internalization of Quest-Romance," in *Romanticism and Consciousness: Essays in Criticism*, ed. Bloom (New York: W. W. Norton & Company, Inc., 1970): 3–24; originally published in *The Yale Review* 58, no. 4 (Summer 1969). In his article, Bloom explains how the initial phase of the romantic quest was basically Promethean (Prometheus was the god of the unfulfilled promise). In this phase, the poet is the hero of an endless iconoclastic rebellion that always ends in an unfulfilled situation. Also, for Bloom as well as for Paul De Man and others, romanticism is a cultural movement that extends from the end of the eighteenth century to the present. These critics believe that all efforts to truly overcome the basic romantic premises or objectives have failed.

22. For a study of the importance of classical texts in Spanish American autobiography, see Sylvia Molloy, *At Face Value: Autobiographical Writing in Spanish America* (Cambridge: Cambridge University Press, 1991).

of sexual marginality. Arenas's national story is arguably an epic of the oppressed. Although nationalism in itself is not rejected in principle, in Arenas's text despotism is furiously denounced, specifically the despotic machismo so prevalent in the formation of nationalism (especially the nationalism of socialist Cuba). Arenas began to publish in the 1960s, but it was his posthumous autobiography that has given him a much wider visibility in the non-Spanish-speaking world, especially in the United States. The translation of *Before Night Falls* into English has introduced Arenas to many English-speaking readers, particularly, as one might expect, to gay readers in the United States. Undoubtedly, the undermining of modern master narratives in postmodern societies, with their well-known space for marginal discourse, has made room for this dissident and transgressive text.

Thus far, our study has led us to the idea that Arenas's autobiography exists in a space created by a crisis of authority; a crisis that manifests itself on the personal, social, and institutional levels. On the personal level, there is a crisis in relation to the father figure, and on the social and institutional levels, one finds the absence of an established model of conduct and of government. This discourse is radically dissident and transgressive from both ethical and political perspectives, but not in terms of aesthetics (at least not intentionally so). The struggle between marginal sexual desire and political power in *Before Night Falls* implies an ideology in which desire is an instinctive and natural force whose ultimate aspiration is to liberate itself from all forces of power. Thus, there is an implicit desire in this text that is perceived as a presocial force, the fullest expression of which is achieved only when all the pressures of power are absent. In accordance with this position, it is in "pure desire" that the individual's true authenticity resides, and this individuality expresses itself through writing.

Moreover, the autobiographical persona of *Before Night Falls* seeks to convey the extraliterary truth of his life, something that the reader must believe as an established historical fact. All this means that, although in other works Arenas stylistically implies a decentralization of subjectivity and a questioning of the realist mimesis or representation, in *Before Night Falls* he returns to realism—at least on the level of the ideology proposed in the text.[23] It is not a text that questions subjectivity and mimetic representation, but rather a text that, due to the nature

23. I want to emphasize that several of Arenas's texts prior to his autobiography constitute, as is well known, radical questionings of the realist foundation. Nevertheless, *Before Night Falls* is a different kind of text in this respect. His objective seems to be more ethical than aesthetic.

of autobiographical writing, clearly insists on an extraliterary *truth*. So in this autobiography Arenas approaches an ethical rather than an aesthetic transgression, moving toward a position closer to that of André Gide than of Oscar Wilde;[24] closer to the testimonial novel than to the textuality of Lezama or Sarduy.[25] To do otherwise would require a rejection of the principles of naturalness and reality themselves.

The narrative of *Before Night Falls* searches for *the truth*, something which, as Friedrich Nietzsche reminds us, is the ultimate basis of Western metaphysics. Nevertheless, and in spite of the proposed ideology of the text, Arenas's autobiography contains elements such as extreme hyperbole that undermine (perhaps unintentionally) its implicit realism. For this reason *Before Night Falls* alternately takes part in the basic discourse of modernity—in its desperate search for authenticity, truth, freedom, posterity, and history—and offers exaggerations and extreme sexual transgressions that ultimately point to a postmodern condition. Perhaps it is not, after all, sexual transgression that is the greatest rupture in *Before Night Falls*, but rather its constant hyperbole, its drawing near to falsehood and lies; the exaggerations of the text are often hard to believe. The liar is so dangerous because he undermines not only conventional morals, but also the foundation that sustains such morality: the truth, which is the epistemological legitimization of the real. Reality, thus devalued and demystified by the loss of the true, is forced to imitate art, which is rhetorically associated with appearance, style, and falsehood. *Before Night Falls* is a text that represents a rhetorical struggle between prosopopoeia, the figure that gives voice and face to the dead and the absent, and hyperbole, the figure that undermines the prosopopoeia by means of exaggeration. A face is given and simultaneously taken away as the narrator-protagonist desperately attempts to survive in his own writing—a survival that is betrayed over and over again by the very act of writing. All these relentless paradoxical tensions make *Before Night Falls* one of the most dramatic and compelling autobiographies ever produced in Latin America.

24. For a comparison between Gide's and Wilde's ethical and aesthetic positions, see Jonathan Dollimore, *Sexual Dissidence: Augustine to Wilde, Freud to Foucault* (Oxford: Clarendon Press, 1991).

25. I studied the antirealist aesthetics of José Lezama Lezama and Severo Sarduy in chapters 6 and 7 of this book.

★ NINE ★
Attempting a Difficult Rectification

The Cuban film *Fresa y chocolate* (Strawberry and chocolate), with screenplay by Senel Paz and direction by Tomás Gutiérrez Alea and Juan Carlos Tabío, generated a great deal of excitement around the world after its release in 1994. In addition to winning the prestigious Silver Bear prize in Berlin, *Fresa y chocolate* was the main attraction at film festivals in Argentina, Brazil, Colombia, Italy, Japan, Mexico, and Spain, and was released in other countries as well. Most surprising, however, was the film's monumental success in socialist Cuba, where it won not only the country's Critics' and People's Choice Awards but also the Catholic Church's OCIC *(Organización Católica Internacional de Cine)* Award for exemplary films. (Perhaps the Catholic Church's award was more in recognition of the film's implicit defense of religious freedom in Cuban society than of its explicit defense of gay and lesbian rights.) So much interest was generated by the screening of *Fresa y chocolate* in Havana and throughout the provinces that crowds outside theaters pushed and shoved in competition for tickets. Finally, in September 1994, *Fresa y chocolate* arrived in the United States. Following its initial screening at the Latin American Film Festival in New York, it was distributed with English subtitles throughout most of the country.

The most extraordinary aspect of *Fresa y chocolate* was neither its cinematographic quality nor its theme of homosexuality per se, but rather that it was produced and released in socialist Cuba and dealt with the rights of homosexuals in that society. Of course, had it been a poorly made film, the theme and country of origin by themselves would not have given rise to such success. *Fresa y chocolate* was well made; the acting was excellent (with Mirta Ibarra truly exceptional in the role of Nancy), and, above all, the human warmth of certain scenes (especially those in which David and Diego communicate through an understanding that is progressive and complex) captured the attention and sensibilities of many audiences, especially gays and liberals.

There is little doubt, however, that within the context of 1994 Cuba, the film offered a drastic proposition by implying the acceptance and integration of homosexuality in the concept of Cuban nationality. Such an idea would not have been so surprising had it not been proposed by a Cuban writer committed to the revolution. Senel Paz is the son of peasants who, thanks to the Cuban Revolution, escaped his marginal condition to achieve national and international acclaim as a fiction writer and screenwriter. But in *Fresa y chocolate* (as well as in his short story "El lobo, el bosque y el hombre nuevo" [The wolf, the woods and the new man], on which the screenplay was based), this revolutionary implies that Cuban socialism and nationalism must fully integrate the gay (and, by implication, the lesbian) members of society.[1]

Beyond a nominal treatment of the theme of homosexuality in Cuban socialist society, the script invites interpretations that take into account the complex tension between heterosexuality and homosexuality, nationalism and antinationalism (the latter signifying treason within the ideology of the film), socialism and antisocialism (i.e., capitalism), and power and desire. To all of this must be added a religious aspect, inasmuch as the film's plot deals (although not centrally) with the topic of Diego's religious beliefs and David's atheistic convictions. These relationships are further complicated not only by the historical period in which the action takes place (about 1979, as indicated by a TV news broadcast that announces Anastasio Somoza's departure from Nicaragua—that is, at the culmination of the Sandinista Revolution), but also by Cuba's entire modern history up to the present.

At the beginning of the film, David possesses all the characteristics deemed positive by traditional, hard-line Cuban socialism: he is heterosexual, an atheist, a socialist, and a nationalist. Diego, on the contrary, possesses most of the negative characteristics, with the exception of antinationalism. (Diego insists that he is profoundly

1. Senel Paz, *El lobo, el bosque y el hombre nuevo* (The wolf, the woods and the new man) (Mexico City: Ediciones Era, 1991).

nationalistic.) From this point of view, the shared ideological code that draws David and Diego together is nationalism, but of two types founded upon very different political principles: David is a socialist who belongs to the proletariat, while Diego is antisocialist and has upper-class tastes and values. Within the semantic context of the film, it is one thing to be a nationalist/socialist (a revolutionary) and quite another to be a nationalist who not only opposes the revolution (in spite of momentary doubts), but also wants to flee the country as a political exile. How, then, is it possible for these two characters to maintain a friendship that grows steadily despite their having such antithetical characteristics? I believe that one of the keys to their progressive friendship is the slow "conversion" that Diego brings about in David. Primarily ethical (but also political), this conversion enables a common ground to be established between Diego's nationalism and David's. Diego constantly "preaches" an ethic to David that presents gays as worthy of inclusion in the concept of Cuban nationalism and as dignified persons capable of heroism.

Diego's "sermon" could be called the ethic of the oppressed, which corresponds to the notion of resentment that Nietzsche applied to the ethic of primitive Christianity. Here, the oppressed try to convince the oppressor that it is imperative to be compassionate and generous toward them—that the oppressed must have the right to participate in the world of the oppressor—while accepting that they are in the hands of the dominant ideology, which protects the privileged position of the oppressor.[2] It is important to remember that at the beginning of the film, and especially in his relationship with Diego, David is weak and indecisive. From this perspective, one can infer a certain envy on David's part with respect to Diego's strength and decisiveness. But, having assumed the ethic of the oppressed by means of what psychoanalysis calls transference, David is transformed, relatively speaking, into gay rights activist.

Moreover, although the relationship of envy/resentment between David and Diego does not seem at first to arise from class differences, it could be argued that the film at least implies class conflict in an obscure or transformed manner, inasmuch as Diego's preparation of fine foods and his social and political values can be associated with a certain sector of the Latin American intellectual bourgeoisie. Yet

2. Here I follow Fredric Jameson's adaptation of Nietzsche's notion of resentment in *The Political Unconscious: Narrative as a Socially Symbolic Act* (Ithaca, N.Y.: Cornell University Press, 1981).

homosexuality is not, strictly speaking, a class phenomenon (however frequently it may be utilized in class struggles as a political weapon, as in "homosexualizing of the enemy").[3] If this interpretation is correct, *Fresa y chocolate* presents a gay character from a social class inherently opposed to the film's basic ideology. Although the film makes an overture toward other social perspectives, the fact that the gay character is identified with a bourgeois class while the revolutionary is heterosexual implies a distancing—albeit partial and subtle—from a more committed gay politics. As a result, one cannot help but consider the wealth of possibilities entailed by a work that includes a gay man of the Cuban proletariat and/or of *campesino* (peasant) origins (like some of the characters in Reinaldo Arenas's narratives, for example).[4] Moreover, as the critic José Quiroga asserts, Diego and *Fresa y chocolate* in general attempt "to relate the homosexual to the intellectual in one body, seen and narrated by another who is not torn between the contradictions of sex and culture but between two versions [of culture] (the official and the 'dissident')."[5] Quiroga convincingly argues that in this film homosexuality and culture are essentialized in a nonorganic relationship to each other: "as a transmitter of culture but nevertheless not organic in relation to it, the homosexual is deracinated from a context, outside nature."[6]

Although Nietzsche considered resentment an ideological trick by which the weak corrupt the strong in order to rob them of their properly aristocratic arrogance, vitality, and aggressiveness, in *Fresa y chocolate* something akin to an inversion of resentment's inversion takes place. This dialectic deals with a proletariat that, having been weak and oppressed under the former regime, is now in a position of power, so it is David who has to undergo conversion to the ethic of the oppressed. On the other hand, in the specular plane of this relationship, Diego (the character with upper-class attributes) must exercise the tactic of resentment with David (the proletariat character). The solution offered by the film in the face of this dilemma is a mutual understanding that points toward a utopian view of society.

3. For a detailed and ambitious history of this question, see David F. Greenberg, *The Construction of Homosexuality* (Chicago: University of Chicago Press, 1988).

4. Some of Arenas's writings, as we have studied in chapter 8, are autobiographical, so the main character of his narratives is often a Cuban homosexual of humble peasant origins.

5. José Quiroga, "Homosexualities in the Tropic of Revolution," in *Sex and Sexuality in Latin America*, ed. Daniel Balderston and Donna J. Guy (New York: New York University Press, 1997), 141.

6. Ibid., 138.

An alliance between Diego and David—between the gay and the revolutionary—enables an interpretation of *Fresa y chocolate* based on a more global perspective. That is, if within the Cuban context of the film the socialist discourse seems dominant and oppressive, this discourse may be considered profoundly marginal and isolated from a world perspective at the dawn of the twenty-first century. For this reason the dialogue between David's socialist and Diego's gay position can be interpreted as two oppressed positions aspiring to a utopian alliance in the face of the hegemonic power of capitalism. One well-known symbolic means of liberation from an intolerable situation is the creation of utopian solutions.[7] Therefore, as Fredric Jameson has observed, cultural critics must adopt a dialectic method that goes beyond "the positive" and "the negative"; that is, they must develop a cultural critique in which the *effectively ideological* is at the same time the *necessarily utopian*, and vice versa.[8] From this point of view, a cultural artifact such as *Fresa y chocolate* operates not only as an effective concealment of an ideology of domination but also as a necessary utopian compensation for it, which enables alternative options to be raised in the face of an otherwise intolerable situation.

Although the debate over the status of gays is foregrounded in *Fresa y chocolate*, the ideology of the film prevents it from becoming a full-blown treatise on repression. As in most works of this nature, once a problematic issue for the dominant ideology is brought into focus, it becomes a question of *managing* (to use, in an ideological sense, what Norman Holland describes as the need *to manage* repressed desires in the artwork)[9] the potentially subversive effects of the dialogue (or struggle) with a marginal discourse. This is how the film represses even as it illuminates some of the problematic aspects of the relationship between homosexuality and Cuban nationality.

One repressed aspect of the film that emerges after a careful analysis is the nature of the friendship between David and Diego. While it is not necessary to sexualize all such relationships, this homosocial friendship, as a national allegory of ideological and political struggles from the historical subtext, does not dare to be more radical, which it would be if the characters had a sexual relationship (as occurs in Manuel Puig's *Kiss of the Spider Woman*, for example). The love affair between Nancy and David at the end of *Fresa y chocolate*, however,

---

7. What I mean by *utopia* here is a social order free of conflicts.

8. See Jameson, *Political Unconscious*, especially chap. 6.

9. See Norman Holland, *The Dynamics of Literary Response* (New York: Oxford University Press, 1968), 243–61.

goes to the other extreme—a conventional happy ending for the heterosexual lovers, with the young man finding the woman he has long needed and searched for. Meanwhile, Diego is left in disgrace and solitude. David's extreme joy as he tells Diego (who is about to go into exile) of the wonders of making love to a woman seems dissonant with the tone and objective of the film at other moments. The happy ending for David and Nancy is, in my opinion, a double strategy of containment that both facilitates an ideological closure and obscures other possible resolutions, such as a sexual relationship between David and Diego and the implications of such a relationship.

In an interview that I conducted with Senel Paz about *Fresa y chocolate*, he spoke to this issue, saying that if David had been a closeted gay (i.e., if Diego had managed to draw David out of a repressed homosexuality), the film would have been weakened, because the intention was to portray a straight character who could understand a gay person and his situation in Cuban society. Moreover, another consideration was how far a film produced and released in Cuba could go with its subject matter at that time without meeting rejection not only from officialdom (as I interpret Paz's comments on the matter) but from the Cuban public.[10] While these points have certain validity—inasmuch as both possibilism (the possibility of producing and performing a work in any given place and time) and the notion of a straight who can understand the gay Other are real issues in certain contexts—I would argue this point with Paz nonetheless.

Kiss of the Spider Woman, for one, has a different resolution than that of *Fresa y chocolate*. Puig's character, Valentín, is not someone who "awakened" to his "true identity" as a result of Molina's attentions; that is, he was not necessarily a homosexual (depending on how the term is defined). The issues examined by Puig's film are much more complex. His work is a meditation on, or investigation of, the porosity of sexual definitions and attitudes and a radical questioning of the artificial barriers (in the sense of social constructs) that constrain sexual behavior, as well as a conceptualization of "marriage" between the gay and the revolutionary. As for the possibilism of *Fresa y chocolate*, perhaps a more radical resolution would have made the film taboo and led to its censure by officialdom and the public—but perhaps not. As demonstrated by its success, there seems to be a fairly high level of tolerance, even avidity, in Cuban society for works that address the topic of homosexuality. That society might have been more willing to

10. Senel Paz, interview by author, Boulder, Colo., 27 March 1994.

take up the problematic issues in *Fresa y chocolate* than the filmmakers had anticipated.

The other part of the strategy of containment effected by the happy ending for David and Nancy pertains more to the character of Nancy. How should her role in this national allegory be interpreted? The answer that would be consistent with the film's implicit ideology is that Nancy is another type of marginal person whom the Cuban Revolution must recover in the process of political "rectification." But Nancy's character is very complex and rich. She is akin to what Marxists call *lumpen* in that she does not work, she is promiscuous, and she lives off sales made in dollars (which, in the late 1970s, when the story takes place, was prohibited in Cuba). But as Nancy herself says, "There is something in me very clean that no one has been able to dirty," so the film reclaims for this "lumpen" a degree of social integration.

I believe, however, that a much darker and more problematic interpretation of Nancy's character is possible. When Nancy attempts suicide by slashing her wrists, it is in the hospital (where David donates blood to save Nancy's life) that Diego and David establish the true bonds of their friendship—and a relationship of donation toward Nancy. Both contribute to her wellbeing and happiness: Diego takes care of her after the suicide attempt and later does everything possible to further the relationship between Nancy and David, while David gives her his blood and finally his love. Perhaps one way to read all this would be that Nancy is that part of the Cuban nation which desperately needs to be saved from self-destruction. Accordingly, the friendship between Diego and David would represent an alliance needed to bring about Cuba's "utopian salvation." In contrast, their relationship could be viewed as a truncated and impossible resolution, since this alliance is never completely realized. Ultimately, the two men go their separate ways, and Diego goes into exile.

All of the main characters in *Fresa y chocolate* can be seen as engaged in acting out a national allegory.[11] Miguel, David, Diego, and Nancy play symbolic roles: Miguel obviously portrays the repressive revolutionary who must constantly shout "The enemy is only 90 miles away!" to justify the system's many abuses. Unlike the more complex and interesting Ismael in "El lobo," Miguel is a highly stereotypical character.[12] He tries to persuade David that gays (and especially Diego) are not worthy of the slightest consideration within the revolution and

11. See Doris Sommer, *Foundational Fictions: The National Romances of Latin America* (Berkeley and Los Angeles: University of California Press, 1991).

12. On Ismael, see my "Senel Paz: homosexualidad, nacionalismo y utopía," *Plural* 269 (February 1994): 58–65.

that if David doesn't follow the Party line, the enemy "90 miles away" will take advantage of the situation to pursue its own interventionist interests.

In his struggle with Diego for control over David, Miguel appeals to the coercion of slogans, clichés, and threats that sound more worn-out and less effective the more they are repeated. Ironically, Miguel and Diego's intense competition for David at times has homoerotic overtones, such as in the school bathroom scene between Miguel and David, especially when Miguel gives the half-naked David a slap on the buttocks and compliments his "little buns." This suggests that Miguel's fury against the (homosexual) Other is not so much antagonism toward the distant and the strange as it is an aggressive display of fear in the presence of the proximate and the familiar.[13] Similarly, the violent scene at Diego's apartment, where Miguel struggles with Diego and David, resembles a love-triangle fight more than a political argument. In addition to an implied class struggle, the relationship between Diego and David thus implies class attraction as well. Is Diego's attraction to David related to their differences of class and/or sensibility? In other words, is David attracted to Diego's sophistication in a homoerotic sense?

Whether sexual or otherwise, their mutual attraction is more complex than a "naked desire" that confronts the inherent obstacles of a *machista* society. For example, Diego is called *la loca roja* (the red queer) by his friends because of his relationship with the militant Communist David, thus revealing the paradoxical intertwining of passion and politics, desire and difference. Similarly, David's conversion to the ethic of the oppressed and transformation into a relative activist for gay rights occurs not just as a result of developing a shared ideological code (that of nationalism) but as a manifestation of the complex relationship between power and pleasure. Perhaps David also undergoes this conversion because of an attraction to the difference, or otherness, that he perceives in Diego—an idea that raises questions about the structure of desire itself. Desire and power are not simply opposites, and the Freudian "hydraulic model" of desire as a naturally polymorphous instinctual flux, which institutionalized power uses to produce creativity through sublimation, is highly questionable today. It is more likely that desire occurs through power—not just in spite of it.[14]

13. For the concept of the *proximate* in relation to homophobia, see Jonathan Dollimore, *Sexual Dissidence: Augustine to Wilde, Freud to Foucault* (Oxford: Clarendon Press, 1991).

14. As is well known, Michel Foucault believed that desire is far from being a polymorphous flux whose only obstacle to expression comes from institutionalized power. Desire, for Foucault, is expressed only through power, which continually molds and remolds desire.

According to the film's ideology, David's role is quite clear: he is the idealistic revolutionary of a generation born precisely at the triumph of the Cuban Revolution, who, while supporting the nationalist/socialist system, insists on a new vision of the nation and the revolution. Within the semantics of *Fresa y chocolate*, David represents the complex term: the utopian horizon of the film's implicit ideology. However, as already noted, we must take into account the idea that all cultural artifacts propose a solution that both reveals and obscures the problem. That is, this artifact's utopian proposition is revealing insofar as it portrays the new revolutionary (David) as one who accepts the marginal elements in his society and tries to broaden the concept of nationality to include them. At the same time, however, it obscures those aspects of the problem that the ideology of the work cannot handle, such as the implications of the relationship among David, Diego, and Nancy, as well as the need for an effective way to "liberate" the gay and lesbian members of Cuban society. David initially follows the line propounded by Miguel, but his idealism and honesty soon lead him to conclude that the true revolution must be one that dignifies and accommodates someone like Diego. David's capacity to deliberate honestly—dramatically registered in his succinct query "Damn it! Am I turning into a son of a bitch?"—is his greatest virtue. This new, all-embracing attitude that David develops requires an anti-*machista* sensibility. Indeed, this aspect of David's character is so important to the film that from the beginning he is portrayed as being quite different from the typical Cuban macho (i.e., by the scene with Vivian in the hotel and by the fact that at twenty he is still a virgin).

But *Fresa y chocolate* goes even further in deconstructing machismo. Regarding sex and gender roles, early in the film David observes a woman making love in an "active" position. This scene exposes the binary woman/passive-man/active relationship as merely conventional, thereby disarticulating the social constructs that establish the codes of relation among sex, gender, and sexuality.[15] Similarly, in the short story "El lobo," Diego, in describing his classification of different Cuban sexual types, refers to men so obsessed with "perpetual fornication" that "they can go to the Post Office . . . and on the way screw one of us 'girls' without damaging their virility."[16] That is, in this typology, these extremely virile men can have sexual relations with a

15. The deconstruction of traditional definitions of sex, gender, and sexuality has become known as queer theory and transgender politics. Among works on the topic, see Judith Butler, *Bodies That Matter: On the Discursive Limits of "Sex"* (New York: Routledge, 1993).

16. Paz, *El lobo, el bosque y el hombre nuevo*, 12.

homosexual "without damaging their virility"—without being defined as homosexual.

This manner of classifying and conceptualizing sexuality can certainly be found in other Latin American countries. For example, among some Mexicans, a man who is represented as "active" (i.e., exclusively "active") in his sexual relations with another man is considered very macho, while Chicanos (under the influence of attitudes prevalent in the United States) usually define men involved in any type of homoerotic relationship as homosexual.[17] The prevailing definition of the homosexual in Cuba (at least among certain individuals and groups) is therefore closer to that of Mexicans than to that of Chicanos, which illustrates the relativity of these classifications. Moreover, the view of sexual "passivity" as degraded often stems from heterosexism in a society in which women, supposedly "passive" in *machista* rhetoric, occupy an inferior social position. It is on these grounds that the term *effeminate* has been applied to homosexual men as an insult. Within this logic, the plight of gays is frequently lumped together with that of women; that is, the social status or condition of the homosexual is almost always related to gender—to the definitions and roles historically assigned to each (biological) sex.

Of the characters in *Fresa y chocolate*, the most interesting and complex, not to mention contradictory, is Diego. As stated earlier, he succeeds in "converting" (or, as the film says, "winning") David to a greater understanding of the Cuban gay's condition by means of the strategy of resentment. In this strategy a member of the oppressed (Diego, in this case) implants in a member of the oppressor class (David, in his initial role of homophobic revolutionary) an understanding, often with a strong burden of guilt, of the plight of the oppressed that leads to his actively supporting the latter's liberation. But Diego is not only a gay man who demands the right to full participation in his society; he also represents a complex ideology of class and personal characteristics that intertwine with his sexual orientation but that could never be reduced to sexual orientation alone. Moreover, Diego is both an oppressed gay man and a character who has internalized some of the other prejudices of the society that discriminates against him. For example, he expresses racist sentiments, such as when he amuses himself by thinking about his superiority in drinking tea from French

17. See Tomás Almaguer, "Chicano Men: A Cartography of Homosexual Identity and Behavior," in *The Lesbian and Gay Studies Reader*, ed. Henry Abelove, Michèle Aina Barale, and David M. Halperin (New York: Routledge, 1993), 255–73.

cups, while outside "the blacks are shouting." He also says that tea is for civilized people, while coffee is for the unrefined—especially for black people. (Diego ironically sings a song called "All of Us Blacks Drink Coffee" when arguing this point with David.) When David, repeating slogans from the Cuban Revolution rather mechanically, answers that blacks and whites are equal, that "we all came from Africa," Diego reacts strongly, retorting, "Not you and I." Here Diego affirms the Spanish legacy while denying the African—a truly contradictory stance for a character claiming to be a believer in Afro-Cuban religion.

Diego's already complex nationalism is also mixed with an intense Eurocentrism, which is established in several ways, but particularly through his contrasting tea with coffee: sophisticated Europeans (Britons, in particular) drink tea, whereas vulgar Cubans drink coffee. This attitude conflicts with his explicit endorsement of "Cubanness" (an exquisite "Cubanness," to be sure) and his assiduous study of Cuban cultural figures. In fact, Diego instills in David a great appreciation of Cuban culture, especially of music, literature, and the architecture of Havana.[18] All of this indicates that, besides being a sophisticated gay man who represents the struggle for inclusion of gays and other marginal groups disenfranchised by the Cuban socialist system of that time, Diego exhibits a series of contradictions typical of a Cuban gay man from a certain class and with certain personality traits. The sexual politics that Diego represents, with its corresponding illumination and alienation, is of the class that could be called the nationalist bourgeoisie.

One of Diego's characteristics that illustrates his ideology is his attitude toward art, that is, the implicit value system informing his opinions on art and literature. His conversations with David at the beginning of the film reveal that despite an impressive range of reading (from John Donne to José Lezama Lima), his attitude toward literature often suffers from a certain superficiality. For example, he is more interested in imagining that one of the chairs in his apartment is "the chair of John Donne" than in trying to understand the work of that great seventeenth-century English writer, who dared to relate sex to sanctity. By the same token, Diego is more inclined to fetishize the

18. On both the novel and the film, see Emilio Bejel, "Nacionalidad y exilio en la narrativa cubana contemporánea (Reflexiones sobre la narrativa cubana a partir de 1959)," *Confluencia* 9 (spring 1994): 73–87, especially p. 77. Diego's Eurocentrism is reminiscent of that of Sergio, the main character in *Inconsolable Memories* by Edmundo Desnoes (New York: New Maerican Library, 1967). The movie based on this work was directed by Gutiérrez Alea, a codirector of *Fresa y chocolate*.

figure of Lezama Lima by means of a "Lezamian lunch" in the *style* of the latter's novel *Paradiso* than to study his theory of image and metaphor or the "poetic system of the world" elaborated in his work. Thus Diego's "chair of John Donne" and "Lezamian lunch" exemplify his fetishistic perspective on art and literature.

But Diego's reaction to an exhibit of Germán's sculptures and his indignation when Nancy says that the works "do not transmit anything" reveal his aesthetic: a passionate conviction that art must not make any concessions to politics or yield to any type of censorship or coercion. Decidedly in favor of unconditional artistic freedom, he reacts negatively to "propagandistic art" and art that "transmits" something. Art must not "transmit" ("Let the National Radio transmit," he says), but rather should "incite thinking and feeling." However, Diego never makes clear exactly what is to be *thought* and *felt* about art; what it means to "think" and "feel" in relation to art. Are not thoughts and feelings, then, transmitted by art? Although expressed in a very contradictory and confusing manner, his attitude seems to be one of "art for art's sake" (as opposed to an explicit, socially committed art): an art sufficiently abstract so as to conceal its ideology, an art that emphatically promotes a sharp, if untenable, division between poetry and politics.

Diego implies that he favors an art that aspires to a pretended autonomy, resisting any definition of it in terms of other forms of knowledge: the political, the social, the psychological. Diego's attitude toward art and literature causes a typical dilemma: on the one hand, he preaches (in his "sermons" to David) an activist politics of gay liberation, while on the other, he defends an art that is apolitical. From this contradiction arises the logic of art as fetish, for if art cannot be political or allowed to "transmit" anything, it can at least pretend to be a lifestyle—an elegance of the spirit. Both the "chair of John Donne" and the "Lezamian lunch" are ideologically related to Diego's passion for French cups, Indian tea, and Japanese kimonos.

It is important to emphasize here (and thus put Diego's implied aesthetic into perspective) what historical materialism has insisted upon: that so-called art for art's sake, despite its claiming to be apolitical, actually entails an implicit ideology whose aesthetic rests precisely on a systematic separation of art from politics. Indeed, this aesthetic actively obscures the representation of ideological conflicts within the system. Fredric Jameson has argued that the modernism of the late nineteenth century, with its insistence on an apolitical art, was a symbolic solution to the conflict produced by the radical restructuring and expansion of the major political powers during that period. One of the most important results of this restructuring (from a cultural perspective) was the great difficulty that the dominant ideology experienced in attempting to represent the new world order (or disorder); that is, the hegemonic ideology found itself in the difficult position of not being able to represent its "new otherness": an emerging third world identity.[19] In terms of *Fresa y chocolate*, Diego's implicit aesthetic not only has a highly specific history and "ideology of form"[20] related to a dominant aesthetic of the late nineteenth century, but it also runs counter to the ideology of the film itself, which is a national allegory with an obvious political position.

19. See Fredric Jameson, "Modernism and Imperialism," in *Nationalism, Colonialism, and Literature*, ed. Terry Eagleton, Fredric Jameson, and Edward Said (Minneapolis: University of Minnesota Press, 1990), 43–66.

20. The term *ideology of form* is Jameson's adaptation of Louis Hjelmslev's *content of form*. See Hjelmslev, *Prolegomena to a Theory of Language* (Madison: University of Wisconsin Press, 1961).

★ TEN ★

(Un)Veiling Machismo

At the end of the twentieth century—especially since 1988—works having a gay, lesbian, or queer theme (depending on how those terms are defined and how the texts are read) were published in Cuba with frequency. This phenomenon is even more striking considering the extremism and institutionalization of homophobia in modern Cuban society. But as I have insisted throughout this study, extreme homophobia is frequently a symptom of the Cuban nationalist discourse's dependence on the definition of *homosexuality*. In this discourse homosexuality forms an integral part, by negation, of the very definition of *nation*. This is why the meaning of the phrase "coming out of the closet" implies that the repressed element was always there, menacing and ready to reemerge when the right circumstances arose; from this image comes the phrase's constant spectral expression. Apparently, this is what happened in Cuban society. Although by the end of the 1960s texts by authors whose lives and/or works were clearly related to homoeroticism began to distinguish themselves as part of the opposition to the culture of revolutionary Cuba (Virgilio Piñera, José Lezama Lima, Severo Sarduy, Calvert Casey, and Reinaldo Arenas, for example), the great public explosion of such works, published with the tacit approval of Cuban authorities, is more characteristic of the period from the late 1980s onward (it must be remembered that Reinaldo Arenas published most of his writings outside Cuba and without official approval).

In the introduction to this section I mentioned a series of texts published beginning in the mid-to-late 1980s and in which the representation of homoeroticism is resignified. But I must qualify this by maintaining that such a transformation always brings with it some form of imitation of the oppressing system. Therefore, the texts I will analyze in this chapter can be read as diverse discursive strategies that, in spite of their avowed antimachismo, often reproduce—and sometimes even affirm—the postulates of the system they claim to redress.

Of the most notable and well-known texts on the gay theme written in Cuba at the end of the twentieth century, *El lobo, el bosque y el hombre nuevo* (The wolf, the forest and the new man) by Senel Paz stands out. Published in 1991, this text was excerpted in *Bohemia* magazine in 1990 and formed the basis for the script of the 1993 film *Fresa y Chocolate* (Strawberry and chocolate), which I studied in chapter 9. Other stories on the homoerotic theme that have had appreciable resonance in contemporary Cuba are "La carta" (The letter) and "El retrato" (The portrait) by Pedro de Jesús López Acosta; "Por qué llora Leslie Caron?" (Why is Leslie Caron crying?) by Roberto Urías; "El cazador" (The hunter) by Leonardo Padura Fuentes; "Monte de Venus" (Mound of Venus) by Mercedes Santos Moray; and "Mi prima Amanda" (My cousin Amanda) by Miguel Mejides, among others. The novel *Máscaras* by Leonardo Padura Fuentes also has enjoyed great popularity there. In 1998 López Acosta (the pen name used for his latest publications has been simply Pedro de Jesús) published his first collection of short stories in Spain; some of these stories also have been published in Cuba. Titled *Cuentos frígidos* (Frigid tales), practically all of the stories deal boldly with homoerotic situations. Among the texts having specifically lesbian themes, the stories "Sombrío despertar del avestruz" (Dark awakening of the ostrich) and "Dos almas perdidas nadando en una pecera" (Two lost souls swimming in a fishbowl) by Ena Lucía Portela Alzola stand out, as do the poems of Odette Alonso and Damaris Calderón.

Among the deceased gay Cuban writers, José Lezama Lima and Virgilio Piñera are the ones most frequently considered heroes or martyrs by the young Cuban writers on the island who address the gay theme, while Reinaldo Arenas has this distinction for Cuban writers in exile. I noted in chapter 8 Reinaldo Arenas's autobiography, *Antes que anochezca* (Before night falls), in which he names Piñera as his inspiration. I also mentioned in chapter 9 how Diego, the gay character in *Fresa y chocolate*, pays homage to Lezama. In the present chapter I shall analyze how Leonardo Padura Fuentes (1955–) constructs in his novel *Máscaras* (Masks) a character called Alberto Marqués, who closely resembles the persona of Virgilio Piñera. Among the young "Virgiliano" Cuban writers, I must mention Pedro de Jesús López Acosta (1970–), who named his latest collection of stories *Cuentos Frígidos* (Frigid tales) in obvious reference to Piñera's *Cuentos Fríos* (Cold tales). Piñera, who was called El Diablo (The devil) by his political and literary enemies, today reappears as a ghost who takes revenge on his critics. This highly iconoclastic literary, social, and political rebel has emerged as the return of the repressed gay spirit who must be reckoned with, since his entire work and life have become a symbol of resistance from a posture of marginality, while at the same time, ironically, he has become the most appreciated of the Cuban literary fathers.

The Masks of Máscaras

Of all the texts mentioned in the previous paragraphs, I have chosen to begin with a reading of *Máscaras* (Masks) (1997) by Leonardo Padura Fuentes, since it can be read as a summarized history of Cuba's worst homophobic moment during the revolution.[1] The story tells of a summer's day in 1989 when a transvestite named Alexis Arayán Rodríguez is found dead in a Havana park known as the Bosque de La Habana (The Havana forest). The murder investigation is assigned to Lieutenant Mario Conde, who, besides being a policeman and detective, also aspires to be a writer. It is precisely his affinity for fiction writing that leads Conde to develop a whole series of theories about who killed the transvestite. These theories are fairly similar to those elaborated by characters in some of the short stories of Argentine writer Jorge Luis Borges in that they (re)construct the murder based more on inferences and literary intuitions that on concrete evidence. Lieutenant Conde's extraordinary investigative dedication and zeal lead him to discover an entire marginal queer world.

As part of his investigation, Conde interviews an old gay writer and playwright named Alberto Marqués, who has long been a victim of the homophobic system institutionalized by the Cuban Revolution. Although the story makes it clear that by 1989 Alberto's political situation has improved quite a bit, he still feels very bitter and resentful toward the Cuban regime that humiliated him and stifled his opportunities for expression and publication. Alberto was a friend to Alexis, the murdered transvestite, so Conde must interrogate him. After an interesting series of adventures, we learn that Alexis Arayán's murderer

1. Leonardo Padura Fuentes, *Máscaras* (Masks) (Havana: Ediciones Unión, 1997).

is his own father, Faustino, who killed his son out of homophobia and also to silence him after he discovered something unsavory about Faustino's past. The fact that Faustino wishes to hide is that after the triumph of the revolution in 1959, he had forged some documents so as to make it appear that he had belonged to the urban revolutionary resistance movement in the late 1950s. Based on this lie he had risen in position and privilege in the revolutionary government and become an ambassador.

The novel ends with a love scene between Mario Conde and Poly, a young woman whom he had met a few days earlier at a queer party. Both the resolution of Conde's investigation as well as the final scene of the novel are very disappointing. In the murder investigation, the novel's plot seems to promise a much more interesting ending up until the very moment of the denouement. The theme of corrupt bureaucracy is quite common in Cuban literature, and therefore it is not very original. In the last scene of the novel, which relates the heterosexual relations between Conde and Poly, it also seems to me that this is a strategy of containment from what the novel seems to promise at other points in the narrative. Such a restrained ending to *Máscaras* leads me to conclude that an ideological conflict has hindered its most daring possibilities. After bringing the theme of homosexuality and the abuse of gays to the surface, the text ultimately opts for a solution that is contained and ideological (in the worst sense of the term), reinstalling and reaffirming the heterosexism that it had challenged earlier.

In spite of this weak ending, the rest of the novel is notable due to Padura Fuentes's narrative skill. Lieutenant Conde's every step is told in a very seductive series of details and plot twists. It is, of course, a detective novel with a rich narrative and a plot that at each crossroads leads us to believe that the investigation is uncovering the crime, yet frequently leads us to new crossroads to maintain our interest. Another interesting aspect of this novel is the number of situations representing Havana society at the end of the 1980s. This was precisely the crucial period in which the Soviet Union was on the point of dissolving, and Cuba, highly dependent on Soviet economic and military strength, entered into an unprecedented time of hardship that from 1989 onward has been known officially as *el período especial* (the special period). But what stands out in Padura Fuentes's novel is not history with a capital *H* but rather the daily trials endured by the average resident of Havana. In spite of the representation of such hardships, however, the narration frequently seems to lean toward a vision that alleviates the gravity of Cuba's situation at the time.

All narratives contain a dialogue of voices in conflict, each struggling to be heard. Accordingly, various subjective positions enter into dialogue and argue amongst themselves in *Máscaras*. Padura Fuentes clearly wants to present the novel as a critique of the most repressive period of the revolution. The narration of Conde's investigation makes a series of commentaries not only on the period following the murder (1989), but also on the years of the worst institutionalized homophobia in Cuba, namely from the mid-1960s to the mid-1970s. There are moments in which the atrocities of the Military Units to Aid Production (UMAPs) are mentioned, along with the repressive excesses of the 1971 First National Congress on Education and Culture and some of the horrors of the events associated with the exodus of Cubans from the port of Mariel in the summer of 1980.

In narrating this institutionalized homophobia, the novel uses the character of Alberto Marqués as symbol and symptom of the phenomenon. Mario Conde, the police officer, meets Alberto, a gay playwright, in the course of his investigation of the murder of Alexis, a transvestite. Alberto is a great writer whom Cuban officialdom had censored for many years due to his "ideological deviations." In his case these "deviations" are considered to be his homosexuality and his defiant attitude toward the official mandates directed at artists and writers during the most repressive decade of the revolution. The official reports on Alberto are said to classify him as "a homosexual of vast predatory experience, politically apathetic and ideologically deviant, a trouble maker and provocateur who socializes with foreigners, an elitist, secretive, a possible user of marijuana and other drugs, a protector of stray faggots, a man of dubious philosophical affiliation, full of petite bourgeois and class prejudices, noted and classified with the undeniable assistance of a Moscow manual of techniques and procedures of socialist realism."[2]

The character of Alberto Marqués is an obvious adaptation or interpretation of the persona of Virgilio Piñera (1912–79). Of course, since this character is alive in 1989, ten years after Piñera's death, the novel is taking poetic license. But several of the other characteristics of Piñera's personality, including his physique and even what has been said of his

2. Spanish original: "un homosexual de vasta experiencia depredadora, apático político y desviado ideológico, ser conflictivo y provocador, extranjerizante, hermético, culterano, posible consumidor de marihuana y otras drogas, protector de maricones descarriados, hombre de dudosa filiación filosófica, y lleno de prejuicios pequeñoburgueses y clasistas, anotados y clasificados con la indudable ayuda de un moscovita manual de técnicas y procedimientos del realismo socialista." Ibid., 37.

sexual habits, are incorporated into the representation of Alberto. This character is described as effeminate, having a very delicate physique, and showing a sexual preference for black men (whom he sometimes pays to pretend to come to his house and rape him). He is witty but embittered over the abuses that have been committed against him. All these characteristics have been attributed to Virgilio Piñera. Moreover, Alberto, like Piñera, is the author of a play titled *Electra Garrigó* (in which Piñera reinterprets and Cubanizes the Electra myth).

Piñera is mentioned in *Máscaras*, but we are also told that Alberto has met the historical figure and tried to emulate him. The similarities between the two, however, are too many for this to be a coincidence or a simple matter of Alberto's admiration for Piñera. There can be no doubt that with Alberto, Padura Fuentes has not only tried to represent a person like Piñera, but also insisted on the similarities between the fictional character and the historical figure in an often excessive manner. What is more, the first of the three quotations that serve as the prologue comes from *Electra Garrigó*. This quotation ends with a reference to Piñera's Havana: "It is, do not forget, a city in which everyone wants to be fooled."[3]

As this quotation implies and as the very title of Padura Fuentes's novel emphasizes, the text proposes a theory of representation and of life as a series of masks. The novel emphasizes this theory to such a degree that it demands we pay it due attention. It is quite obvious that throughout *Máscaras*, Padura Fuentes occasionally tries to develop a theory of representation, of the mask, that is somewhat similar to José Lezama Lima's and even more so to Severo Sarduy's in his essay *La simulación* (The simulation). Although Mario Conde is the novel's protagonist, this text's theory of representation does not come from him. Conde represents instead a character with ethical principles related to those of certain Cubans having socialist leanings and to their vision of how revolutionary Cuban society ought to be (a sort of good revolutionary, as opposed to a bad one). Also, Conde constantly worries about the meaning of life and death from an existentialist position like that of Albert Camus or the one given in certain early works of Jean-Paul Sartre. As a child Conde was Catholic, but he has now achieved a materialistic concept of life that leads him to view the world as a great void lacking in answers to the meaninglessness produced by death.[4] Of course, the fact that the story deals with the

3. Virgilio Piñera, *Electra Garrigó*, in *Teatro completo* (Havana: Ediciones R, 1960), act 3 p. 68.

4. Padura Fuentes, *Máscaras*, especially pages 24–25.

death of a transvestite lends itself perfectly to reflection not only on death but also on simulation. Thus Conde, in his murder investigation, must constantly reflect on the "reality" that is hidden behind the transvestite's mask or on the theory that everything is a mask hiding other masks—that behind the interminable masks, reality is nowhere to be found.

It is precisely these two theories—that reality must be unmasked and that there is nothing to be unmasked, since everything is a mask—that create in Padura Fuentes's text a paradoxical tension. At times the text seems decidedly inclined toward the second option, that behind each mask is another mask, and so on to infinity. This position occasionally seems to be drawn almost directly from Severo Sarduy's treatises on representation. At one point in the novel, as part of a story Alberto is telling Conde about a conversation among three gay Cuban writers in Paris (Alberto, Recio, and the Other Boy), we read ideas very much like those of Severo Sarduy on transvestism in his essay *La simulación*. Recio says the following:

> [E]l tranvesti humano es una aparición imaginaria y la consecuencia de las tres posibilidades del mimetismo . . . : primero: el travestismo propiamente dicho, impreso en esa pulsión ilimitada de la metamorfosis, en esa transformación que no se reduce a la imitación de un modelo real y determinado, sino que se precipita en la persecusión de una realidad infinita (y desde el inicio del "juego" aceptada como tal). Es una irrealidad cada vez más huidiza e inalcanzable (ser cada vez más mujer, hasta sobrepasar el límite, yendo más allá de la mujer). . . . Segundo, el camuflaje, pues nada asegura que la conversión cosmética (o incluso la quirúrgica) del hombre en mujer, no tenga como finalidad oculta una especie de desaparición, de invisibilidad, *d'effacement* y de tachadura del macho mismo en el clan agresivo, en la horda brutal de los machos. Y por último—dijo el Recio—, está la intimidación, pues el frecuente desajuste o la desmesura de los afeites, lo visible del artificio, la abigarrada máscara, paralizan o aterran, como ocurre con ciertos animales que utilizan su apariencia para defenderse o para cazar, para suplir defectos naturales o virtudes que no tienen: el valor o la habilidad, no?[5]

> [The human transvestite is an imaginary apparition and the result of the three possibilities of mimeticism . . . : First: transvestism itself, imprinted in that unlimited impulse of metamorphosis, in that transformation that cannot be reduced to the imitation of a real and specific

5. Ibid., 44–45.

model, but which throws itself into the pursuit of an infinite reality (and which is accepted as such from the beginning of the "game"). It is a more and more fleeting and unattainable unreality (to be more and more of a woman, until surpassing the limit, going beyond the woman). . . . Second, the camouflage, since nothing assures that the cosmetic (or even surgical) conversion from man to woman won't have as a hidden end a sort of disappearance, invisibility, effacement and crossing out of the very maleness in the aggressive clan, in the brutal horde of men. And finally . . . there is intimidation, since the frequent lack of adjustment or ill-fittingness of the makeup, that which is visible of the artifice, the multi-colored mask, paralyzes or terrifies, such as occurs with certain animals who use their appearance to defend themselves or to hunt, to compensate for natural defects or for virtues they lack: valor or ability, right?]

Nevertheless, and in spite of the text's emphasis upon and apparently preference for expounding ideas like those of Severo Sarduy, at other points, in the mouths of other characters, the text attributes the idea of representation as an endless process to José Lezama Lima, who during his lifetime was known as *el Gordo* (the fat man) because of his girth; Padura Fuentes's texts uses this same epithet in referring to him. Lezama Lima's writings repeat Blaise Pascal's principle that "since true nature has been lost, everything can be natural,"[6] affirming a philosophical position that, although containing religious vestiges (the idea of a nature that "has been lost" refers to the loss of Paradise, an idea that Sarduy rejects), points nevertheless toward a radical questioning of any "natural" base or stability.

The association between the theory of representation as a mask without limits appears as part of the story within the story about Alberto's life in Paris during part of his youth. Alberto recreates this account for Mario Conde based on a conversation between himself, Recio, and the Other Boy:

> —"No. El travesti no imita a la mujer"—comentó entonces el Recio, como si estuviera dictando una conferencia, con esa voz y esas palabras suyas de saberlo todo-todo. Siempre usaba oraciones largas, estratificadas, barrocas y lezamianas como caricaturas del pobre Gordo—. "Para él, *à la limite* no hay mujer, porque sabe (y su tragedia mayor es que nunca deja de saberlo) que él, es decir, que ella es una apariencia que su reino y la fuerza de su fetiche encubren un insalvable defecto de las otras veces sabia naturaleza."[7]

6. See my discussion of this idea in chapter 6.
7. Padura Fuentes, *Máscaras*, 43.

["No. Transvestites don't imitate women," said Recio, as if he were giving a lecture, with that voice and those know-it-all words of his. He always used long sentences, stratified, baroque and Lezamian, like cartoons of the poor Fat Man. "For him, *à la limite* there is no woman, because he knows (and his greatest tragedy is that he can never stop knowing it) that he, that is to say, that she is an appearance, that her kingdom and the strength of her fetish cover up an irreparable defect of an otherwise wise nature."]

Although at first glance it may seem that Recio's statement affirms the theory of representation as an endless simulation, the last sentence reveals a shift toward an opposite interpretation. The phrase "her kingdom and the strength of her fetish cover up an irreparable defect *of an otherwise wise nature*" denotes another theory, another voice, that threatens to emerge in opposition to the first one. If nature can sometimes have "an irreparable defect" while at others it can act differently, in a "wise" fashion, we are faced with a very basic contradiction. Has nature committed an error with the gay and the transvestite? Has nature stopped being "wise" in the case of the homosexual? This struggle between two worldviews on representation is constant throughout Padura Fuentes's entire text.

A list of examples of this contradiction in *Máscaras* would be extensive. Of course, in pointing out these contradictory positions I am not trying to invalidate Padura Fuentes's work; rather, I am underlining the dialogical tensions of the text and their possible implications in order to make reference to other paradoxes having ideological and political consequences. It can be argued that if the theory of the essential and natural character of the genders is not uprooted, it is very difficult to arrive at emancipatory political positions, insofar as the socially constructed differences in human sexuality are concerned. If there is still vacillation within this theory between whether the genders are stable categories endowed by "wise nature" or whether they are social constructs produced by repressive discourses, it is difficult to deconstruct all the homophobic prejudices and their sustaining structures.

I believe that *Máscaras* has many masks, both in the sense of ontological ambivalence concerning the theory of representation and in its political implications. Even though the novel obviously tries to represent itself as a radical mea culpa for the homophobic abuses of the Cuban Revolution, especially for the period from the mid-1960s to the mid-1970s, this act of contrition leaves much to be desired. Although *Máscaras* seems to be a very different work from the film *Fresa y chocolate*, it shares some of its virtues and several of its questionable aspects. In fact, I consider both works to have many more similarities than might be apparent at first glance: both represent a protagonist espousing basically socialist ideas who, through his vocation of (mediocre) writer, seems to achieve an understanding of homosexuals and the abuses they have suffered in Cuba. Moreover, in both works the gay man appears as a strange being, as someone weird in relation to the other characters, despite being looked upon with some compassion; and in both works, although much is said about homosexuality and the abuses of the *machista* socialist Cuban society, only heterosexual sex scenes between the protagonist and a woman are represented, thus reaffirming heterosexism. In short, both works are admirable for the transformation they at times represent in the situation between the Cuban regime (and *machista* Cuban culture in general) and homoeroticism, but both end with a heterosexist (and also socialist) reaffirmation once "the homosexual problem" is raised. The internal ideological conflict that the central theme of these texts brings out is very noticeable, especially at the end of both works.

The struggle of voices found in *Máscaras* can be read not only in terms of the contradiction between the theories on representation and political vacillation in relation to homosexuality, but also from a queer perspective. Throughout the entire novel I note a traditional definition of the homosexual, that is, that person is defined exclusively in terms of his or her sexual orientation. Thus defined, sexual identity is very cut and dried, and the limits of the definition seem certain: the homosexual is the opposite of the heterosexual; they are two clearly different types of persons. Although at various points in the novel it is decidedly put forth that one should have compassion for the homosexual (here meaning only gay men), he is undeniably represented as someone very different from the norm and perhaps from what is "natural." Nevertheless, and despite the prevalence of this definition in Padura Fuentes's novel, there is another voice that I would like to point out, or to make speak in this text: a certain queer voice that emerges at one point in spite of the gravitational force exerted by the thinly veiled heterosexism of the narrative.

As it is to be expected in a novel about a transvestite, the queerness of certain characters in the text is ontologically related to the theory of representation described earlier. Thus there are no natural limits between the constructs of sexuality and other social formations. The most revealing part of the queer voice in Padura Fuentes's text appears in the conversation between Conde and Poly. Both are at a queer party

to which Alberto has brought Conde, who expects to uncover some
revealing information about the murder of Alexis. Poly, who after the
party will have her first sexual relations with Conde (the second and last
encounter occurs at the end of the novel), tells him that the attendees
(some thirty people) have multiple definitions. She explains that not
only among themselves but within each person there exist several of
the subjective positions which she goes on to define:

—Dios, qué horror, si aquí hay de todo—dijo ella, mirando los
ojos del policía, como si se tratara de una confesión y el Conde supo
que en aquella sala de La Habana Vieja había, como primera eviden-
cia, hombres y mujeres, diferenciables además por ser: militantes del
sexo libre, de la nostalgia y de partidos rojos, verdes y amarillos; ex-
teatristas sin obra y con obra . . . maricones de todas las categorías y
filiaciones: locas . . . cazadores expertos en presas de alto vuelo, buga-
rrones por cuenta propia de los que dan por culo a domicilio . . . almas
desconsoladas sin consuelo y almas desconsoladas en busca de consuelo,
sobadores clase A-1 con el hueco cosido por temor al SIDA, y hasta
aprendices recién matriculados en la Escuela Superior Pedagógica del
Homosexualismo . . . ganadores de concursos de ballet, nacionales e
internacionales; profetas del fin de los tiempos, la historia y la libreta
de abastecimiento; nihilistas conversos al marxismo y marxistas con-
vertidos en mierda; resentidos de todas las especies: sexuales, políticos,
económicos, sicológicos, sociales, culturales, deportivos y electrónicos;
practicantes del budismo zen, el catolicismo, la brujería, el vodú, el
islamismo, la santería y un mormón y dos judíos; un pelotero del
equipo Industriales . . . admiradores de Pablo Milanés y enemigos de
Silvio Rodríguez; expertos como oráculos que lo mismo sabían quién
iba a ser el próximo Premio Nobel de Literatura, como las intenciones
secretas de Gorbachov, el último mancebo adoptado como sobrino
por el Personaje Famoso de las Alturas, o el precio de la libra de café
en Baracoa; solicitantes de visas temporales y definitivas; soñadores y
soñadoras; hiperrealistas, abstractos y ex-realistas socialistas que ab-
juraban de su pasado estético; un latinista; repatriados y patriotas;
expulsados de todos los sitios de los que alguien es expulsable; un
ciego que veía; desengañados y engañadores, oportunistas y filósofos,
feministas y optimistas; lezamianos—en franca mayoría—, virgilianos,
carpenterianos, martianos y un fan de Antón Arrufat; cubanos y ex-
trajeros; cantantes de boleros; criadores de perros de pelea; alcohólicos,
siquiátricos, reumáticos y dogmáticos; traficantes de dólares; fumadores
y no fumadores; y un heterosexual machista-estalinista.

—Ese soy yo . . . ¿Y travestis? ¿No hay travestis? —preguntó [Conde], clavándole en el pecho su mirada de cazador de vampiros.

—Mira [dice Poly], al lado de la puerta del balcón; esa es Victoria, aunque le gusta que le digan Viki, pero de verdad se llama Víctor Romillo. Es de lo más bonita, verdad? Y aquella, la trigueña que se parece a Annia Linares: por el día se llama Esteban y por la noche Estrella, porque ella es la que canta boleros.

—Dime una cosa: aquí hay como treinta personas . . . ¿Cómo puede haber tantas cosas como me dijiste?

Poly sonrió, inevitablemente.

—Es que practican el multioficio. . . . Mira, mira, el que está al lado de Estrella se llama Wilfredito Ínsula, y es como diez de las cosas que te dije.[8]

["My God, what a fright, there's something of everything here," she said, looking at the policeman's eyes, as if it were a confession and Conde knew that in that room in Old Havana there were, as primary evidence, men and women, who could be further differentiated as: card-carrying members of the free sex party, of the nostalgia party and of the red, green and yellow parties; ex-playwrights both with an oeuvre and without it . . . faggots of every type and affiliation: *locas* . . . hunters specialized in high-flying prey, independent-minded Top Men who make ass-service house calls, disconsolate souls without consolation and disconsolate souls looking for consolation, A-1 masseurs with their holes sewn shut out of fear of AIDS, and even recently enrolled apprentices in the Upper Division Normal School for Homosexuality . . . winners of ballet competitions, both national and international; End Times prophets, history prophets and prophets of ration coupon books; nihilists turned into Marxists and Marxists turned into shit; resentful people of every sort: sexual, political, economic, psychological, social, cultural, sporting and electronic; practitioners of Zen Buddhism, Catholicism, Witchcraft, Voodoo, Islam, Santería and one Mormon and two Jews; a baseball player from the Industriales team . . . fans of Pablo Milanés and haters of Silvio Rodríguez; oracle-like experts who just knew who would win the next Nobel Prize for Literature, what Gorbachev's secret plans were, who the last bachelor adopted as a nephew by the Famous Character of the Heights or the price of a pound of coffee in Baracoa; solicitors of visas, temporary and permanent; dreamers; hyperrealists, abstract expressionists and ex-social realists who had forsworn their previous esthetic; a

8. Ibid., 130–31.

Latinist; patriots and the repatriated; those expelled from anywhere anyone can be expelled from; a blind man who could see; the enlightened and the deceivers, opportunists and philosophers, feminists and optimists, followers of Lezama Lima—the clear majority—and followers of Virgilio Piñera, of Alejo Carpentier, of José Martí, and one fan of Antón Arrufat; Cubans and foreigners, Bolero singers; pit-bull breeders; alcoholics, psychiatrists, rheumatics and dogmatics; money launderers; smokers and nonsmokers; and a *machista*-Stalinist heterosexual.

"That would be me . . . And transvestites? Aren't there any transvestites?" asked [Conde], pinning her in the chest with his vampire-hunter's gaze.

"Look [said Poly], beside the balcony door: that's Victoria, although she likes it when you call her Viki, but her real name's Víctor Romillo. She's really beautiful, isn't she? And that one, the dark blonde who looks like Annia Linares: by day she's called Esteban and by night Estrella, because she's the one who sings Boleros."

"Tell me something: there are about thirty people here . . . How can there be as many things as you told me?

Poly smiled, inevitably.

"They all work extra jobs. . . . Look, look, that one who's beside Estrella is called Wilfredito Ínsula, and he's about ten of the things I told you."]

Besides the intentional humor of this section of the novel, the multiplicity of definitions and subjective positions attributed to the people at the party is so overwhelming that a lack of limits is implied, resulting in a queer vision that questions the very stability of any definition of sexual, artistic, or political identity. With this queer voice the text seems to deconstruct several of its own postulates about the homosexual. Nevertheless, in the section immediately following I will undertake a reading of some texts that can be considered more radically queer than *Máscaras*.

The Search for an Elided Voice

The never-ending search for a subjectivity that undertakes many thematic and narrative techniques for veiling and unveiling identities can be read in *Cuentos Frígidos* (Frigid tales) (1998) by Pedro de Jesús.[9]

9. Pedro de Jesús López Acosta, *Cuentos frígidos* (Frigid tales) (Madrid: Olalla Ediciones, 1998).

The two most frequent strategies employed by these texts in the search for such a subjectivity are the staging of homoerotic sexuality and the play of narrative voices. The latter is characterized by what I could call a transvestism of narrative voices, since we often read that the narrator presents him- or herself as feminine and then as masculine, sometimes heterosexual and other times gay, lesbian, or bisexual. The gender play of the narrative voices becomes very complicated at times, and we must read another story in the collection to obtain a temporary idea of who is narrating and what his or her gender identity is. The answer to this gender question is frequently what could be called *entendido* or queer, since the sexual and narrative identities of the narrators and characters themselves are frequently oblique and blurred. All this narrative complexity is closely related to the themes of the stories that are told in these texts; these stories frequently deal with homoerotic relations between "men" and between "women," and at times between people of different sexes who also have lovers of the same sex. Perhaps it is precisely this ambiguity of gender and sexual object, along with the constant and radical rearticulation of subjectivity at all levels, that characterizes not only the stories of Pedro de Jesús but also those of a great many texts by young Cuban writers born after the triumph of the revolution (some quite a few years after).

In the case of Pedro de Jesús, some of his texts published in Cuba are at the very limit of what that society allowed to be published for many years in terms of (homo)sexual stories. For example, in his story "El retrato" (The portrait), Pedro de Jesús narrates the erotic scenes between Ana, a "heterosexual" painter, and Jorge, a "heterosexual" chauffeur, in great detail, as well as those between Gabriel and Héctor, two "homosexual" lovers, and Héctor and Jorge, one of the "homosexual" lovers and the supposedly "heterosexual" chauffeur. This is one of the author's best stories, and in it some of the most outstanding characteristics of his other texts can be noted: the use of ingenious narrative strategies, the combination of narration with highly intuitive reflections on love and/or sexual relations between people of different sexual orientations and identities, and the extraordinary changes in time and narrative voice.

All of the stories in *Cuentos Frígidos* are very interesting and imaginative, full of dark humor and subtle insights. "El retrato" stands out among them, along with "La carta" (The letter) and "Maneras de obrar en 1830" (Manners and customs in 1830). These last two texts have interwoven plots, since "Maneras de obrar en 1830" deals with someone (anonymous at the beginning of the story) who has read

"La carta" and sent the author a letter praising him for that text and asking that he appraise one of her stories. The story within the story (which at the same time makes reference to "La carta") deals with a supposedly autobiographical character named Claudia, who is having sexual relations with a friend named Laura; at another point with a recent acquaintance, a young woman with the nickname Rocky; and at the same time as Rocky, with a young man named Jorge Ángel. Laura, the friend and lesbian lover, tells Claudia the details of her sexual relations with a young man named Carlos. The story also refers to the behavior and love relations among some young lesbians in the student dormitories who have formed a group known among the students as *Las Vikingas* (the Viking women).

The narrative structure of the story within the story becomes further complicated with a series of letters exchanged between the male author of the story we are reading and the female author of the inner story. This complex game of who is narrating and what the identity of the author and the narrator is reaches its climax in the relationship between the text of "La carta" and that of "Maneras de obrar en 1830" (the reference to 1830 clearly indicates that Pedro de Jesús is emulating Henri Beyle Stendhal, especially his novel *The Red and the Black*; Pedro de Jesús's story takes its title from a chapter in this novel). The Stendhalism of these two stories lies above all in the many pseudonyms of the narrative voices (which leads to a confusion and dissemination of the narrators' identities), the communication via letters that frequently leads to a confusion of motivation and meanings, the erasure of the limits between life and art, and the confusion of who is narrating and what his or her identity or identities are.[10]

Let us examine this narrative complexity one step at a time. "La carta" presumably depicts a love triangle between a him, a her, and a dancer. The identity of each of these characters is deliberately ambiguous and blurred, since although it is frequently said or implied that she is the narrator and he is the object of desire, another voice actually emerges to tell the adventures of him and her; also, we do not know exactly who the dancer is, or what part he plays in this love triangle. The mystery regarding who is speaking and what his or her identity or identities are is compounded by a letter that she (or the narrator) is supposed to have written him, but in the end it is not clear who really

---

10. For a study of Stendhal's narrative techniques and characteristics, see Gérard Genette, "'Stendhal,'" in *Figures of Literary Discourse* (New York: Columbia University Press, 1982), 147–82.

wrote it—nor is it clear for whom it was written or why. What is more, the evasive identity of the dancer is very difficult (perhaps impossible) to determine in this story, since this character is only mentioned at the beginning and at the end, which seems at times to allow the narrator "to at least preserve the illusion that my story was not so trivial and common."[11] The narrator also says that "had the dancer not existed, I would have lost my memory, the ability to ask myself questions" (ibid.).[12] In other words, the creation of the dancer seems to be a narrative ploy to add to "the ability to ask myself questions," which can be interpreted as the ability of the text to allow itself to be read in many ways, to permit a questioning of the construction and destruction of the narrator's identity and of the limits between life and art, between the sexes and gender roles of the characters—in other words, of the (de)formation of subjectivity itself.

The text says that "[t]he letter shouldn't have been a letter, a text for others, but rather for me, to understand myself and then to love or horrify myself" (ibid.).[13] In fact, even the gender identity of the narrator is in doubt from very early on, since the descriptions of the erotic scenes between her and him seem to constantly indicate that it is not a relationship between a woman and a man but rather between two gay men. The most noteworthy sex scene in the story is that which describes how "she" inserts her finger into "his" anus while "he" has his legs up in the air and open to "her." Furthermore, the matter of his homosexuality is mentioned more than once in the story ("It didn't matter to me that he was a homosexual" [ibid.],[14] says the narrator), as is that of the dancer, who is implied to be his lover at the end of the story.

To further complicate the questioning of the subjectivity and sexual objects of the characters, allusions are made to the Kensey scale in the story. What is his, or at times her, number? Would it be 1 ("exclusively heterosexual") or 6 ("exclusively homosexual") or 5 ("predominantly homosexual, on occasions heterosexual")? Can a person go from one number to another? Can one "switch" from one number to another due to a specific sexual experience? These are the questions constantly appearing, explicitly and implicitly, in the story, although they are

11. López Acosta, *Cuentos frígidos*, 19.

12. Spanish original: "De no haber existido el bailarín, hubiese perdido la memoria, la capacidad de interrogarme."

13. Spanish original: "La carta no debió ser una carta, un texto para otros, sino para mí, para entenderme y luego amarme u horrorizarme por mí misma."

14. Spanish original: "No me importaba que fuera homosexual."

frequently asked in a humorous fashion, parodying the entire matter of "sexual orientation" and "identities." At the end of the story, when it seems that a clear, definite answer will at last be given to the matter of the letter, there is a dialogue supposedly between him and her in which a heated discussion between her and him (or perhaps the dancer) ensues. This discussion takes place because the letter has unleashed a series of negative reactions toward her, since it had fallen into the hands of one of the lovers (him or the dancer), causing problems in the love triangle. The story ends by repeating some of the sentences and thoughts that it opened with, leaving us without any clarification of the identity of the characters, who wrote the letter we never read, or why the letter had been written.

In "Maneras de obrar en 1830," some points from "La carta" are "clarified," while others are made murkier still. Basically, the story involves the author of "La carta" (s/he now states that "he" is masculine), who has received an anonymous letter from an admirer who insists on keeping her identity secret and asks for his opinion on a story she has written. There then develops an intense correspondence between the author of the story and the anonymous author of the letter. As can be easily verified, "Maneras" undoubtedly supports a Stendhalism of narrative techniques, since the letters between the narrator-protagonists in this story are at times signed "Stendhal" and at others "Julien Sorel," and the two authors refer to each other with names from *The Red and the Black,* such as Mathilde and Madam Rínal. Of course, a narration based so heavily on an exchange of letters also could make reference to the work of Choderlos de Laclos or Juan Valera, but here the reference to Stendhal is direct and insistent.

The story ends with the revelation that the "admirer" of the author of "La carta" was not a woman but a beautiful mulatto dancer, who at times cross-dresses as a "blond woman"—which supposedly explains, at least partially, the role of the dancer in the story. The admired author has a sexual encounter with this mulatto man just as the story ends, therefore drawing him nearer to the identity of the character from "La carta" named "him." Since the anonymous story within "Maneras" is untitled, the author of the main story suggests to the author of this inner one that he call his work "Maneras de obrar en 1830," thus bringing about a complex game of narrative juxtapositions and interweaving that even includes the very title of the story we are reading. These interweavings are related to the play of narrative voices with their ambiguity of gender and identity, since both techniques imply a resistance and a destabilization of the accepted codes of power.

In Pedro de Jesús's stories the tale of erotic relations is the element that seduces the reader, but the issue that seems to dominate these narratives is always the search for that voice which had been elided by dominant discourse, a *queer* voice that insists on (de)constructing itself on a slippery semantic slope that is never totally defined or determined. The queer voice finds itself, not in order to be defined as gay, lesbian, or homosexual, but precisely as that voice that resists being classified and trapped into rigid or "frigid" definitions. There is a simultaneous denaturalization of the genders and their respective roles and a resignification of their subjective possibilities in Pedro de Jesús's stories. Although any search for subjectivity has to make use of the mediation of the Other (and therefore participates in a form of replicating the system of power), the implicit reversibility of the "identity" of these characters points toward a greater flexibility of identity and an elastic construct of subjectivity. This construct insists on situating itself in the gaps between subjectivity and otherness, thus giving rise to a means of resistance based on pointing out the incoherence and tensions in the accepted definitions.

Since the relationship of oneself as an Other allows discursive otherness to intervene as an instrument of one's own intelligibility, the subject that turns the gaze on him- or herself practices a relationship of power. He or she determines a field of tension between power and resistance that allows her or him to stay within the discourses that have been imposed by his or her culture and which are a necessary condition for that culture's discursiveness. But the techniques of destabilization in Pedro de Jesús's stories, by situating themselves in the gaps of subjectivity, are able to make a show of resistance that affirms homoerotic desire as being somehow authorized. Nevertheless, I cannot help but ask myself at this point who or what the "authorized" voice is in these stories that permits the queer one to name the object of its desire. Perhaps this authorized or authorizing voice is a certain literary canonicity, which in the stories of *Frigid Tales* is represented by the name Stendhal. The obvious and explicit Stendhalism of these tales may serve as an authorizing discourse allowing for the naming of the object of desire, which can only be materialized by means of the discourse of the other. Nevertheless, I believe that there is another authorizing voice besides Stendhalism in *Frigid Tales*. Again, as in Arenas's *Antes que anochezca*, it is the invocation of the figure of Virgilio Piñera, the "impossible father" (in contemporary Cuban culture he represents an extremely iconoclastic attitude), who despite his iconoclasm keeps emerging in the literary and political paternity of several Cuban writers dealing with the queer theme today.

Pedro de Jesús invokes Piñera with both the title of his collection and the first story in it, which contains a direct reference to Piñera. Titled "Instrucciones para un hombre solo" (Instructions for a single man), this story explicitly cites Virgilio's name as a sort of Virgil (in the Dante-esque sense) searching for the expression of the narrative voice in his quest to name the object of his desire, which in the end is clearly named: "A beautiful man who doesn't swish too much, he must be free and bold in sex, and his prick must go from normal to painfully swollen" (15).[15] Also in this story (so revealing of the search for the identity of the narrator/alter ego of the character/author) is a character named René. This name, for those familiar with Cuban literature, clearly refers to the main character in Virgilio Piñera's novel *La carne de René* (René's flesh), one of the few Cuban novels with homosexual implications to be produced during the 1950s.

In "Instrucciones" we are told that "Pedro de Jesús" meets "Virgilio," who is introduced by "the very nice boy from the agency" as René (ibid.).[16] Here the texts says that Pedro de Jesús tries at these moments not to show that he is profoundly saddened, and that he should take this encounter "as a joke, a revelation or an amusing remark after which he'll leave us alone again" (ibid.).[17] Next, Virgilio says, "Not until now did I realize that we were made for each other" (ibid.).[18] The story ends by making the judgment that this search for a narrative voice to remedy his loneliness has failed, since the search as well as the date with Virgilio has been "like someone who returns from one void to another void" (16).[19] Pedro de Jesús's text, like Arenas's autobiography before it, has called on the paternity of Virgilio Piñera, yet has immediately realized the improbability of that paternity—something that Arenas's text does not seem to emphasize. Then the narrative goes even further by rejecting its own writing. At the bottom of the page is a note that

15. Spanish original: "Bello, que no tenga muchas plumas, que sea libre y osado en el sexo, que su pinga transcurra de la normalidad al dolor."

16. Spanish original: "El muchacho amabilísimo de la agencia."

17. Spanish original: "Como una broma, una revelación o una gracia tras la cual se nos dejará otra vez solos."

18. Spanish original: "Nunca hasta ahora me di cuenta de que éramos ideales el uno para el otro."

19. Spanish original: "Como quien regresa de un vacío a otro vacío."

tries to cross out the very act of writing: "NOTE: Don't write the story, not that one nor any other one. Put an end to the bad habit" (ibid.).[20]

I believe that there might be a discursive connection between Stendhal and Piñera, between "Stendhalism" and "Piñerismo," that allows the texts of *Cuentos Frígidos* to name the object of their desire, to participate in the unsuccessful search for identity, to create literature, to write and at the same time unwrite or cross out what has been written (a typical gesture of Piñera and Stendhal alike). Of course, we can always ask ourselves, what meaning do the shows of resistance in these stories intend, and what debt do they owe to the systems of authority that allow them to name themselves and to name their object of desire? As in the case of Reinaldo Arenas in *Antes que anochezca*, Piñera's literary paternity is quite precarious and problematic, since a writer who insisted on a total lack of literary paternity, in the most iconoclastic gesture, can scarcely be made to be a Father. In any case, the figure of Virgilio Piñera, both for Arenas and for Pedro de Jesús, is a paradoxical symbol that on the one hand affirms, fortifies, and authorizes their supporters and followers, but on the other insists that the instability of the discourse of rebellion, the queer discourse, should be maintained at all cost, even if the Father must be slain instead of used as a prosopopoeia.

Writing Lesbian Desire

Ena Lucía Portela Alzola, a young Cuban writer born in 1972, has written several stories and a novel employing interplay between the narrative levels, connections between the narrators, and intertextualities that point toward an (un)veiling of machismo. She does so in a somewhat different fashion than Pedro de Jesús, even more so than Padura Fuentes. I will examine two stories by Portela Alzola here: "Dos almas perdidas nadando en una pecera" (Two lost souls swimming in a fishbowl)[21] and "Sombrío despertar del avestruz" (Dark wakening of the ostrich).[22] Like the stories of Pedro de Jesús, and to a certain extent the novel of Padura Fuentes, the writings of Ena Lucía Portela Alzola

20. Spanish original: "NOTA: No escribir el cuento, ni ése, ni ningún otro. Ponerle fin al vicio."

21. Ena Lucía Portela Alzola, "Dos almas perdidas nadando en una pecera" (Two lost souls swimming in a fishbowl) (Havana: Editorial Extremaduros, 1990).

22. Ena Lucía Portela Alzola, "Sombrío despertar del avestruz," (Dark awakening of the ostrich), in *El cuerpo inmortal. 20 cuentos eróticos cubanos*, ed. Alberto Garrandés (Havana: Editorial Letras Cubanas, 1997), 113–23.

deal with prohibited sexualities; in her case, the not very hidden theme is lesbianism. Keeping the ghost of excluded otherness in its nonplace is the never-ending job of the dominant system, and lesbian desire has been so excluded from the dominant discourse in Cuban culture that its literary expression is scarce. As I said at the beginning of this section, at the end of the 1980s and the beginning of the 1990s several gay, lesbian, and queer voices emerged in Cuban literature. Portela Alzola's is perhaps the youngest of these and one of the most original, or sui generis, of the writers who address lesbianism and bisexuality as a persistent and central theme in their work.

"Dos almas perdidas nadando en una pecera" is one of the earliest texts from this writer (this story and "Sombrío despertar del avestruz" were probably written before Ena Lucía reached the age of twenty), yet some of the narrative and artistic characteristics developed in her later works can be noted here. "Dos almas" is a work that on the one hand employs the style of a children's story or a fairy tale, and on the other deals with two themes that are very much prohibited and scandalous from the point of view of Cuban culture: lesbianism and suicide.

The story tells of the strange and conflictive relationship between two very young women (one of them states that she is eighteen, and it is implied that the other is about the same age). Their names are given as Mónica and la Rojita (little Red); in the story within the story they are called Mery and Misu, and they later name themselves Mónica and la Rojita. The inner story is a sort of fairy tale (at least in terms of its narrative tone) in which two girls leave their homes because they feel unhappy and lonely. They meet each other by coincidence, and it seems that each has found in the other the type of person she was seeking. Nevertheless, the main story tells how a young woman nicknamed la Rojita is in love with a girl named Mónica, but Mónica rejects la Rojita's advances and la Rojita commits suicide. There is a moment in the story when la Rojita kisses Mónica passionately on the lips:

> —Mónica . . . te amo y como un animalito que nunca ha sido mal-tratado, cierra los ojos, se inclina y la besa en los labios. La pelirroja, un rato después, contempla en el espejo el estigma de los cuatro dedos en el rostro. " 'No lo entiendo.' ¿Cómo pudo ser tan mala? Yo sólo quería que ella . . . bueno, pero a lo mejor es culpa mía: me pareció que sólo estaba asustada, que por fin ella y yo . . . ¿me habré engañado? . . . tantas ilusiones . . . ¡qué tonta he sido! Ahora lo he perdido todo. No

puede ser, no puedo perderla. La llamaré, le pediré perdón . . . haré lo
que ella quiera . . . Mónica . . ."[23]

["Mónica . . . I love you and like a poor little animal that's never
been mistreated, she closes her eyes, leans forward and kisses her on the
lips. The redhead, a little while later, gazes in the mirror at the stigmata
of the four fingers on her face. "I don't understand. How could she have
been so bad? I only wanted her to . . . well, but maybe it's my fault: I
thought she was only frightened, that finally her and I . . . Have I been
deceiving myself? . . . so many illusions . . . how stupid I've been! Now
I've lost everything. This can't be, I can't lose her. I'll call her, I'll tell
her I'm sorry. . . . I'll do whatever she wants . . . Mónica . . ."]

After la Rojita's suicide over her rejection by Mónica, Mónica is left
with an overwhelming feeling of guilt, and an obsession for knowing
herself better. It seems that the lesson of la Rojita's suicide has caused
Mónica to reflect on her own feelings, but it's too late to save la Rojita
now. Of course, the name *la Rojita* and the fairy-tale style of the
narrative suggest that this is a story like that of Little Red Riding Hood
but without the wolf—or rather, in which Little Red Riding Hood is
herself a sort of wolf.

The story's reflections on the search for self and therefore on the
ability to name the object of desire seek their authorization with
a quotation from the Argentine writer Jorge Luis Borges, used as
the epigraph to the story: "What can I do to keep you . . . I offer
you explanations of yourself, theories about yourself, authentic and
surprising news about yourself."[24] It is as if the young lesbian voice
had to appeal to the authority of certain literary discourses in order
to be able to articulate the object of its desire. Also, the childlike
discourse of fairy tales is the means by which the homoerotic lesbian
desire tries to (un)veil itself in this story. That is, on the one hand
we have the fairy-tale style that indicates an innocent narration, and
on the other is an entire thorny problematic concerning suicide and
homoeroticism between women that is somewhat hidden by this
childlike tone. Moreover, it is suggested in this story that Mery and
Misu (the characters from the fairy tale within the main story) are
perhaps not two people but rather two parts of Mónica, and therefore

23. Portela Alzola, "Dos almas," 55.
24. Spanish original: "¿Con qué puedo retenerte? . . . Te ofrezco explicaciones de ti
misma, teorías de ti misma, auténticas y sorprendentes noticias de ti misma." Ibid.

the title of the fairy tale is "Las dos Mónicas" (The two Mónicas). This is clearly a search for the sexual and emotional identity of a young woman who realizes that her behavior and the "orientation" of her feelings fall outside of that which is allowed.

Ena Lucía's "Sombrío despertar del avestruz" is a text of greater stylistic maturity and narrative skill. A greater control of narrative techniques and language can be noted here. This "maturity" can also be seen in the comments and reflections on the articulation of lesbian desire. This story, too, deals with lesbian relations between two young women. The technical control of the story is notable in that it articulates the object of lesbian desire much more clearly than in "Dos almas." As in the narratives of Pedro de Jesús, these two stories are intertextually interwoven, since the first is mentioned in the second. The plot of "Sombrío despertar del avestruz" involves a tense and difficult sexual relationship between the female narrator and a young woman named Laura, who greatly admires the narrator's story "Dos almas nadando en una pecera"; this admiration recurs several times in the text. It is precisely Laura's admiration for the narrator that unites these two young women, first in friendship and then in a lesbian relationship.

Unlike "Dos almas," where lesbian desire is somewhat obscured by the fairy-tale style and the childlike details, in "Sombrío" lesbianism is finally proclaimed clearly and repeatedly, although at times Ena Lucía attempts to hide this desire behind certain narrative and linguistic games:

> ¡Hay que ver la cantidad de mentiras que nos dijimos! Fui a la cocina a preparar jugo de naranja y le propuse que se quitara la ropa para sentir menos el calor (ventilador roto). Cuando regresé con el jugo me desvestí yo también. Lo agradable de todas nuestras mentiras era que ambas presentíamos lo poco efectivo del engaño.
>
> Le ofrecí el vaso, enorme y amarillo, y encendió un cigarro. (A la sombra de los reflejos tornasolados del dominó sobre su boca, como transcribió luego al dorso de una pedante mitología, torpe intento de extirpar un poema a las brutalidades del sexo.) La vista fija en sus senos puntiagudos. (Un estilete el delicioso disimulo de ella para mirarme a mí.) Yo no acertaba a sentir una intensidad en lo inverosímil de la situación, nada más estremecimientos "donde yo sé" disuelto en algo parecido al deseo.
>
> Se acostaron abrazadas para sentir menos el frío. . . . Pero Laura tenía miedo. En sus incursiones de invasora y en su juego por conocer si yo era

o no era eso mismo que nunca mencionaba delante de mí [claro, esta es una referencia que apunta a la palabra *lesbiana*] creí haber llegado demasiado lejos. Cerró los ojos a la manera de hipotéticas avestruces. . . . Pero mientras le acariciaba esa parte del cuello donde está el nacimiento de su pelito y sentía sus pezones, duros contra mi piel, la exploración de sus manos por la línea de la espalda y el cálido riachuelo (qué forma tan tonta de decirlo!) saliéndose a las dos, no podía casi pensar.

Un desastre: casi mordidas en su cuello, flores rojas, besaba sus hombros, sus senos, una vuelta despacio para acariciarle las nalgas y la espalda, diciéndole aún lo que no recuerda con tal de esconder su miedo poco a poco, al tiempo que ejercía una búsqueda de oraciones efectivas como liturgia de este cuento. Pero, falso fracaso, la única traducción de ese cáncer, su mente, era que el cuerpo de Laura, más que lindo, estaba riquísimo y con eso veinte obsenidades más, por cierto, bastante directas.[25]

[You should see all the lies we told ourselves! I went to the kitchen to make some orange juice and I said that maybe she should take her clothes off to not feel so hot (fan broken). When I got back with the juice I undressed, too. The nice thing about all our lies was that we both felt how ineffective the trick was.

I offered her the glass, huge and yellow, and lit up a cigarette. (In the shadow of the sunflower reflections of the domino above her mouth, as she later transcribed to a boring mythology, a clumsy attempt to extract a poem from the brutalities of sex.) My gaze fixed on her pointed breasts. (A stiletto her delicious excuse to look at me.) I was unable to feel an intensity in the falseness of the situation, just shudders "I know where" dissolved in something like desire.

They lay down with their arms around each other to feel the cold less. . . . But Laura was afraid. In her incursion as invader and in her game to find out if I was or wasn't that same thing that she never mentioned in front of me [this is a veiled reference to the word *lesbian*] I thought I had gone too far. I closed my eyes like the hypothetical ostriches. . . . But while I stroked that part of the neck where the little hairs start and felt her nipples, hard against my skin, the exploration of her hand along the line of my back and the warm stream (what a stupid way to say it!) flowing out of both of us, I almost couldn't think. . . .

A disaster: almost bites on her neck, red flowers, I kissed her shoulders, her breasts, a slow turn to caress her buttocks and back, telling

25. Portela Alzola, "Sombrío."

her something I still can't remember so as to hide her fear bit by bit, while I undertook a search for effective sentences like a liturgy of this story. But, false disaster, the only translation of that cancer, her mind, was that Laura's body, more than beautiful, was absolutely delicious and with that twenty obscenities more, and, of course, pretty direct ones.]

Nevertheless, in spite of such a passionate sex scene, the story tells that something interrupted relations between the two women, and at a certain point Laura told the narrator, "you're a joke, a great big bastard . . . I *do* like men!" to which the narrator says, "I do too, a little bit" (ibid.).[26] But Laura is very upset and in the middle of her aggressive outburst names the unnamable: "I don't have to be depending on you, you fucking lesbian" (ibid.).[27] We don't know with absolute certainty if this angry scene occurs minutes after the love scene, or if, on the contrary, the narrative is referring to another, later moment in the relations between the two women; this last possibility seems the most plausible. At any rate, although we are told of the struggle between the two women in their relationship, there can be no doubt that the object of desire has been unequivocally and unabashedly lesbian; the lesbian desire has been clearly articulated in very contemporary terms. It now remains to be asked by means of what discourses of authority the articulation of this prohibited desire has been made possible—that is, by means of what discourse of power does this previously elided body materialize.

First, we should note that in this story various foreign artists and writers are mentioned or quoted: there is an epigraph by Saint-John Perse, and Baudelaire is mentioned, as are Marguerite Duras, Alain Resnais, Albert Camus, Raymond Radiguet, Norma Jean, and Pink Floyd (they had also been mentioned more than once in "Dos almas"), along with several quotations in French and English. More important than the ideas that are attributed to these writers and artists, I believe, is the fact that they are quoted, that so many are mentioned and that they are all foreigners in relation to Cuba. Not one Cuban writer or artist makes the list. It is as if none of the national figures carried enough weight to authorize the text's discourse, the writing of Portela Alzola. The lesbian desire expressed in the text seems to require the authority of foreign voices; otherwise, it could not be written.

26. Spanish original: "'eres una farsante, tremenda hija de puta. . . . A mí sí me gustan los hombres!'"; "'A mí también, un poquito.'"
27. Spanish original: "'No tengo por qué estar dependiendo de ti, lesbiana de mierda.'"

Nevertheless, and in spite of the obvious need for the authority of foreign figures, a certain narcissistic affirmation leads the narrator to describe herself physically and at times mentally:

> Prometí una vez no hablar de mí ni de las relaciones con las muchachas que me han impresionado. Pero las promesas no se hacen para ser cumplidas (yo no sé para qué se hacen las promesas) y así pues, afirmo que soy delgada, nerviosa, tengo una cara bastante bonita (y vulgar), no soy virgen, ni buena deportista, tengo supersticiones con las arañas, fumo cantidad y en diciembre cumpliré veinte años. (Ibid.)

> [I once promised I'd never talk about myself or about my relations with the girls I've liked. But promises are made to be broken (I don't know why people make them at all) and so, let me state that I'm thin, nervous, have a fairly pretty (and ordinary) face, I'm not a virgin, nor good at sports, I have some superstitions about spiders, I smoke like a chimney and I'll be twenty in December.]

This description, which is possibly the author's self-portrait, shows some independence from the "authorizing" and "authorized" foreign voices in the narrator's self-examination. It is a sort of self-affirmation that aspires to create its own body, which has been erased from intelligibility by the dominant discourse. But in order to be written, every self-examination demands the discourse of the Other. This text, in addition to the quotations and allusions to foreign writers and artists, calls on the image of the *writer*, on the authority that being able to write represents. Very near the end of "Sombrío despertar" the narrator remarks, "Being a writer is a wicked vice. Sticking both hands all the way into the slaughtering of blank pages, in turn defenseless against the platen of great-grandma Remington, months later, in order to remember all of Laura without reproach. . . ." (ibid.)[28] Writing is represented as an act of penetration into the "blank pages" with the same hands that only recently were used in the text to represent the sex act, the lesbian desire to penetrate Laura. The "foreign" discourse and the discourse on the "role of the writer" give meaning and authority to the textuality of these two stories by Portela Alzola. It cannot be precisely determined which has supremacy or whether in fact the two

---

28. Spanish original: "Vicio infame el de ser escritor. Meter las dos manos hasta el fondo en la matanza de páginas en blanco, por turno indefensas ante el rodillo de bisabuela Remington, meses después, para recordarte toda Laura sin reproches."

authorizing discourses are allies or enemies in their role as producers of this textuality, which represents lesbian desire with such passion. Diverse voices in the text struggle for systemic supremacy, and that struggle occasionally allows for cracks through which the phantom of excluded otherness, demanding a place in the public imagination of the subjects who inhabit the nation, emerges. Nevertheless, Portela Alzola's stories, with their insistence on seeking authority from exclusively foreign sources, seem to suggest a great national failure. In terms of nationalist discourse, it is as if these stories imply that in order to name the prohibited lesbian desire, one must forget, or at least avoid, everything national—as if everything related to the nation lacked authority to name the unnamed, to name the lesbian desire.

★ ELEVEN ★
Gender Trouble in the
Land of the Butterflies

*T*he relationship that equates citizenship with heterosexuality is
based on a sexuality constructed on the naturalized alignment of
sex, gender, the object of sexual desire, and nationhood. But since these
categories are not naturally or biologically necessitated, the norms that
the heterosexist system demands never manage to completely control
that system's own insubordination. Therefore, when the hegemonic
subject calls someone *afeminado* (effeminate), *maricón* (faggot), or
loca (very effeminate faggot), it is expressing its fear of losing "proper"
gender as it regulates sexuality by policing gender and shaming gender
infractions. Thus I continue my reflection on the relationship between
heterosexuality and citizenship in contemporary Cuban culture with
the following question: if the identity of an individual is born into
Cuban social life by means of an injurious interpellation, how can that
person, coming from such a formation, transform the terms of her/his
violation? In other words, if a person has acquired at least part of her/his
identity based on being called *afeminado*, *maricón*, or *loca*, how can
such a person resignify those interpellations into something positive?
This is a basic question that I will address in examining "homosexual
transvestism" in Cuba at the end of the twentieth century. With this
objective in mind I will refer specifically to the documentary *Mariposas*

Author's note: In Cuban culture, as well as in other Hispanic cultures, the word *mariposa*
(butterfly) is sometimes used with a homosexual connotation. I want to clarify from the
outset that the main topic of this chapter is male-to-female transvestism, and therefore I
will not refer on this occasion to either lesbianism or female-to-male transvestism.

en el andamio (Butterflies on the scaffold) by Luis Felipe Bernaza and Margaret Gilpin, filmed in 1995 in the La Güinera neighborhood on the outskirts of Havana.[1]

The interpretation privileged by *Mariposas en el andamio* is quite apparent: in spite of the machismo and homophobia that still predominate in Cuban society, there exists in La Güinera a transvestite movement that has not only brought about tolerance of transvestism by area residents, but also transformed it from something detestable and repressed into an event almost entirely integrated into community life. Married couples and even many children in the neighborhood regularly attend the transvestite shows, and community leaders, with the exception of the chief of police, have encouraged the transvestites to continue with their performances and have fostered their inclusion in the community. Even the parents and other family members of the transvestites accept them and support them to a certain extent, both in their artistic endeavors and their homosexual orientation. Although this interpretation has a great deal of validity in terms of the relationship between the transvestites and the La Güinera neighborhood, several aspects of this documentary require careful consideration.

When a male-to-female transvestite comes onstage dressed as a woman, s/he is playing out a complex drama that almost always brings with it consequences and implications related not only to gender but also to nationality, race, and class. In addition, the problems posed by transvestism can lead to an examination of the very formation of human subjectivity. In *Mariposas en el andamio*, two thematic lines are clearly articulated: one that deals with the transvestites during their performances and while changing in the dressing rooms, and another that details their private lives, their families, and the community in which they live. Let me begin my analysis with the shows themselves.

In their performances the transvestites of La Güinera demonstrate little originality. The luxurious pretensions of their presentations, the invariably tragic and even tacky songs, and their exaggerated wardrobe are no different from other transvestite shows the world over. Like most transvestites in Western countries, those of La Güinera, far from imitating ordinary women in everyday attire, seek to imitate actresses or singers in their performances. Theirs is the imitation of a certain highly exaggerated and fantastic ideal (or idealized) woman; it is as if transvestism were a sort of attraction to and envy of glamorous women.

1. Luis Felipe Bernaza and Margaret Gilpin, *Mariposas en el andamio* (New York: Kangaroo Productions, 1996).

But the transvestite has no stable referent to imitate; his/her phantas-magoria is dominated by excess, and this excess can be theorized. The theory on transvestism by Cuban writer Severo Sarduy is relevant here. In his book-length essay *La simulación* (The simulation), he says that "[t]he transvestite does not imitate woman. For him, *à la limite*, there is no woman. He knows—and perhaps, paradoxically, he is the only one who knows—that she is an apparition, that her kingdom and the power of her fetish conceal a defect. . . . The transvestite does not copy or simulate since there is <u>no norm to invite</u> and magnetize the transfor-mation or to determine the metaphor: it is rather the non-existence of that which is imitated that constitutes the space, region or support of that simulation."[2] In another of his essays, "Writing/Transvestism," Sarduy says the following:

> Transvestism . . . is probably the <u>best metaphor</u> for what writing is . . . not a woman *under whose outward appearance* a man must be hiding, a cosmetic mask which, when it falls, will reveal a beard, a rough hard face, but rather *the very fact of transvestism itself* . . . the coexistence, in a single body, of masculine and feminine signifiers: the tension, the repulsion, the antagonism which is created between them. . . . Painted eyebrows and beard; that mask would enmask its being a <u>mask</u>. (Italics in the original.)[3]

In this sense Sarduy is in full agreement with Marjorie Garber, since both insist that transvestism is not merely a <u>mask of one gender or the other,</u> but something that must be theorized on its own, as transvestism per se.[4]

Perhaps the transvestite dresses flamboyantly so as to make his/her body <u>visible</u> in the public space from which it has <u>been displaced, rejected, or erased.</u> The transvestite's most common tactic is to dress in a way that greatly exaggerates a certain <u>idealized female image.</u> And here I must again bring up Marjorie Garber's argument that we should

2. Severo Sarduy, *La simulación* (Caracas: Monte Ávila Editores, 1982), 13. Spanish original: "El travestí no imita a la mujer. Para él, *à la limite*, no hay mujer, sabe—y quizás, paradójicamente sea el único en saberlo—, que *ella* es una apariencia, que su reino y la fuerza de su fetiche encubren un defecto. . . . El travestí no copia; simula, pues no hay norma que invite y magnetice la transformación, que decida la metáfora: es más bien la inexistencia del ser mimado lo que constituye el espacio, la región o el soporte de esa simulación."

3. Severo Sarduy, "Writing/Transvestism," *Review* 9 (Fall 1973), 33.

4. Marjorie Garber, *Vested Interests: Cross-Dressing & Cultural Anxiety*, 2d ed. (New York: Routledge, 1992; reprint, New York: HarperPerennial, 1993), 1–17.

look not only through but also *at* cross-dressing. Garber insists that the figure of the transvestite should not be subsumed within one of the two traditional genders, that we must see the transvestite as a transvestite, and "not . . . see cross-dressing except as male or female manqué."[5] Transvestism's contribution to a critique of the accepted norms is its deconstruction of the binary categories, thus introducing a crisis into the thinking behind those categories. This explains Garber's idea that "*transvestism is a space of possibility structuring and confounding culture*" (Italics in the original).[6]

But perhaps the symbolism of the transvestites' exaggerated wardrobe also indicates a certain hidden, uncontrollable desire for liberation. But what kind of liberation is this? What is the possible meaning of these extreme adornments, of this compulsive effort to obtain extravagant clothing, false eyelashes, and fabulous wigs in the midst of such great scarcity in Cuba? Perhaps it has to do with the desire to imitate the idealized image of a woman who, based on exaggerated elegance, beauty, and fame, achieves a certain feeling of liberation from discrimination, prejudice, and poverty. This is an idealized image, since the transvestite's transformation may demonstrate a fundamental error in logic: if the objective is freedom and social power, women are not the ideal objects of imitation, since their place is subordinate to that of men in dominant society. This is why male-to-female transvestism implies a whole series of contradictory emotions and symbolisms: the transvestite imagines a woman freed and subjugated at the same time; a rich, famous woman unhappy in love as well as in other aspects of her life.

It is true that, in general and also from a certain viewpoint, women's social status is superior to that of gays. But the transvestite's mostly unconscious impulse to imitate an actress as a means of acquiring some sort of symbolic liberating power is at the very least questionable, since women also suffer from discrimination and abuse at the hands of a characteristic *machista* society. Of course, by imitating an actress rather than an ordinary woman, the transvestite channels her/his and the audience's desire through the stage, with all of its artificiality and frivolity. Moreover, if we study the lyrics of the songs the La Güinera transvestites lip-synch, we will note that many of them are dedicated to the masochistic love that the female singer supposedly feels toward her man, who is frequently tyrannical, domineering, unfaithful, or physically separated from the woman. In this sense the transvestite, instead

5. Ibid., 9–10.
6. Ibid., 17.

of transgressing the basic rules of the society that has discriminated against her/him, is affirming and reactualizing them; s/he is exaggerating the power of the male and the male's subjugation of women. By employing these attitudes of subjugation, transvestites are exaggeratedly repeating the same terms that society has used to subjugate them and women as well.[7] This may be one of the reasons that many male-dominated societies permit and even encourage transvestite shows. Here we should remember Oscar Montero's argument that "drag may become so incorporated into the fabric of a culture . . . may answer so precisely that culture's own desire that it ceases to provoke and becomes entertainment."[8]

It can be said that, in a certain way, the transvestite performance is the compulsive and exaggerated repetition of a trauma that is both personal and social, a trauma that in Cuban society dates to at least the moment when modern nationality was formed. What the transvestites are imitating, then, is an integral and basic part of the system of oppression. Nevertheless, and despite this replication of the dominant system, transvestism offers the possibility of an affirmative response to this trauma. It is precisely where the violation has become traumatic that the force of repetition can be used as the very condition of an affirmative reply against the initial violation.[9]

When I reflect on the La Güinera transvestite shows, I note that they act out norms pertaining to accepted culture while questioning those norms. This is why the transvestite has two faces: one that imitates women out of the desire to become an idealized woman, and another that imitates women in such a highly exaggerated manner that it implies a possible questioning of gender norms. Let me make this last point clear: the wardrobe and "feminine" mannerisms of the transvestites are so exaggerated that their shows may very well call into question femininity itself, along with it its discursive complement, masculinity. Transvestism, through the practice of cross-dressing, uncovers the artificiality of the genders, and underscores femininity (and therefore masculinity) as a social construct. As one of the transvestites from *Mariposas* says: "Ya me estoy convirtiendo en toda una mujer. Dentro de breves minutos me convierto en Maridalia" [I'm becoming

7. See Judith Butler, *Bodies That Matter: On the Discursive Limtis of "Sex"* (New York: Routledge, 1993), especially chap. 4.

8. Oscar Montero, "Lipstick Vogue: The Politics of Drag," *Radical America* 22, no. 1 (January–February 1988), 41.

9. Butler, in *Bodies That Matter*, develops the psychoanalytic idea of traumatic repetition as the chance for an affirmation in the face of an initial violation.

a real woman now. In a few short minutes I'll turn into Maridalia.][10]
That is, this person who by day "passes" for a "man," during the show
"passes" for a "woman." The question then becomes, is s/he a "man,"
or is s/he just passing for one? Is s/he a "woman," or is s/he simply
passing for a woman? And here begins a questioning of the genders.

Transvestism tests the unstable boundaries of the genders, and
this is something the heterosexual system fears: that gender will be
discovered to be a social construct. This destabilization of gender is
important because it contributes to a questioning of the naturalization
of heterosexuality, which is one of the main repressive principles of
dominant Cuban culture. Thus it is revealing that in *Mariposas* the
chief of police is the most critical of the transvestite shows and also
the one who worries the most about trying to stop their gender blur-
ring. His words demonstrate *homosexual panic* as well as an obsession
with patrolling the unstable boundaries of the genders. Referring to
transvestism in La Güinera, he says,

> Esas cosas para mí, yo no quisiera, en el plano personal, que se incre-
> mentaran. . . . Al contrario, que disminuyan. Y considero que los niños
> yendo allí y viendo una persona que realmente es un hombre en la
> vida normal, o anda como un hombre en la vida normal, y luego en
> un momento determinado en una actividad lo veas vestido de mujer,
> lo veas vestido de otra forma. . . . Pienso que los niños después van a
> querer experimentar, y no es nuestro deseo.[11]

> [In my opinion, I personally don't want to see these things increase. . . .
> On the contrary, I want them to decrease. And I feel that with kids going
> there, and seeing a person who is really a man in real life, or who goes
> around as a man in real life, and then at some point during an activity
> you see him dressed as a woman, you see him dressed in a different
> way. . . . I think that then the kids are going to want to try it, and that's
> not what we want.]

With these comments, the police chief is establishing himself as
guardian of gender limits. He is expressing a *panic* that requires the
reinforcement of the borders of accepted sexuality and gender roles.
At one point he speaks of "a person who is *really* a man in real life,"
and then immediately deconstructs his own sentence by implying the
opposite: "or who *goes around as* a man in real life." He also fears that

10. Bernaza and Gilpin, *Mariposas en el andamio.*
11. Ibid.

children will "try out" these ambiguities. What the officer implies, probably without knowing it, is that to be a man is perhaps not a direct result of having certain anatomical parts that differ from those of women, that having a penis is not enough to maintain a stable platform for the gender roles. What one has does not necessarily define what one is. The verbs *to have* and *to be* are not synonymous. If the genders were firmly or essentially anchored to a physical referent, there would be no need for so many precautions, for so many normative practices. Heterosexualized gender norms bring about unattainable idealizations, and therefore heterosexuality itself operates by means of the compulsive regulation of norms, which produce exaggerated versions of what is a "man" and what is a "woman."[12] As with all required norms, the heterosexist norm is dubious and frequently full of ambiguities, hence the police chief's anxiety as macho guardian of heterosexualized norms.

Everything we have just studied about the transvestite shows suggests that their exaggeration of gender approaches parody and excess, and is far from mimesis. Furthermore, mimesis that attempts to equalize the genders is undermined by the instability inherent in synecdoche: possessing or lacking a physical appendage cannot entirely sustain the totality of being a man or a woman. Judith Butler, following Jacques Lacan, explains that the phallus functions as a synecdoche by being a figure of the penis, and as such constitutes itself as an idealization and reduction of one part of the body; this body part then appears to be endowed with the corporeal power of the symbolic law. According to the symbolic order of a society, a gender is taken on by approaching a synecdochic reduction. Therefore, in accordance with this logic, the sexual integrity of the entire body paradoxically depends on an identification with its reduction to the idealization of a body part. This means that men become men to the extent that they "have a phallus"; in other words, they are obligated to assume a "position" that stems from the synecdochic collapse of masculinity in one of its parts (the penis), along with an idealized corollary of the synecdoche as the symbol governing the entire symbolic order. This symbolic order tries to impose a law that always goes beyond the desired limits. The excess produced by the same law brings about the possibility of deviation or transgression. This basic failure of all performative power of the law, this fundamental error between the order and the desired effect, is what allows for the opportunity for transgression.[13]

12. Butler, *Bodies That Matter*, 237.
13. Ibid., 139.

And here I must repeat my initial question from a different perspective: How can a "creative transgression" be established in this system of interdependence between law and disobedience? And how can we mobilize the power of an offense rooted in a transgression that is in turn rooted in that same offense? I believe that in this situation one must examine those sites of gender ambivalence that appear in a specific society, in this case Cuban society. To deal with these questions we will look specifically at another aspect of *Mariposas:* the transvestites' transformation in their dressing rooms.

The entire process of transformation that the camera of *Mariposas* invites us to peep in on is of special interest to my analysis. This "candid camera" seduces us with the vision of those most private moments of dressing and undressing. These are the great moments of gender ambiguity: one minute we see bodies we identify as male, and a few minutes later we see people usually identified as provocatively dressed women. The gender signifiers are confused and twisted here, and gender ambiguity is seen in all its splendor. At these moments the materiality of the bodies and the instability of the gender "identities" are tested more intensely. In the end, revealing that instability is the contribution of transvestism, perhaps its great contribution. It is here that the butterflies are in their cocoons and that cultural gravity loses all weight, revealing the fictionality that underlies these seemingly solid genders. These moments of transformation also indicate the very formation of human subjectivity as being a construct rather than an essence. As has been noted earlier, transvestism promises to expose the flaw in heterosexism's insistence on achieving complete and absolute control of its own ideals. Nevertheless, it is not so much that transvestism is opposed to heterosexuality, or that its proliferation will do away with heterosexism. Instead, together with the questioning of gender categories, transvestism tends to allegorize heterosexuality and its associated melancholy.[14]

The La Güinera transvestites, like those in other parts of the world, usually change their own names to female ones: Paloma, Maridalia, Imperio, Sussy, Marie Antoinette, Sandra. This name changing is very important for the change in identity. The birth name is perhaps the most fundamental gender marker society imposes on a newborn; it is what begins to define the child. It is the place where the differences in name, pronouns, and all of the linguistic apparatus begin to exhibit their centuries-old, powerful ideology. It is also the place where a series

14. Ibid., 238.

of roles and expectations that extend throughout the child's life begin to be implied. Due to its radical importance, it is logical that if a change in identity is to be made, it is the name that should be changed first. This is the first time that the transvestites have been able to choose their names, a privilege most people will never know. Through this name change, the transvestite destabilizes the very center of gender identification or identity.

Of course, this name changing is not unique to the transvestites of La Güinera. Nevertheless, *Mariposas en el andamio* shows a degree of innovation related to naming. I am referring to the transvestite who plays the part of "La loca" in one of the shows. In this scene, this transvestite sings a song titled "La loca" while portraying an obviously crazed character. The scene is interesting for two reasons: first of all, this transvestite, unlike the others, is dressed in a poor and disheveled fashion; and second, the name "La loca" has multiple connotations. Two meanings of the word *loca* immediately come to mind: that of *a crazy woman*, and that of *a very effeminate gay man* (in Cuban culture this is a very common meaning of *loca*). Through this word, femininity, homosexuality, and madness are combined into one injurious term that is constructed as a "deviation from the norm" and as a multiple rejection on the part of society. Dominant culture establishes the term *loca* in order to strictly delineate the boundaries of that which is permitted and to stigmatize those bodies that, being perceived as outside the accepted gender norms, must be rejected or erased from the national body.

Upon seeing how tragic the "La loca" lyrics are, along with the transvestite's performance, I can only view this moment in the documentary as basic to the symbolism of the pain of a person vilified by an injurious interpellation. This is a key metaphor of the entire documentary, or at least of that terrible aspect that sees the transvestite as something detestable. Curiously, in order to stage such an eloquent scene, the transvestite must shed all of the luxurious attire and appear to be disheveled and in despair. Perhaps behind all of the luxurious dresses and the fabulous display of the transvestites lies the image of someone traumatized by the ignominy of a society that insults him/her. But a violation that becomes madness and leads to a destructive compulsion can use the force of that repetition as the very condition of a creatively resistant response, thus shifting the violation from its initial objectives. By singing "La loca," an injurious term is being repeated, but as both a protest and an accusation.

In examining the relationship of the La Güinera transvestites to their community, I must begin by emphatically stating that the accord established by these transvestites is indeed highly peculiar. This is important to note because it constitutes the opening of a social space at the grassroots level for the queer bodies of the nation. From the beginning of the documentary this aspect of the transvestites is emphasized. According to what some of those interviewed say, it seems that La Güinera is a relatively recently established neighborhood (dating from the beginning of the Cuban Revolution in 1959) where there has been a great deal of community cooperation. Also, judging by what can be learned from the documentary, La Güinera is a marginal zone. Perhaps the sense of community in La Güinera and its marginality in relation to the central power of the country have favored a less discriminatory treatment of the transvestites. It seems certain that this acceptance and integration have taken root in a truly generalized fashion in La Güinera. Judging by the statements of some of the transvestites, in the late 1980s their activities were initially almost clandestine, but bit by bit, with the assistance of some prominent members of their community, such as Fifí, "homosexual transvestism" and everything that it implies became increasingly more accepted. The community reformulation in *Mariposas* is perhaps the most subversive element of this process of integration, since it implies that although this reformulation is related to the power that it opposes yet is part of, its consequences are not easily reducible to those dominant forms of power.

What is even more radical and important in this entire process is that the acceptance of the transvestites has not been limited to their shows, but has also been extended to their "homosexual identity." They are all openly homosexual, and the community has reevaluated positively this highly taboo aspect of Cuban society. As we know, transvestism is not synonymous with homosexuality, nor vice versa. Nevertheless, not only do all of the transvestites of La Güinera identify themselves as homosexual, but their comments and those of other residents show an unmistakable identification of transvestism with homosexuality. Here we should consider what Marjorie Garber says regarding this issue: "The story of transvestism in western culture is in fact . . . bound up with the story of homosexuality and gay identity, from 'drag' to 'voguing' to fashion and stage design, from the boy actors of the English Renaissance stage to Gertrude Stein and Divine."[15] But

15. Garber, *Vested Interests*, 4.

Garber adds that although it would be a mistake to ignore the role played by homosexuality in the social and cultural implications of cross-dressing, it is also wrong to limit cross-dressing to the context of modern gay and lesbian identity. Homosexuality and transvestism, she says, "belong to quite different lexicons of self-definition and political and cultural display."[16]

It should be noted that one of the young people interviewed in the documentary declares an identity somewhat different from that of the other interviewees. When asked if he is a transvestite (and, following the logic of the documentary, also homosexual), he says that although he might try being a transvestite someday, for the moment he is not, but adds that he is gay.[17] Homosexuals calling themselves gays is a phenomenon also taking place in other Latin American countries in recent years.[18] One frequently encounters "homosexuals" in Latin America and in Cuba who call themselves gays, implying that they identify themselves as subjects who besides being sexually oriented toward others of the same sex, consider their identity to be something positive and perhaps connected (either in reality or symbolically) to an international liberation movement.[19] This seems to be another means of transforming or changing the injurious interpellations to which homosexuals are subjected in Cuban society, as well as in other societies having similar attitudes.

It is also interesting that this documentary shows most of the transvestites to be black or mulatto and all of them to be seemingly poor, even within the generalized poverty of the Cuban nation at the time. Several of them, however, during their moment of transformation for the show, demonstrate a preference for blonde or light-colored wigs and for makeup that lightens the color of their skin. Moreover, the typical wardrobe of these transvestites strives for a highly luxurious look. If we take all of this into consideration, it is not difficult to conclude that this transvestism (and in fact the majority of transvestism in other countries) is a phenomenon that implies a transformation not limited to gender, but that also has racial and class connotations. It is

16. Ibid., 5.
17. See Stephen O. Murray and Manuel G. Arboleda, "Stigma Transformation and Relexification: *Gay* in Latin America," in *Latin American Male Homosexualities*, ed. Stephen O. Murray (Albuquerque: University of New Mexico Press, 1995), 134–44.
18. Ibid.
19. For a fairly recent study on the political situation of gays and lesbians in Cuba, see Ian Lumsden, *Machos, Maricones and Gays: Cuba and Homosexuality* (Philadelphia: Temple University Press, 1996), especially chap. 9.

a phantasmatic transformation in the nexus between gender, race, and class, in which the gender transformation serves as a point of articulation in the search for legitimacy at various levels of social meaning.[20] As resistance, these performances are symbolic attempts to break free from homophobia, from machismo and racial and class discrimination. And as replication, this transvestism is a reactualization of the values of another sexual "identity" (heterosexual), another race (white), and another class (the wealthy).

Another curious aspect of the La Güinera transvestism is related to the wealthy class, symbolically represented by the performers' dresses. If working-class transvestites imitate rich women in a capitalist country, it becomes a sort of metaphor for the consumer culture of a privileged class that, although very different from the class the transvestites belong to, is part of the social context beyond their shows.[21] But in La Güinera rich women such as those imitated by the transvestites cannot be found offstage. La Güinera is not a social metaphor but an ellipsis, a comparison with a world that is elided (on the national plane, at least) but implicit. Perhaps the only fabulous women to be found beyond the stage of the La Güinera transvestite show would be those on television and at the nightclubs. In this sense, Cuban transvestites—like most transvestites in Western countries—are somehow related, directly or indirectly, to the tourist industry.

Let me now examine the relationship between the camera, the transvestites, and the audience in *Mariposas en el andamio*. It seems that the filmmakers have sought to make their documentary a recreation of the transvestites' world (their shows as well as their community). The filmmakers' point of view becomes reduced to an occasional voice or hand that comes out from behind the camera as if by chance or mistake. It is as if they were playing the part of ethnographers in a study of a non-Western society's tribal customs. This perspective implies a great sympathy for the transvestites (the natives) and their wellbeing. It also gives rise to an omniscient vision or a sort of blind eye that does not appear in the film. This is why we have the initial impression that the documentary takes as its only theme the interviewees, giving the interviewers a privileged and hidden position. Nevertheless, in *Mariposas*, although there is a great deal of this ethnographic camera work, it could certainly be argued that the point of view of the filmmakers, or at least their ideological position in relation to homosexuality,

20. Butler, *Bodies That Matter*, 121–40.
21. See Ibid.

becomes a theme to an extent, given the participation of the Cuban director Enrique Pineda Barnet, whose appearance frames the entire production.

Pineda Barnet's on-camera participation initially doesn't seem to fit with the other content of the documentary. While he speaks of the great discrimination that still exists toward homosexuals in Cuban society, his remarks are general and not directly related to the La Güinera transvestism. He never directly mentions what goes on in the La Güinera neighborhood. So we must ask ourselves, what is his role in this documentary? I believe that his participation represents, whether intentionally or not, the ideological position of the filmmakers. Instead of appearing in person to make their judgments about the relationship between Cuban society and homosexuality, which would expose their viewpoints and ideological position, they have chosen to express their ideas through the words of Pineda Barnet. Thus their position becomes, indirectly, another theme of the film. Pineda Barnet's participation may also come to reveal, at least in part, the sort of audience for which the documentary is principally intended: it should ideally be international in perspective and liberal in mindset. Thus the documentary has a strong element of narcissism, as is common in these sorts of productions; the filmmakers make their presentation to an audience who thinks and feels as they do. And here we can ask an even more daring question: who benefits more from this documentary, the transvestites or the filmmakers?

Perhaps *Mariposas* represents the real situation of transvestism in La Güinera (and, by implication, in other regions of Cuba, where similar events have occurred). But the documentary's ability to make these transvestites internationally famous is very doubtful. Perhaps it is rather a case of popular culture being recycled in a modern communications medium for an international audience and with political objectives, since this documentary is almost unknown in Cuba. Nevertheless, the camera emerges with a seeming promise of international fame for the participants. It not only films but also seduces both the viewer and the participants. Phallic power is on the side of the camera (as well as on the side of the critic who expresses these judgments in analyzing and interpreting the documentary). In its gaze, the camera creates a specular and narcissistic image of itself. At the same time, it conceals its own process, hiding itself behind a voice that remains unseen, refusing to reveal itself clearly. But one suspects that desire exists behind these masks, along with the search for phallic power, just as I, as a critic, also seek to hide myself behind masks to veil my desirous and highly involved participation. The filmmakers and the critic are not unlike the transvestites in their respective moments of filming, dressing, and making themselves up. We are all trying to put on and take off costumes that construct and deconstruct a subjectivity that is not only the desire for power, but also a ceaseless demand whose fantasy consists of nothing less than subjugating the meaning of the things of this world.

As a final thought about this documentary, let me point out that there is always a certain basic implication of "authenticity" in the logic of the transvestites interviewed in *Mariposas*. They (and their supporters) continually imply that they are more authentic as transvestites precisely because they are expressing who they "really are." As Jonathan Dollimore argues regarding the political use of the concept of authenticity by marginalized peoples and groups, the paradox of this argument is that these transvestites are making use of the dominant society's fundamental categories—that is, they are using the principles of authenticity and naturalness in favor of the cause of the marginalized, who have been victims of precisely such principles on the part of the hegemonic culture, which is based on the categories of the real, the natural, and the true. The greatest tyranny that hegemonic society imposes on its members is frequently committed in the name of the natural. Freeing the cultural from the natural, and the gender-related from the biological, is to make visible the political unconscious of a sexual culture. When the transvestites or any other marginal group of people claim to be more authentic and natural than others, they are appropriating part of the dominant ideology. There also exists another, even more radical means of resistance: that of marginality exercising its subversion through a radical critique of the dominant system, and questioning the same basic categories of naturalness, authenticity, truth and reality.[22]

Nevertheless, one must make the proviso that essentialism is not always a conservative philosophy, but frequently finds itself in the service of revolutionary positions. In the struggle to achieve legitimacy, the subordinated cultures frequently appeal to essentialist concepts that are central to the dominant culture. This is what happens in La Güinera: almost all of those interviewed base their complaints on principles of individual authenticity and honesty instead of rejecting, sabotaging, or displacing those principles. The injurious interpellation

22. Jonathan Dollimore, *Sexual Dissidence: Augustine to Wilde, Freud to Foucault* (Oxford: Clarendon Press, 1991), 307–25.

not only gives rise to a subjugated subject; it also demands that the subject form its subjectivity based on that interpellation. For this reason, the subjugated subject is frequently forced to use the colonizer's categories in establishing the possibility of a dissident identity that leads to a solution of the conflicts. It is for this reason that the attraction of a show like the La Güinera transvestites and the documentary *Mariposas en el andamio* lies to a large extent in its capacity to form a specific utopian promise. It is in the midst of this promise that a conflictive situation in the society being examined can be perceived. The path we thought we were following naturally and of our own free will, we were following because we were socially programmed to do so; by deviating from it, alternative paths to alternative futures can be discovered.

★ TWELVE ★

Crossing Gender and
National Boundaries

In this final chapter I have decided to return to the initial theme of the book: the relationship between Cuba and the United States in terms of representations of nationalisms and homosexualities. But this time the problem is not reduced to a single figure in Cuban politics, nor is it limited to the city of New York (in chapter 1 I discussed some of José Martí's texts written in New York City). The texts studied in this chapter come almost exactly a century after the article "Do We Want Cuba?" and Martí's reply, both from 1889. Written by three authors of Cuban origin who hold American citizenship, the texts that I discuss deal with matters related to homoeroticism, Cubanness, and the question of American "ethnic identities" by narrating stories set in Los Angeles, Chicago, New York, Miami, and even Havana.

First, I wish to examine the novel *Crazy Love* (1989), by "Cuban-American" Elías Miguel Muñoz (1954–). This text tells of the conflict of national and sexual identity experienced by a Cuban-American character living in Los Angeles. In this work the dissemination of Cuban identity and the ambivalence of sexual identity are complicated by the enormous pull of American consumerism and mass culture. Another author studied in this chapter is Achy Obejas (1956–), whose collection of short stories is titled *We Came All the Way from Cuba So You Could Dress like This?* (1994). Several of the conflicts seen in *Crazy Love* also appear in Obejas's stories, but this time the main character is a Cuban-American lesbian living in Chicago who feels very much a part of U.S. ethnic and urban lesbian culture. From that position she must deal with the conflict of older Cuban relatives who have clung more tightly to the customs and values of another time and place, of another nationality. Also in Obejas's texts, there is a social and political redefinition of mainstream America as well as of socialist Cuba; in this way these stories both affirm and break American and Cuban-American stereotypes.

Finally, I undertake a reading of the short story collection *Las historias prohibidas de Marta Veneranda* (The forbidden stories of Marta Veneranda) (1997), written in Spanish by Cuban-American Sonia Rivera-Valdés (1937–). These stories problematize not only national and ethnic identity, but also sexual and even linguistic identity: although written and frequently set in New York, some of the stories' characters travel to and from Cuba, speak Spanish and English, mingle with characters of other nationalities, and often question their sexual identities. Moreover, they invite a queer reading that indicates a destabilization of the socially prescribed limits that rigidly maintain stereotypes. To complicate things even more, *Las historias prohibidas de Marta Veneranda* was honored with a literary award in Cuba by the Casa de las Américas in 1997 and was published in Havana in 1998. The success of these texts, both in Cuba and elsewhere, seems to carry implications of dissemination and synthesis, of exile and of return. Reading Rivera-Valdés's works and those by Muñoz and Obejas does not resolve the question of nationalities and homosexualities; instead, it opens new horizons and crossroads on these issues.

Dissemination, Consumerism, and New Stereotypes

In 1989 Elías Miguel Muñoz published *Crazy Love*, a semiautobiographical novel that was his first work in English.[1] The story takes place in Los Angeles, where young Julián (later spelled without an accent as "Julian") lives. The novel's main theme is the relationship between the opposing forces of the Cuban culture left behind and the new American culture taken up. The latter is driven by what could be called an ideology of success, which is articulated in the novel mainly through popular music; hence the title *Crazy Love*, after the well-known Paul Anka song. In fact, Julian becomes a pop musician during the course of his first-person narration. The story of Julian, a Cuban who as a child left his country with his family and now lives with them in Los Angeles, consists of fragments. Each part respectively

1. Elías Miguel Muñoz, *Crazy Love* (Houston: Arte Público Press, 1989).

relates Julian's memories of life as a child in Cuba, his journey to the United States, and his personal, professional, and erotic (including homoerotic) development in California.

One of the main conflicts presented in this novel is the dilemma between the past and the present, between the pull of the culture of origin and the temptations and obstacles of the adoptive culture. In the novel, Julian's grandmother is the figure who best and most radically represents the Cuban past. She purports to faithfully maintain the customs and values of the Cuban middle class of the 1950s, along with the family's unity and "Cubanness" in their present situation in Los Angeles. Her demands are often out of place in relation to the values of U.S. society. Faced with his grandmother's demands, Julian desperately asks himself, "Why won't grandmother let go of the past?" and "Why can't she realize that we're far, so far from Cuba?" (104).

Through the narrative it becomes clear that Julian's strongest desire is to achieve large-scale success in U.S. society. The more focused this desire becomes in Julian's personality, the more he realizes that the values of his Cuban past constitute obstacles to his dreams. But Julian's drive toward commercial achievement finds other obstacles as well: his homosexual practices conflict with both Cuban and American cultural norms. Therefore, it becomes necessary for him to resolve not only the dilemma between Cuban and American cultures, but also the conflict between homosexuality and heterosexuality. The most noteworthy gay practices in the narrative are those referring to the homoerotic relationship between Julian and Lucho, another young Cuban-American musician in the same band. Well along in the story, however, a new character emerges: a young American woman named Erica Johnson, who quickly becomes the vocalist, organizer, and highly efficient agent for Julian's musical group, "L.A. Scene." Erica ends up not only taking control of the group, but also of Julian's feelings, since he falls in love with her and discontinues his relations with Lucho. In this way, at the end of *Crazy Love* almost all of the basic story elements change or are radically inverted from what they were at the beginning. Erica has been the principal catalyst of the peripetia of the narrative: from this point in the story the group's music becomes increasingly Americanized and therefore successful on a large scale. In addition, Julian becomes increasingly well adapted to the customs and values of the United States (much to the scorn of his grandmother), abandons his homosexual practices, and surrenders himself completely to his heterosexual relationship with Erica.

In my reading of the story, Erica symbolizes dominant American discourse, which brings with it both the highly prized commercial and consumerist success and the socially approved heterosexual relationship (in this sense, both cultures coincide). The novel ends with a letter from Geneia, Julian's younger sister, in which she approves of her brother's decisions and tells him not to sacrifice himself: "Don't give up your life" (ibid). This appeal by Geneia as well as many other inferences in the text seems to imply that Julian's conflict is between a tyrannical Cuban past and a "freedom" that can only be achieved by adapting to mainstream American values (with a heavy dose of consumerism and heterosexism). Nevertheless, the problem is not that simple. With the conversion of Julian's musical group from a Cuban/Latino beat to a rather Americanized type of music, he, along with his fellow Cuban artists, is able to free himself from a tyrannical past and adopt a new and no less tyrannical set of rules and cultural stereotypes. Julian discovers that the course of his life shows a rejection of Cuban values and customs along with a progressive acceptance of American stereotypes, symbolized in expressions such as "American Success Story," "Hispanic rocker," and "The best thing to come along since Ricky Ricardo" (144–52).

To attain commercial success, Julian's Cuban cultural heritage has been almost totally defeated by the powerful postmodern American discourse. The cultural values of his homeland have been disseminated and practically eliminated, but the new consumerist American values have not brought with them any real sense of freedom. Indeed, in his desire to adapt himself to the mainstream values of his adopted society, Julian has even renounced his gay practices. *Crazy Love* attempts to offer a solution to the dilemma of Cuban versus American values and of heterosexuality versus homosexuality, but the result has been another dilemma, in which the new values are a kind of trap. The appeal of Muñoz's text lies precisely in this realization, because it is not a story of "pure success" but rather an invitation to reflection, dialogue, and debate on Cuban and American values (both homophobic) of the past half century and what they mean for a Cuban-American like Julian.

Another thought-provoking aspect of *Crazy Love* is the dilemma between writing a narrative text (a pseudo-autobiographical novel in this case) and writing popular music. The work is a novel, not a chart-topping pop music hit in the U.S. market. *Crazy Love*, although enjoying some success among Latino and Cuban-American readers, is far from being the large-scale commercial success enjoyed by such popular artists as Paul Anka. Not only did the book fail to become a commercial success in the U.S. market, but it also failed to compete with another novel by a writer of Cuban origin: Oscar Hijuelos's *The Mambo Kings* (1989), which was published the same year as *Crazy Love* and awarded the Pulitzer Prize.[2] Are works like *The Mambo Kings*— works that completely fulfill the stereotypes American society maintains and encourages for Hispanics and Latinos in the United States— the novelistic equivalent of the *I Love Lucy* television program? Perhaps the concessions *Crazy Love* makes to the U.S. market have been insufficient both in content (too many references to Cuban and Cuban-American worlds and to homosexual practices?) and in form (lack of polish and of the specific literary techniques and marketing niche that the U.S. literary market demands of a best-selling novel, or even of a novel well received by mainstream readers). It seems that *Crazy Love* is consumed by the values of the postmodern consumerist society, yet the sacrifices of language, style, content, and sexual orientation have not been enough. One of the main questions left after reading this novel is that perhaps there are other "solutions" to the cultural and sexual dilemmas that Muñoz presents.

Nostalgia for the New Home

The "solutions" that can be derived from Achy Obejas's short story collection, *We Came All the Way from Cuba So You Could Dress like This?* (1994),[3] have some similarities with and notable differences from those of *Crazy Love*. Obejas's stories, like Muñoz's novel, were originally written in English, and like the protagonist of *Crazy Love* some of the characters in this collection struggle against the values and customs of their Cuban parents. Also, several of both authors' characters engage in homoeroticism. Nevertheless, there are many important differences between Muñoz's novel and the short stories of Obejas. For example, although at the end of *Crazy Love* Julian seems to have adopted the values of the American consumer society, he still shows constant concern for his Cuban roots. He has cast them off, but not without great difficulty and second-guessing. Also, Julian ends up abandoning homosexual practices, giving himself over to heterosexual relations with Erica Johnson, who represents the values of the "American Way of Life." In contrast, most of Obejas's characters

---

2. Oscar Hijuelos, *The Mambo Kings* (New York: Harper & Row Publishers, 1989).

3. Achy Obejas, *We Came All the Way from Cuba So You Could Dress like This?* (Pittsburgh: Cleiss Press, 1994).

seem to be Hispanics or Latinos who have become part of American "ethnic minorities" and whose conflicts are not at all directly related to the values of their homeland or to a sense of nostalgia for its loss. If they feel nostalgia at all, it is not for Cuba or even for Miami, but rather for the city of Chicago. Also, almost all of Obejas's characters are strongly associated with the gay and lesbian identities and politics typical of the post-Stonewall world.

The details and daily worries of American society in the 1980s and 1990s are depicted so thoroughly in Obejas's stories that only a reader well versed in these matters can understand most, if not all, of the narratives. They touch on matters including automobile insurance, the Chicago mass transit system, postmodern consumerism, TV dinners, the sort of relationships that develop between lesbians in major American cities, recent films, typical feminist attitudes, police behavior, therapy sessions, the sharp differences between gay, lesbian, and straight, drug addiction, and relations with those who have AIDS.

The majority of the main characters in Obejas's works are clearly and openly lesbian, although a "gay" male couple are the main characters in one of the stories. In that story, "Above All, A Family Man," the narrator-character Tommy Drake identifies himself as a gay man sick with AIDS who has relations with Rogelio, an illegal Mexican immigrant living in the United States. The effects of his illness are truly terrible and their description very characteristic of the suffering of AIDS victims. But the title of the story refers to Rogelio, who despite having a sexual and loving relationship with Tommy and showing great patience, understanding, and even tenderness toward his partner, never perceives himself as "homosexual" or as "gay." As the text says, Rogelio "does not consider himself even vaguely homosexual. Instead, he thinks of himself as *sexual*, as capable of sex with a cantaloupe as with a woman or a man." Rogelio "is no less married, no less a parent—in fact, he is, above all, a family man—and how he manages to juggle it all has always amazed me."[4] All of this "identity" or lack thereof in Rogelio points to the instability or lack of a real referent in terms like *homosexual* or *gay,* and therefore to the variety of identifications that those of different cultures acquire in relation to their sexual behaviors. What also stands out in this story is Tommy's nostalgia for Chicago. When he and Rogelio are in St. Louis, Tommy thinks nostalgically of Chicago as his "hometown."[5]

4. Ibid., 53.
5. Ibid., 59.

The descriptions of those living with AIDS and of homosexuals, gays, and lesbians in somewhat difficult socioeconomic positions, as well as of drug addicts, lead to images in these stories that are often marginal in relation to mainstream America. Also, these images refer to a marginal world quite typical of any great U.S. city, in this case Chicago. Nevertheless, it is repeatedly mentioned that one of these characters is a writer, specifically a Hispanic journalist quite well known in Chicago (sometimes it is implied that she is Cuban, at other times Puerto Rican or simply Hispanic/Latina). Perhaps the scenes that most typify this world of the great American city are the descriptions of this journalist traveling on the Chicago mass transit system amidst great crowds of people. Not only does the novel tell us that she is a journalist, but the style of narration and description is frequently journalistic, with short, precise sentences; insightful, detailed descriptions; and penetrating observations.

It should be noted that the title of the last story in this collection is also that of the entire book, which is somewhat deceptive, since this story is quite different in style and content from the others. Judging from the title of the collection, Obejas's stories seem to imply a central struggle between a certain Cuban character and his parents. Nevertheless, this only takes place in the last story, the only one in the collection that covers the life of a narrator-protagonist from childhood to the present, emphasizing her Cuban roots. This text generally deals with two moments in the narrator-protagonist's life: her arrival from Cuba at the age of ten in a small boat with her parents, and thirty years later (assumed to be the present of the narrative), when she is reflecting on the past during her father's wake in Miami. The protagonist, who now lives in Chicago, is a lesbian, a feminist, and in several other ways the opposite of her parents, especially in terms of social and political values. In fact, her political ideas could be called leftist in regards to socialist Cuba, since she has reconsidered her political position in this respect and has established a sort of rapprochement with Cuba.

Some of the situations and commentaries in this story seem to imply that her political changes have come about as a result of the attitudes and values of feminism and the U.S. gay/lesbian liberation movement rather than from any Cuban influence. The two key moments from "We Came All the Way from Cuba" imply that all or most of the other stories in the collection take place between these two moments. The story mentions a number of historical events and political figures related to the United States and Cuba: the Vietnam War, the Kennedys and the protagonist's father's opinion of them (he is a stereotypical

Cuban anticommunist), the Bay of Pigs invasion, and Fidel Castro. Her father views all of these issues with an intense and often exaggerated patriotism. But little by little he starts to get used to the idea that a return to Cuba as a result of a U.S.-backed overthrow of Castro is not imminent, and so he begins to try to adapt himself to American life. But while his adaptation is minimal and comes politically from the extreme right, the protagonist's adaptation seems to be quick and from an iconoclastic, rebellious, leftist position. Her coming out of the closet as a lesbian seems to have some influence on her coming out politically as a left-wing liberal. All of the changes and conflicts of this last story lead the narrator-protagonist to reflect on her life, past and present, and even on what would have happened had her parents not come with her to the United States or had the 1959 Cuban Revolution failed. These questions are left unanswered, but returning to Miami for her father's wake allows her to put everything that has happened to her as a journalist, lesbian, feminist, and activist into perspective. Perhaps the death of her father can be read as the end of a Cuban-American stereotype. The representation of the protagonist implies another sort of person who on the one hand lends herself to new stereotypes (the typical urban lesbian in present-day America) yet on the other is able to break molds and limits, allowing for an interpretation that includes a possible resistance to the dominant power system.

An Aesthetics of Destabilization

In January of 1997 the Special Prize for Hispanic Literature in the United States[6] was awarded by Cuba's Casa de las Américas to Sonia Rivera-Valdés for her collection of short stories *Las historias prohibidas de Marta Veneranda* (The forbidden stories of Marta Veneranda).[7] This was a truly special occasion, since it was only the second time in more than thirty-five years that the Casa de las Américas had so honored a Cuban-American. The first was Lourdes Casal, who in 1981 won the Poetry prize for her *Palabras juntan revolución* (Words gather revolution). Rivera-Valdés, like Casal, identifies herself as a "Cuban-New Yorker," but unconditionally accepts her literature as being more within American "ethnic literature" than "Cuban literature."

6. Premio Extraordinario de Literatura Hispana en los Estados Unidos.

7. Sonia Rivera-Valdés, *Las historias prohibidas de Marta Veneranda* (The forbidden stories of Marta Veneranda) (Havana: Ministerio de Cultura, Colombia/Casa de las Américas, Cuba, 1997).

This gives rise to some complex questions about categorization: is *Las historias prohibidas* part of "Cuban literature," or is it of "American ethnic literature"? My answer comes from my conviction that the delimitation of what is Cuban, American, Cuban-American, or Ethnic is often the product of political and discursive struggles more than of ontological realities. Of course, there are elements of identification and shared memory that help to construct a "national identity" or group, but I think that even the concept of nation is a category in a constant state of change, which serves as the battleground for several opposing discourses, since the limits of a nation are not real but "imagined" (in the sense that Benedict Anderson uses the term).[8] The very instability and porosity in the parameters of the concept of nation are what lead many citizens to try to mark the boundaries that determine (or try to determine) where this idea called "our nation" begins and ends. This dissemination of national borders does not, in my opinion, imply that we should not take seriously the political position of citizens who adopt a defensive attitude toward other nations or powers when they deem it necessary. Rather, I wish to draw a distinction here between a category's ontological implications and the political and strategic needs of a group of people in the face of another at a given point in time.

Rivera-Valdés distinguishes between her "personal identity" and her "literature." She was born and raised in Cuba, but has lived most of her life in the United States, almost entirely in New York, and has been a U.S. citizen for many years. The themes and influences in her literature are closely related to the "ethnic literatures" of the United States, above all to the work of feminists Cherríe Moraga and Gloria Anzaldúa. This is not to say that Cuban literature, both past and present, has not influenced her work; indeed, her texts are always written initially in Spanish, never in English; and the characters of *Las historias prohibidas* are almost all Cuban women living in New York, although there are also Peruvian, Puerto Rican, Indian, Italo-American, and Anglo-American characters. The more one might try to categorize these texts, the more reductive the results would become. Many elements would be left out of such a classification and therefore the classifications themselves would become obviously arbitrary.

The struggle for classification (and also for the process of assimilation/rejection) is at times obvious and at others quite veiled in

---

8. Benedict Anderson, *Imagined Communities: Reflections on the Origin and Spread of Nationalism*, rev. ed. (London: Verso, 1991).

Rivera-Valdés's work. Although *Las historias prohibidas* was honored in January of 1997, it was not published until the end of that year and only came out in Havana at the beginning of 1998. Published by the Cuban Casa de las Américas and the Colombian Ministry of Culture, the book's front and back covers were designed by Cuban artist Félix Antequera Amaral. Even with these covers, various discourses try to assimilate Rivera-Valdés's text into an artifact of "Cuban culture." Antequera Amaral's back-cover photo shows a young woman with black hair, dressed in a somewhat punk style: hair slightly frizzed; wide, striped pants coming to below her shoes; wide, black, long-sleeved blouse. This blouse is open to below the navel, exposing part of her breasts, and she is posed dramatically against a crumbling wall typical of certain places in Old Havana (the photo is from a collection by Antequera Amaral titled *Habana siempre viva* [Havana: always alive]).

The seduction offered by the young woman's open blouse (her image could also be interpreted as the representation of a person having characteristics of a certain lesbian stereotype or of the new Cuban generation) takes on new possibilities with the front cover. This cover shows a head-and-shoulders close-up of the young woman in a two-by-two-inch square at the viewer's lower right, superimposed over a larger, somewhat muted photo of a street in Old Havana. This street is wide in the foreground but narrows as it recedes to the upper left, finally disappearing altogether in the brightness of the space beyond. If the seduced vision of the observer had previously been fixed on the torso and barely covered breasts of the young woman in the back-cover photo, this attention is now reoriented toward the receding of a wide street in Old Havana. The representation of a modern young woman seems to have seduced us into a "Havana-ization" of our gaze, initially lascivious and now nostalgic. There has been a contention for the initial libido by a reorientation toward a vision of *Habana siempre viva*. The nostalgic possibilities of the background photo of Old Havana seem to have been the objective (or at least part of the objective) of the photograph's seduction: relocate the lesbian body within the stereotypical frame of Old Havana. The observer of the book (before he or she has become its reader) has already been nostalgically Havana-ized or Cuban-ized.

But like any cultural artifact, the front- and back-cover photos permit several readings, whose possible interpretations become dispersed before the viewer's gaze. So another possible reading of this photo is that it symbolically connects the texts of *Las historias prohibidas* with the most recent generation of Cuban writers and artists. The connection is not entirely absurd, since from a certain viewpoint of Cuban culture at the end of the 1990s, what could be more like these texts full of scenes of lesbian eroticism, of marginal situations of liberated women who escape from their husbands to live an independent life, of intense bisexuality . . . than a clever image of the newest generation of Cubans? So the front- and back-cover photos may establish a link to the culture of resistance of this newest Cuban generation (above all, to the image that some of its members have projected). It also may be interpreted as an assimilation of marginal eroticism (specifically lesbian eroticism) to everything that is stereotypical of Havana and intensely nostalgic. But the texts of *Las historias prohibidas* are constructed by an image that destabilizes all attempts at clear and precise definition; its aesthetic conspires against all processes of institutionalization or naturalization of the accepted limits.

The intended assimilation of *Las historias prohibidas* becomes much more obvious in the note appearing on the back cover. It states that in these "forbidden stories" "the revival of the most traditional concepts and stereotypes of citizens' conduct is pursued and achieved."[9] It seems to be understood, although not explicitly stated, that this "citizen" is Cuban. It is surprising to read this opinion about Sonia Rivera-Valdés's stories, since they are characterized by precisely the opposite qualities. Can these mostly "lesbian," "gay," and "bisexual" stories of "Hispanic" characters in New York, whose female characters murder their husbands when they can find no other escape from *machista* abuse, be said to be "the revival of the most traditional concepts and stereotypes of citizens' conduct"? It is rather difficult to discern what is meant by this note, but what seems obvious to me is that, apart from the intention of these opinions, the note implies a marked effort to contain the subversive possibilities of these texts. They deal with all kinds of "forbidden stories"; they are all forbidden precisely from the point of view of the official history of the nation, of traditional morals, and of the "stereotypes of citizens' conduct."

All this leads me to believe that the dynamic of these texts projects a dissemination that a certain conservative ideology is trying to contain by encapsulating it within stereotypes. What characterizes these texts is not their stereotypical nature but rather their constant crossing of the lines of accepted codes, and their insistent questioning of the limits

9. Spanish original: "[se] persigue y logra la reanimación de los más tradicionales conceptos y estereotipos de la conducta ciudadana." Rivera-Valdés, *Las historias prohibidas.*

of stereotypes. That is why I would like to orient the critical reading of *Las historias prohibidas* toward an aesthetic of destabilization—that is, toward the representation of the transgression of national, cultural, sexual, and authorial codes. But this aesthetic does not imply that such a transgression leads to a utopia outside the realms of power. There is no accessible space that transcends oppression; it is, rather, an illusory effect of the very discursive structures that this "outside" claims to overcome.[10] Rivera-Valdés's texts question the mechanisms of homophobia and situate themselves in the place where various conflicting codes intersect. But, like all cultural artifacts, they still participate in some way in those same mechanisms of power and acquire their force of resistance from the structures of domination they hope to overcome.

Las historias prohibidas is a collection of eight short stories and a "clarifying note."[11] This introductory note frames the stories, and "clarifies" that these forbidden stories have been compiled by Marta Veneranda, a Cuban woman who attended college in New York and now holds a Ph.D. in literature. Her American professor, Arnold Haley, deceased by the time the note was written, had sent her to make an ethnographic or "scientific" study of the relationship between what people consider shameful about their lives and the very deeds for which they feel shame. Marta resists Dr. Haley's method, since he comes to represent the American patriarchy with its discursive power of science. She prefers to approach the matter through literature. Of course, it is supposed that the eight forbidden stories the other characters tell Marta are real, but she does not make use of the scientific method for her study. These stories are more like therapeutic confessions that the narrator-characters tell to the narrator Marta. From this initial moment the rupture of numerous codes begins to appear. Marta Veneranda resists scientific discourse and the tutelage of an American man. A Hispanic or Latina woman residing in New York appropriates authority to choose both the method as well as the informants for her stories, and with this gesture starts what I could call a project of reclamation in which certain power structures are decentered to open a public space for marginalized persons.

10. See Annamarie Jagose, *Lesbian Utopics* (New York: Routledge, 1994), 162. For an interesting study of the "project of reclamation of the lesbian body" in Latina artistic production in the United States, see Yvonne Yarbo-Bejarano, "The Lesbian Body in Latina Cultural Production," in *Entiendes? Queer Readings, Hispanic Writings*, ed. Emilie L. Bergmann and Paul Julian Smith (Durham, N.C.: Duke University Press, 1995), 181–97.

11. Spanish original: "nota aclaratoria." Rivera-Valdés, *Las historias prohibidas*.

In spite of the apparent variety of stories in this book, several patterns emerge. Four of the narrator-protagonists, as well as other secondary characters, practice homosexuality (three of them practice lesbianism and one, male homosexuality), but all of the lesbians are or have been married to men and have marital problems. In almost all of the stories there is a sort of alliance among the women that helps them to subvert the established male order. The characters are frequently Hispanic or Latino/a and have experienced poverty, which they have overcome by the time of the narration of the story, to the point that several are professionals and function quite well in American society. Several of the stories tell of exaggerated incidents of sexual passion and cultural transgression, and throughout the entire collection official histories both of Cuba and the United States are notably absent.

Only two of the stories have male narrator-protagonists: "El olor del desenfreno" (The smell of the spree) and "Desvaríos" (Deliriums). In "El olor del desenfreno," Rodolfo, the narrator-protagonist, tells Marta Veneranda of the unexpected passion he felt one day toward a very fat neighbor woman who gave off a "horrible stink" (31).[12] Rodolfo says that it is inexplicable that he has been able to have passionate sex with someone like her, since he considers himself to be very tidy. But I believe that there seems to be an obvious explanation for one aspect of his passion: Rodolfo's unconscious attraction to the smell of the sea (which is not unlike the smell of the neighbor woman). Rodolfo states that as a boy he used to meet his girlfriend on a little bridge in Jaimanitas, near the sea. According to the logic of the story, it is implied that this smell is what lies hidden in Rodolfo's subconscious, only to reemerge with renewed force when he finds himself near the neighbor woman with the sealike stench. This return to his childhood in Cuba in order to explain an adult phenomenon seems to be a psychoanalytic or Freudian interpretation, which, of course, it is; the story's logic leads me to this possible conclusion. But the representation of the Cuban coastal village of Jaimanitas is quite idealized, appearing as a utopian place beyond the problems of the world and its unpleasant realities.

As is customary in these stories, "El olor del desenfreno" avoids all explicit mention of politics and history. These matters can only be perceived through the conduct and emotional conflict of the characters; it is as if Cuban public life were present and had an effect on the characters, but they prefer not to give it explicit or detailed mention. They

12. Spanish original: "fetidez horrible."

are eccentric to official national history. Nevertheless, the narrator's idealization of his childhood village in Cuba, and of his childhood itself, is important to my reading. Jaimanitas, his girlfriend, and the sea odor he associates with them are somehow present in Rodolfo. He retains a subconscious utopian feeling for his homeland that as an adult leads him to do inexplicable things. His exaggerated desire is associated with the utopian Cuba of his childhood, a utopia that leads to exaggeration and excess. But here I should note that the symbolism of his childhood utopia reemerges traumatically (and therefore may be symbolically and compulsively repeated in adulthood) at the very moment his parents are sending him alone to the United States as part of Operation Peter Pan. His childhood ends there, as he sees himself helpless and alone, separated from his parents and thrown into a totally unknown world.

Operation Peter Pan came about as a political ploy of the forces opposed to the Cuban Revolution (principally the U.S. government). Its goal was to frighten Cuban parents with the notion that the Cuban socialist government was going to take their children away from them to be raised by the state. The anxiety of Cuban families was great, and Rodolfo was a victim of this political turmoil. Nevertheless, the reader must be informed about Cuban history in order to understand what Rodolfo is referring to when he says, "That's the way it was, I came with Operation Peter Pan. That Operation hurt so many people" (29).[13] For all of these reasons, I can say that both his utopian childhood and the "Peter Pan trauma" mark Rodolfo in this story. Thus, Cuba is present in his (sexual) desire, conditioning it but not subjugating it, since in this and the other stories the conditioning is always restructured toward a new meaning. The childhood utopia and the "Peter Pan trauma" serve as symbolic sources of Rodolfo's adult passions.

In "Desvaríos" the narrator-character is named Ángel, information that we draw from the other stories, since the narrator does not tell us his name in the course of this one. All of the characters in these stories are linked by friendship and give subtle clues for the reading of the other stories. Although Ángel identifies himself as gay or homosexual, the story has certain structural similarities to "El olor del desenfreno." In "Desvaríos" the explanation privileged by the story is quite obviously psychoanalytic, and the utopian place is a little village near the Mayabeque River in the province of Havana, where

13. Spanish original: "Así mismo fue, vine con la operación Peter Pan. Esa operación desgració a más gente."

Ángel lived during his childhood. The first thing Ángel tells Marta Veneranda is that "[f]or more than twenty years . . . I haven't had sex with a woman. Always with men, and black men" (53).[14] But Ángel, who is an adult and a math teacher at the time of his confession to Veneranda, hesitates between two mental symbols imposed during his youth that seem to have a paradoxical effect on the objects of his desire: Teresita and Sandokan. Curiously, these two characters from his childhood are poor, and their status is that of servants or children of servants from Ángel's household.

Teresita was a housemaid in the home where Ángel was brought up. His relationship with her was one of dependence and is quite erotic. Sandokan is the young black or mulatto son of a servant. In his childhood, Ángel thought of Sandokan as a kind of superchild, because Ángel was spoiled and overprotected. Among other things, he was not allowed to eat fish with the bones intact (his mother, grandmother, and servant obsessively dissected and deboned each fish before Ángel could begin to eat it), while he saw Sandokan eat fish with the bones, head, and everything else intact. Ángel's idealization of black men stems from this. And here I must add not only the conditioning between sex and race, but also among sex, race, and social class. All of this combined seems to "explain" Ángel's sexual attraction. Nevertheless, and to the surprise of the reader, Ángel's confession to Veneranda is not about homosexuality, nor even about his attraction to black men, since in reality he has very much assumed his gay identity. His "secret" is that in spite of his gay identity or identification, he has heterosexual fantasies that he channels through heterosexual porn videos, which allow him to imagine himself having sex with women. Here the story takes a turn typical of almost all of those in this collection: there is a destabilization not only of the socially accepted limits but also of marginal identities. Not only are the borders of traditional codes crossed toward marginal identities, but they stay crossed for some time. Not even gay identity is stable, and Rivera-Valdés's texts make a gesture that is more queer than gay/lesbian. The destabilizing image that predominates in all of these stories avoids fixed categorizations, even that of gay or lesbian identity.

Another type of destabilization that indicates an attack on machismo is shown in "Entre amigas" (Among friends) and "Los venenitos" (The little poisons). In these stories the narrator-protagonists literally kill their abusive husbands. In "Entre amigas" the narrator-protagonist

14. Spanish original: "Hace más de veinte años [. . .] no me acuesto con una mujer. Siempre con hombres, y negros."

tells how she disconnected her dying husband's oxygen tank after realizing how bad he had been to her for so many years. In "Los venenitos" the narrator kills her husband with some poisonous flower pistils that leave no trace of the crime. In both stories the murder is not only justified from a certain point of view, but also committed as a perfect crime. The authorities never discover the truth about these men's deaths, and the wives' friends help to cover up the deeds. Thus the texts situate the reader as an accomplice, perhaps as a "female accomplice." Machismo has been dethroned and no one has come to its rescue, not even the readers' morality, which has been curiously directed or manipulated during each of the texts in order to justify the murders.

In "Los ojos lindos de Adela" (Adela's pretty eyes) the attack on machismo is not a murder but rather something that from the male character's perspective could be called a scene of frustrated seduction. From the female character's point of view, however, it is a scene of symbolic castration. In this story, as in several others in the collection, Cuba is mentioned, but most political or historical commentary is avoided. We are told that the narrator arrived in New York in 1966 during the Vietnam War, but no further mention is made of that great historical event. It is the private lives (made public through the act of telling) that are of interest and not the events of history. Neither the Cuban Revolution nor the Vietnam War form an important part of any of the characters' commentaries.

"Los ojos lindos de Adela" is one of the most touching stories in the entire book. The poverty-stricken lives of two Cuban women in New York are described dramatically and in detail as, in their exile, they work in factories under sometimes unhealthy conditions. Adela, a childhood friend of the narrator's, begins to lose her eyesight due to the microscope she works with in a transistor radio factory. The narrator, who convinced Adela to take the job in the first place, feels guilty. They go to another factory, but Adela is unable to perform adequately and the boss wants to fire her before the Thanksgiving holiday. The narrator takes drastic action to keep Adela from losing her new job. The factory boss is a highly *machista* Italian-American who is constantly trying to seduce the narrator, but she always resists his advances. He is always advertising his masculinity and sexual prowess, but when the narrator decides to have sex with him so that he won't fire Adela, he is unable to achieve an erection—a patently ridiculous scene. The boastful male is unable to even become sexually aroused; it has all been a farce, but an agreement has been made, and he cannot fire Adela. The narrator has symbolically castrated this "supermacho."

In the story "Cinco ventanas del mismo lado" (Five windows on the same side) we see something common to all of these stories: a character who seems to discover her homosexuality but without definitively renouncing her heterosexuality. Mayté, the Cuban narrator-protagonist, lives in New York and is married to a man named Alberto; she also has a lesbian relationship with her cousin Laura, also married, who is visiting from Cuba. The seduction takes place in Mayté's apartment (her husband is away on a trip) while the two women dance to some long boleros that serve as the romantic motivation between them. In her confession to Marta Veneranda, Mayté says that when she was dancing with her cousin she felt a "desire to conquer her, to sexually possess her" (21).[15] It is obvious from the bolero scene and from the confession that lesbian desire here is conditioned by and also erotically reclaimed from heterosexual desire. Mayté has made a gesture both against and within the *machista* code, and one that we see repeated in other characters of the "forbidden stories": the restructuring of a reality achieved by rearranging its components to create a new reality.

The lesbian transgressions may be the most remarkable in the book, due to the repeated and scandalous nature of their rupture and the strictness of the code they transgress. But in this sense I must point out that the figure represented as the "lesbian" maintains an unassuming dependence on the norms of power, from which she seeks to distinguish herself. This aspect of "La más prohibida de todas" (The most forbidden of all) makes it, besides "the most forbidden" story, the most significant. First of all, in this final story there is a reversal of the utopia that appears in the other stories of this collection. If the other stories suggest a utopia situated in the Cuban childhood of the narrator, in "La más prohibida de todas" this utopia is located neither in childhood nor in Cuba. In fact, childhood and Cuba in this story are a destruction of the Cuban utopia and its relation to an idealized childhood. Martirio, the narrator-protagonist, is of very poor Spanish Republican parents from Andalusia. The father was executed during the Spanish Civil War, and the mother was able to leave for Cuba shortly after the end of the war; she was only seventeen years old when Martirio was born just after her arrival. Their life there was one of great misery, and we are told that the mother was a most unfortunate woman, always crying and complaining, and so she gave her daughter the name Martirio (Martyrdom). The mother lived among prostitutes, and from a very young age Martirio had sexual relations numerous

15. Spanish original: "ansias de conquistarla yo a ella, de poseerla."

times with men who were almost always married. At eighteen she became pregnant and had an abortion. All these factors make the representation of the narrator's youth in Cuba exactly the opposite of the utopian idealizations of the book's other stories.

If there is a utopian space in the story of Martirio's youth, it is not that of daily life in Cuba but rather that of American cinema. In this text, the idealization of love in Hollywood movies, with their beautiful women, suffering in the midst of splendor, becomes the place of the first utopian space in this story (another very significant utopian moment will be established later). In those movies "They loved each other as if for the very first time. Their feelings intact, nothing had been able to change that impossible love" (103).[16] In this way American mass culture becomes a decisive factor in the structuring of the narrator's desire, and also in the structuring of the Cuban culture from which she comes. Thus Cuban culture becomes "contaminated" by the American. This means that Martirio's heritage is fundamentally destabilized very early on by American movie culture. This conditioning reaches such an extreme that Martirio confesses that her passion functions largely based on what she has learned emotionally from the American movies that have influenced her so much since her girlhood.

Martirio and her mother left Cuba for New York in 1958 as a way of temporarily distancing themselves from the difficult political situation during the last years of the Batista regime, when Fidel Castro was leading the revolution from the mountains in Oriente. They stayed on and established themselves in New York. From what Martirio says about herself we also know that at the time of narration she is a writer ("author of several collections of short stories" [101])[17] who was once a poor girl with several married lovers. The fact that Martirio is not only an informant at the time of narration (she is one of the characters in Marta Veneranda's stories) but also a writer (as she herself says) destabilizes the narrative levels that had been established in the other stories in *Las historias prohibidas*. Martirio tells Veneranda, "I hope to get *my* own story about the episode from this conversation, that's why I'm going to record it" (102).[18] Also, Martirio states that this story will be part of a collection titled *Historias de mujeres grandes y chiquitas*

16. Spanish original: "Se amaban como la primera vez. Los sentimientos intactos, nada había logrado cambiar aquel amor imposible."

17. Spanish original: "autora de varios libros de cuentos."

18. Spanish original: "Espero sacar de esta conversación *mi* propio cuento sobre el episodio, por eso voy a grabar."

(Stories of women great and small); in fact, this is the title of a still-unpublished collection by Rivera-Valdés.

Martirio says that she wants to establish a distance between the character and the narrator, but in a sense exactly the opposite occurs: the more Martirio insists on this distance the more she looks like Marta Veneranda and the more Marta Veneranda resembles Sonia Rivera-Valdés. Obviously, the narrative levels become subverted by her statements. And Martirio says something that greatly complicates these levels: she tells Marta, "[I want you to listen] from two angles: hearing the story so that you can recreate it, and at the same time listening with a critical sense, as I explain the aesthetic problems that I foresee in the writing of my text and the solutions I've thought of to those problems" (ibid.).[19] With these statements Martirio expresses her intention for this story to have several writerly and readerly perspectives: that of the narrator-character Martirio as an informant, Veneranda as an active and passive listener, and the reader as critic. This entire effort indicates a synthesis of Martirio and Marta as alter egos of Rivera-Valdés's. This process may produce an invitation for the reader as critic, but at the same time it brings the narrator-protagonist (Martirio) closer to the therapist-listener (Marta) and also suggests that the protagonists and characters of the other stories possess certain characteristics of Rivera-Valdés.

But, what is Martirio's "secret"? The narrator-protagonist's attitude in "La más prohibida de todas" is much more affirmative than that of the other protagonists. Martirio tells Marta Veneranda that she believes it is "important to clarify that I haven't come because I think what I'm going to tell you is taboo, in the way you've defined 'forbidden history'";[20] here she admits that she has read or at least knows quite a bit about the other stories in the collection. She adds, "I fully enjoyed what happened, and I take responsibility for it"[21] and "When I analyze it now, I see that within myself I was dedicated to seeking not love but a deception that my subconscious perceived as freedom from my enormous need for affection."[22] But her "forbidden

19. Spanish original: "desde dos ángulos: oyendo la historia para tú recrearla, y a la vez con un sentido crítico, según yo vaya explicando los problemas estéticos que preveo en la escritura de mi texto y las soluciones que he imaginado para sortearlos."
20. Spanish original: "importante aclarar que no he venido por considerar tabú lo que voy a contar, en el sentido que has definido 'historia prohibida.'"
21. Spanish original: "He disfrutado lo sucedido a plenitud, y lo asumo."
22. Spanish original: "En mi interior vivía dedicada a buscar, cuando lo analizo ahora, no el amor, sino una decepción que mi subconsciente percibía como liberadora de mi enorme necesidad de cariño."

confession" seems to be the following: "what I didn't foresee, what I never thought of in the movies, as a girl, is that it wouldn't be_men who would disappoint me in the end, but women. Yes, the greater part of my romantic relationships have been with women, although as a young girl I was fascinated with men" (104).[23] Martirio's statement is clear: she was fascinated with men in her youth (at the time of narration she is fifty-five years old), but later experienced mainly lesbian relationships.

But in spite of her avowed lesbianism, Martirio's sexuality is far from being strictly "homosexual." In fact, she tells how when she was young and already in New York, she met a young man from southern India while both were modeling for a painting school. His name was Shrinivas, and Martirio's sexual-sensual scene with him is the most extraordinary not only of this story but of the entire collection. Their encounter was so exotic and fulfilling, and so delicate and sensual were his caresses, that Martirio, by then "disillusioned with love," resolved that "from then on [she look] for [happiness], certain that it existed" (117).[24] The turning point in the story comes when it is revealed that Shrinivas lives with another man, his lover. In other words, Shrinivas is gay, or at least bisexual (he tells Martirio that he doesn't sleep with women very often). Therefore, the only fulfilling "heterosexual" love scene in the entire collection occurs between a woman who at one point declares her lesbianism, and a man who describes himself as gay. This is typical of the destabilizing ambiguity that appears throughout these stories and that in "La más prohibida de todas" is carried to the extreme.

After her romance with Shrinivas, Martirio tells of a horrible marriage she had with an alcoholic Irishman named Mark, ten years her senior, who mistreated her. After their divorce Martirio "decides" to have only lesbian relationships: the names of her lovers are now Ada, Betina, and Rocío. The initial excuse for her lesbianism comes from a widespread myth that situates lesbian desire as derived from romantic disillusionment with men. Martirio, besides having the excuse of her bad experience with Mark, expresses a sort of lesbian utopia when she explains her reasons for "changing" to lesbian relations: "Woman with woman, without worries of pregnancy, I imagined a relationship free

23. Spanish original: "lo imprevisto, lo que jamás calculé en el cine, de niña, es que no sería de los hombres de quienes me iba a estar decepcionada al final, sino de las mujeres. Sí, la mayor parte de mis relaciones románticas han sido con mujeres, aunque de jovencita me fascinaban los hombres."
24. Spanish original: "en adelante la busqué [la felicidad], segura de que existía."

of inhibitions, total pleasure, absolute intimacy, a perpetual party" (124).[25] Thus conceived, lesbianism is construed not so much as a subversion of machismo but more than anything else as a space of freedom from everything. But lesbianism is also a construct that is never simply a representation that functions as an absolute guarantee of escape from phallocentrism.[26] The lesbian text is also a space in which discursive battles intersect, and the text of "La más prohibida de todas" takes up various aspects of this issue. As for her relations with Ada, Martirio says that "I put up with more from her than from any man"[27] and "[w]ith women everything became even more complicated" (ibid).[28] She finally admits that "[t]he reasons I felt attracted to women were now very distant from the reasons I started seeking them out" (126).[29]

But in spite of the self-deconstruction of the "reasons" Martirio gives for her lesbianism after her divorce from Mark, lesbian utopia does not entirely disappear in this text. In fact the story ends with one that, oddly enough, connects with the sexuality Martirio had learned in her youth during her sexual sessions with older, married men. These Cuban males frequently had a very vocal sexuality: in order to have sex they had to constantly say what they wanted from the woman. What excited them was the mise-en-scène of the woman-child. Among the expressions of these men's "spoken sex,"—possibly the "most forbidden" passages in the collection—the following stands out:

> Ábrete, mami, enséñale a tu papi todo lo que tienes guardadito entre las piernas y que tú sabes es mío aunque te resistas. Déjame ver esa florecita que voy a comerme poquito a poco. Así. Dios mío que cosa más santa estoy viendo. Así . . . así. No puedo creer que todo esto sea para mí solo. Ya verás que no vas a arrepentirte de habérmela dado. Te voy a hacer gozar como jamás te ha hecho gozar nadie. No vas a olvidarme nunca, aunque cien más traten de hacerte lo que yo te estoy haciendo. Nadie va a hacértelo como yo, con este gusto con que te lo hago y a nadie vas a dárselo con el gusto que me lo estás dando a mí. Ven ricura de mi vida, cielo santo. (110)

25. Spanish original: "Mujer con mujer, sin preocupación de embarazo, imaginé una relación libre de inhibiciones, disfrute total, intimidad absoluta, fiesta perpetua."

26. Jagose, *Lesbian Utopics*, 160.

27. Spanish original: "le aguanté mucho más que a cualquier hombre." Rivera-Valdés, *Las historias prohibidas*, 124.

28. Spanish original: "Con las mujeres todo se volvió aún más enredado."

29. Spanish original: "Las razones por las cuales me sentía atraída por las mujeres ahora eran ajenas a aquellas por las que comencé a buscarlas."

[Open up, mama, show your daddy what you've got hidden there between your legs. You know it's mine no matter how hard you resist. Let me see that little flower I'm going to eat out bit by bit. That's it. My God, what a holy thing I'm looking at. That's it . . . that's it. I can't believe all this is for me! You won't regret giving it up to me, you'll see. I'm going to make you scream with pleasure like nobody ever did. You'll never forget me, not even if a hundred other guys try to do you the way I'm doing you. Nobody's going to do it to you like me, the way I like doing it to you, and you'll never like giving it up the way you're enjoying yourself right now. Come here honey child, my little angel.]

At the end of "La más prohibida de todas," Martirio meets up with a young Cuban woman in a bookstore. Her name is Rocío, and early in the conversation she states her inclination toward lesbian relations. Martirio, although attracted to Rocío from the beginning, does not sleep with her immediately, but waits until meeting up with her again in Cuba several months later. Their love scene takes place at Rocío's house in the Malecón District of Havana, and reflects many aspects of Cuban poverty at the time as well as a bit of Havana nostalgia. Martirio and Rocío make love sensuously and tenderly, but Martirio, clearly showing the heterosexual conditioning of her behavior, repeats something very similar to what the men said to her as a girl. She says to Rocío: "Open up, baby, show your mama what you've got hidden there between your legs. You know it's mine no matter how hard you resist. Let me see that little flower I'm going to eat out bit by bit" (140).[30] But to the surprise of the reader and of Martirio herself, Rocío knows perfectly well how the "spoken sex" scene goes. She says to Martirio,

Mírame bien, mi reina, estoy como tú me querías, para ti solita, para que me goces. Ahora tú me vas a dar a mí lo mismo. Deja los dedos donde los tienes y abre las piernas tú, déjame verte yo a ti ahora, fíjate lo buena que soy yo contigo, vas a ser tú igual conmigo, dámelo mami, como yo te lo estoy dando a ti. (Ibid.)

[Take a good look at me, my queen, I'm just the way you want me, just for you, for your pleasure. Now you're going to give the same thing to me. Leave your fingers where they are and open your legs, let *me* see

30. Spanish original: "Ábrete, rica, enséñale a tu mami todo lo que tienes guardadito entre las piernas y que tú sabes es mío aunque te resistas. Déjame ver esa florecita que voy a comerme poquito a poco."

you now. See how good I am with you? You're going to be the same way with me. Give it to me, mama, like I'm giving it to you.]

But in spite of the impression that both Martirio's and Rocío's words copy precisely those said by the men of the narrator's youth, in reality they are not exactly the same. There is a conditioning here, but not a copying; the text requires a restoration of the colonized forms to create a new reality. The strength of the expression comes from the rules of dominance that both women have learned, but this final scene is of a mutual sensuality, of egalitarian understanding. It should be noted that the very fact that Rocío either mysteriously knows beforehand what Martirio is going to say or is simply repeating similar behaviors learned in her youth, is a rupture of sorts in the realism of the text; only at that moment does it appear to be magic or supernatural. The text ends by stating that these relations have been going on for three years, seemingly implying that everything is working out well in the end. The magic moment of repeating the words learned in youth, along with this ending, point to a lesbian utopia. The text, despite the difficulties of failed loves and frustrated passions, ends on this note.

This ending presents a paradox, since on the one hand it underscores the conditioning affected by the power mechanisms of Cuban phal-locentricity, while on the other it makes a utopian gesture indicating a total liberation from those very mechanisms. It is precisely in the intersection of this paradox that we could find the possibility of a more theoretically sophisticated model to analyze both the technologies of control without simply proposing them as derivatives of an un-avoidable monolithic source of power, and the gesture and postures of resistance and subversion without simply attributing them to positions beyond the control system or interpreting them as indicators of the immanent collapse of the system of domination.[31] In this way we avoid falling into unsatisfactory positions that propose either idealistic willfulness ("I make my own reality") or structural determinism ("I am just a victim of the patriarchal/capitalist/colonial world") (ibid.). If we take into account the fact that none of these solutions explains the discourse of emancipation, we will be in a better position to deal with the complex issue of resistance and replication, and we will be able to contribute to a critique of the mechanisms of power and the condition-ing they exercise on the entire liberation process (ibid.). *Las historias prohibidas de Marta Veneranda*, with its destabilizing aesthetic that

31. Jagose, *Lesbian Utopics*, 161–63.

constantly tests the limits both of the established codes as well as the "marginal identities" with pretensions of fixedness, invites a questioning not only of power but also of its liberating responses. Thus, the work constitutes a cultural artifact that not only makes for fascinating reading but also for critical reflection. *Las historias prohibidas* make simultaneous gestures of affirmation and diffusion, of return to the home, and of dissemination and containment. Rivera-Valdés's texts, like the others in this final section of the book, do not put an end to the questions of nationalisms and homosexualities; rather, they open new horizons and crossroads.

BIBLIOGRAPHY

Almaguer, Tomás. "Chicano Men: A Cartography of Homosexual Identity and Behavior." In *The Lesbian and Gay Studies Reader,* edited by Henry Abelove, Michele Aina Barale, and David M. Halperin, 255–73. New York: Routledge, 1993.

Almendros, Néstor, and Orlando Jiménez-Leal, eds. *Conducta impropia* (Improper conduct). Madrid: Editorial Playor, 1984.

Alonso Estenoz, Alfredo. "Tema homosexual en la literatura cubana de los 80 y los 90: ¿renovación o retroceso?" Paper presented at the 2000 Modern Language Association Convention, Miami, Fla., March 2000.

Anderson, Benedict. *Imagined Communities: Reflections on the Origin and Spread of Nationalism.* Rev. ed. London: Verso, 1991.

Arenas, Reinaldo. *Antes que anochezca (Autobiografía).* Barcelona: Tusquets Editores, 1992. Translated by Dolores M. Koch under the title *Before Night Falls (A Memoir)* (New York: Penguin Books, 1993).

Argüelles, Lourdes, and Ruby Rich. "Homosexuality, Homophobia and Revolution: Notes toward an Understanding of the Cuban Lesbian and Gay experience," parts 1 and 2, *Signs* 9, no. 4 (summer 1984): 683–99; 11, no. 1 (1985): 120–35.

Balderston, Daniel. *El deseo, enorme cicatriz luminosa.* Caracas: Ediciones eXcultura, 1999.

Balderston, Daniel, and Donna J. Guy, eds. *Sex and Sexuality in Latin America.* New York: New York University Press, 1997.

Béjar, Eduardo. *La textualidad de Reinaldo Arenas. Juegos de la escritura posmoderna.* Madrid: Editorial Playor, 1987.

Bejel, Emilio. *José Lezama Lima, Poet of the Image.* Gainesville: University of Florida Press, 1990.

———. "Senel Paz: homosexualidad, nacionalismo y utopía." *Plural* 269 (February 1994): 58–65.

———. "Nacionalidad y exilio en la narrativa cubana contemporánea (Reflexiones sabre la narrativa cubana a partir de 1959)." *Confluenica* 9 (spring 1994): 73–87.

———. *"Fresa y chocolate* o la salida de la guarida. Hacia una teoría del sujeto homosexual en Cuba." *Casa de las Américas* 35, no. 196 (July–September 1994): 10–22.

———. *"Colibrí* : homosexualidad, resistencia y representación." *Unión* 7, no. 21 (October–December 1995): 65–69.

———. *"La bella del Alhambra*: seducción, resistencia y representación." *Temas* 9 (January–March 1997): 98–100.

———. *"Strawberry and Chocolate*: Coming out of the Cuban Closet?" *South Atlantic Quarterly* 96, no. 1 (winter 1997): 65–82.

Bergmann, Emilie L., and Paul Julian Smith, eds. *¿Entiendes? Queer Readings, Hispanic Writings*. Durham, N.C.: Duke University Press, 1995.

Bernaza, Felipe, and Margaret Gilpin. *Mariposas en el andamio* (Butterflies on the scaffold). New York: Kangaroo Productions, 1996.

Beverly, John, and José Oviedo, eds. *The Postmodern Debate in Latin America* (a special issue of *Boundary* 2). Durham, N.C.: Duke University Press, 1993.

Bhabha, Homi. "DissemiNation: Time, Narrative and the Margins of the Modern Nation." In *Nation and Narration*, edited by Homi Bhabha, 291–322. London: Routledge, 1990.

Bloom, Harold. "The Internalization of Quest-Romance." In *Romanticism and Consciousness: Essays in Criticism,*. edited by Harold Bloom, 3–24. New York: W. W. Norton & Company, Inc., 1970.

Boone, Joseph Allen. *Libidinal Currents: Sexuality and the Shaping of Modernism*. Chicago: University of Chicago Press, 1998.

Britto García, Luis. "Critique of Modernity: Avant-Garde, Counterculture, Revolution." *The South Atlantic Quarterly* 92, no. 3 (1993).

Bufill, Elio Alba. *Enrique José Varona. Crítica y creación*. Madrid: Hispanova de Ediciones, 1976.

Butler, Judith. *Bodies That Matter: On the Discursive Limits of "Sex."* New York: Routledge, 1993.

Caballero, José Agustín. "Carta crítica del hombre-muger" (Letter in critique to the woman-man). In *La literarura del Papel Periódico de La Habana, 1790–1805*, introduction and edition by Cintio Vitier, Fina García Marruz, and Roberto Friol, 75–78. Havana: Editorial Letras Cubanas, 1990.

Cabrera Infante, Guillermo. *Mea Cuba*. New York: Farrar, Strauss and Giroux, 1992.

Caminha, Adolfo. *Bom-Crioulo: The Black Man and the Cabin Boy*. San Francisco: Gay Sunshine Press, 1982.

Capriles Osuna, Eugenio. *Diccionario razonado de la lesgilación de policía*. Havana: Establecimiento Tipográfico, 1889.

Carrión, Miguel de. *Las impuras* (The impure ones). Havana: Librería Nueva, 1919.

Casal, Lourdes. *El caso Padilla*. Miami: Ediciones Universal, 1971.

Céspedes, Benjamín de. *La prostitución en la Ciudad de La Habana*. Havana: Establecimiento tipográfico O'Reily, Número 9, 1888.

Chatterjee, Partha. *Nationalist Thought and the Colonial World*. Minneapolis: University of Minnesota Press, 1986.

———. "The Nationalist Resolution of the Women Question." In *Recasting Women: Essays in Colonial History*, edited by Kumkum Sangari and Sudesh Vaid. New Delhi: Kali for Women, 1989. Reprint, under the title *Recasting Women: Essays in Indian Colonial History*, New Brunswick, N.J.: Rutgers University Press, 1990.

Chauncey, George. *Gay New York: Gender, Urban Culture, and the Making of the Gay Male World, 1890–1940*. New York: Harper Collins, 1994.

Chiampi, Irlemar. *Barroco e modernidade*. São Paulo: Editora Perspectiva, 1998.

Clavijo, Uva A. "Modernismo y modernidad en la narrativa de Alfonso Hernández Catá." Ph.D. diss., University of Miami, Coral Gables, 1991.

Cristófani Barreto, Teresa. *A Libélula, a pitonisa. Revoluão, homosexualismo e literatura em Virgilio Piñera*. São Paulo: Editorial Iluminuras, 1996.

Cruz, Manuel. *Cromitos cubanos (bocetos de autores hispano-americanos)*. Havana: Biblioteca "El Fígaro," Establecimiento Tipográfico "La Lucha," 1892. Revised with prologue by Salvador Bueno (Havana: Editorial Arte y Literatura, 1975).

Cruz-Malavé, Arnaldo. *El primitivo implorante. El "sistema poético del mundo" de José Lezama Lima*. Atlanta: Rodopi, 1994.

———. "Toward an Art of Transvestism: Colonialism and Homosexuality in Puerto Rican Literature." In *¿Entiendes?, Queer Readings, Hispanic Writings*, edited by Emilie L. Bergmann and Paul Julian Smith, 135–67. Durham, N.C.: Duke University Press, 1995.

Cuba: Cultura e Identidad Nacional. Havana: Cuban Writers and Artists and the University of Havana, 1995.

Davies, Catherine. *A Place in the Sun? Women Writers in Twentieth-Century Cuba*. London: Zed Books Ltd., 1998.

De Jongh, Elena M. "Gender and Controversy: Cuban Novelist Ofelia Rodríguez Acosta." *Journal of the Southeastern Council on Latin American Studies* 23 (March 1992): 23–35.

———. "Femenismo y periodismo en la Cuba republicana: Ofelia Rodríguez Acosta y la campaña feminista de *Bohemia* (1930–1932)." *Confluencia* 11, no. 1 (1995): 3–12.

De Man, Paul. "Autobiography as Disfigurement." *Modern Language Notes*, 94 (1979): 919–30.

D'Emilio, John. *Sexual Politics, Sexual Communities: The Making of a Homosexual Minority in the United States, 1940–1970*. Chicago: University of Chicago Press, 1983.

———. "Capitalism and Gay Identity." In *The Lesbian and Gay Studies Reader*, edited by Henry Abelove, Michele Barale, and David M. Halperin, 467–76. New York: Routledge, 1993.

Desnoes, Edmundo. *Inconsolable Memories*. New York: New American Library, 1967.

D'Halmar, Augusto. *La pasión y muerte del Cura Deusto* (The passion and death of Father Deusto). Madrid: Editora Internacional, 1924. 3d ed., Santiago: Nascimento, 1969.

Diccionario de la literatura cubana. Havana: Editorial Letras Cubanas, first volume, 1980; second volume, 1984.

"Do We Want Cuba?" Philadelphia *Manufacturer,* 6 March 1889. Reproduced in *Our America: Writings on Latin America and the Struggle for Cuban Independence by José Martí,* edited by Philip S. Foner. New York: Monthly Review Press, 1977.

Dubert, Joe L. *Man's Place: Masculinity in Transition.* Englewood Cliffs, N.J.: Prentice-Hall, 1979.

Epps, Brad. "Proper Conduct: Reinaldo Arenas, Fidel Castro and the Politics of Homosexuality." *Journal of the History of Sexuality* 6, no. 2 (1995): 231–83.

Ette, Ottmar. "La obra de Reinaldo Arenas." In *La escritura de la memoria. Reinaldo Arenas: Textos, estudios y documentación,* edited by Ottmar Ette. Frankfurt am Main: Vervuert Verlag, 1992.

Faderman, Lillian. *Surpassing the Love of Men.* New York: Morrow, 1981.

Fanon, Frantz. "On National Culture." In *The Wretched of the Earth,* 174–90. Harmondsworth, England: Penguin, 1969.

Foner, Philip S., ed. *Our America: Writings on Latin America and the Struggle for Cuban Independence by José Martí.* New York: Monthly Review Press, 1977.

Foster, David W. *Gay and Lesbian Themes in Latin American Writing.* Austin: University of Texas Press, 1991.

Foucault, Michel. *The History of Sexuality.* Vol. 1, *An Introduction.* Translated by Robert Hurley. New York: Vintage Books, 1978. Reprint, New York: Vintage Books, 1980. Originally published as *La Volonté de savior* (Paris: Gallimard, 1976).

Fowler, Víctor. *La maldición: una historia del placer como conquista.* Havana: Editorial Letras Cubanas, 1998.

Franqui, Carlos. *Family Portrait with Fidel.* New York: Random House, 1984.

Garber, Marjorie. *Vested Interests: Cross-Dressing & Cultural Anxiety.* New York: Routledge, 1992. Reprint, New York: HarperPerennial, 1993.

García Canclini, Néstor. *Culturas híbridas. Estrategias para entrar y salir de la modernidad.* Grijalbo, Mexico: Consejo Nacional para la Cultura y las Artes, 1989.

García Marruz, Fina. "Amistad funesta." In García Marruz and Vitier, *Temas martianos,* 282–91.

García Marruz, Fina, and Cintio Vitier. *Temas martianos.* Havana: Biblioteca Nacional José Martí, 1969.

Genette, Gérard. " 'Stendhal.' " In *Figures of Literary Discourse,* 147–82. New York: Columbia University Press, 1982.

Ginsberg, Allen. "Interview with Allen Ginsberg." By Allen Young. *Gay Sunshine Interview* (1974): 25–27. Reprinted in Young, *Gays under the Cuban Revolution* (San Francisco: Grey Fox Press, 1981).

Giralt, Pedro. *El amor y la prostitución. Réplica a un libro del Dr. Céspedes.* Havana: La Universal, 1889.

González, Aníbal. "El intelectual y las metáforas: *Lucía Jerez* de José Martí." *Texto crítico* 12, nos. 34–35 (January–December 1986): 136–57.

González, Reynaldo. "Entre la magia y la infinitud." In *Lezama Lima: el ingenuo culpable,* 140–42. Havana: Editorial Letras Cubanas, 1988.

González Echevarría, Roberto. *La ruta de Severo Sarduy.* Hanover, N.H.: Ediciones del Norte, 1987.

———. "Literatura, baile y béisbol en el (último) fin de siglo cubano." *Encuentro* 8, no. 9 (spring–summer 1998): 30–42.

———. *The Pride of Havana: A History of Cuban Baseball* (Oxford: Oxford University Press, 1999).

Goytisolo, Juan. *En los reinos de Taifa.* Barcelona: Editorial Seix-Barral, 1986.

Granma (7 April 1980).

Green, James N. *Beyond Carnival: Male Homosexuality in Twentieth-Century Brazil.* Chicago: University of Chicago Press, 1999.

Greenberg, David F. *The Construction of Homosexuality.* Chicago: University of Chicago Press, 1988.

Gutiérrez Alea, Tomás, and Juan Carlos Tabío. *Fresa y chocolate* (Strawberry and chocolate). Screenplay by Senel Paz. 97 min. Canberra: Ronin Films, 1993. VHS videocassette.

Hasson, Liliane. "*Antes que anochezca (Autobiografía)*: una lectura distinta de la obra de Reinaldo Arenas." In *La escritura de la memoria,* edited by Ottmar Ette, 165–73. Frankfurt am Main: Vervuert, 1991.

Hernández, Librada, and Susana Chávez Silverman, eds. *Reading and Writing the Ambiente: Queer Sexualities in Latino, Latin American, and Spanish Culture.* Madison: University of Wisconsin Press, 2000.

Hernández Catá, Alfonso. *Cuentos pasionales* (Passional stories). Madrid: M. Pérez de Villavicencio, 1907.

———. *La juventud de Aurelio Zaldívar* (Aurelio Zaldívar's youth). Madrid: Biblioteca Renacimiento, V. Prieto y Compañía, 1911.

———. *El ángel de Sodoma* (The angel of Sodom). Madrid: Mundo Latino, 1928.

———. *El sembrador de sal.* In *Los frutos ácidos y otros cuentos,* by Alfonso Hernández Catá. Madrid: Aguilar Ediciones, 1953.

Hijuelos, Oscar. *The Mambo Kings.* New York: Harper & Row Publishers, 1988.

Holland, Norman. *The Dynamics of Literary Response.* New York: Oxford University Press, 1968.

Hulme, Peter. *Rescuing Cuba: Adventure and Masculinity in the 1890s.* College Park: University of Maryland, 1996.

Jagose, Annamarie. *Lesbian Utopics.* New York: Routledge, 1994.

Jambrina, Jesús. "Sujetos *queer* en la literatura cubana: hacia una (posible) genealogía homoerótica." Paper given at the Modern Language Association Convention, Miami, Fla., March 2000.

Jameson, Fredric. *The Political Unconscious: Narrative as a Socially Symbolic Act.* Ithaca, N.Y.: Cornell University Press, 1981.

———. "Modernism and Imperialism." In *Nationalism, Colonialism, and Literature,* edited by Terry Eagleton, Fredric Jameson, and Edward Said, 43–66. Minneapolis: University of Minnesota Press, 1990.

Kaplan, Caren. *Questions of Travel: Postmodern Discourses of Displacement.* Durham, N.C.: Duke University Press, 1996.

Lechner, Norbert. "A Disappointment Called Postmodernism." In *The Postmodern*

Debate in Latin America, edited by John Beverly and José Oviedo, 122–39. Special issue of *Boundary* 2. Durham, N.C.: Duke University Press, 1993.

Leiner, Marvin. *Sexual Politics in Cuba: Machismo, Homosexuality and AIDS.* Boulder, Colo.: Westview Press, 1994.

Lezama Lima, Eloísa. "Mi hermano." In *José Lezama Lima: textos críticos,* edited by Justo Ulloa, 11–17. Miami: Ediciones Universal, 1979.

———. "Vida, pasión y creación de José Lezama Lima: fechas claves para una cronología." In *Paradiso,* by José Lezama Lima, edited by Eloísa Lezama Lima, 16–40. Madrid: Cátedra, 1980.

Lezama Lima, José. "Respuesta y nuevas interrogaciones. Carta abierta a Jorge Mañach." *Bohemia* 40 (2 October 1949): 77.

———. *Paradiso.* 3d ed. Mexico City: Ediciones Era, 1973. Edition by Eloísa Lezama Lima, Madrid: Cátedra, 1980.

———. *Oppiano Licario.* 2d ed. Mexico City: Ediciones Era, 1978.

———. *Cartas (1939–1976).* Edited by Eloísa Lezama Lima. Madrid: Editorial Orígenes, 1979.

———. *Imagen y posibilidad.* Edited by Ciro Bianchi Ross. Havana: Editorial Letras Cubanas, 1981.

López Acosta, Pedro de Jesús. *Cuentos frígidos* (Frigid tales). Madrid: Olalla Ediciones, 1988.

———. *El retrato* (The portrait). *La Gaceta de Cuba* (January–February 1998): 7–12.

Lugo-Ortiz, Agnes. *Identidades imaginadas: Biografía y nacionalidad en el horizonte de la guerra (Cuba 1860–1898).* San Juan: Editorial de la Universidad de Puerto Rico, 1999.

Lumsden, Ian. *Machos, Maricones, and Gays: Cuba and Homosexuality.* Philadelphia: Temple University Press, 1996.

"Los maricones" (The faggots). *La Cebolla,* 9 September 1888, vol. 1, no. 1.

Marcos, Miguel de. *Lujuria: Cuentos nefandos* (Lust: abominable stories). Havana: Jesús Montero, 1914.

Martí, José. *Obras completas.* 2d ed. 27 vols. Havana: Editorial de Ciencias Sociales, 1975.

———. "A Vindication of Cuba." In *Our America: Writings on Latin America and the Struggle for Cuban Independence by José Martí,* edited by Philip S. Foner, 234–41. New York: Monthly Review Press, 1977.

———. *Amistad funesta* (Fatal friendship). In *Obras completas* 18:185–272. Havana: Editorial de Ciencias Sociales, 1975.

———. "Oscar Wilde." In *Obras completas* 15:361–68. Havana: Editorial de Ciencias Sociales, 1975.

Martin, Robert K. "American Literature: Nineteenth Century." In *The Gay and Lesbian Literary Heritage,* edited by Claude J. Summers, 25–30. New York: Henry Holt and Company, 1995.

Martínez-San Miguel, Yolanda. "Sujetos femeninos en *Amistad funesta* y *Blanca Sol*: el lugar de la mujer en las novelas latinoamericanas de fin de siglo XIX." *Revista Iberanoamericana* 62, no. 174 (January–March 1996): 27–45.

Mazzotta, Giuseppe. *Dante, Poet of the Desert*. Princeton, N.J.: Princeton University Press, 1979.

Mejides, Miguel. "Mi prima Amanda" (My cousin Amanda).Manuscript, 1984. Havana: Unión de Escritores y Artistas de Cuba, 1988.

Méndez Rodenas, Adriana. *Severo Sarduy: El neobarroco de la transgresión*. Mexico: Universidad Nacional Autonóma de México, 1983.

———. Review of *Colibrí*, by Severo Sarduy. *Revista Iberoamericana* 51 (1985): 399–401.

Menéndez, Nina R. "No Woman Is an Island: Cuban Women's Fiction in the 1920s and 1930s." Ph.D. diss., Stanford University, 1993.

———. "*Garzonas y Feministas* in Cuban Women's Writing of the 1920s: *La vida manda* by Ofelia Rodríguez Acosta." In *Sex and Sexuality in Latin America*, edited by Daniel Balderston and Donna J. Guy, 174–89. New York: New York University Press, 1997.

Molloy, Sylvia. *At Face Value: Autobiographical Writing in Spanish America*. Cambridge: Cambridge University Press, 1991.

———. "Too Wilde for Comfort: Desire and Ideology in Fin-de-Siecle Spanish America." *Social Text* 31–32 (1992): 187–201.

———. "His America, Our America: José Martí Reads Whitman." *Modern Language Quarterly* 57, no. 2 (June 1996): 369–79.

Molloy, Sylvia, and Robert McKee Irwin, eds. *Hispanisms and Homosexualities*. Durham, N.C.: Duke University Press, 1998.

Montenegro, Carlos. *Hombres sin mujer* (Womanless men). Mexico: Editorial Masas, 1938.

Montero, Oscar. "La periferia del deseo: Julián del Casal y el pederasta urbano." In *Carnal Knowledge. Essays on the Flesh, Sex and Sexuality in Hispanic Letters and Film*, edited by Pamela Bacarisse, 99–111. Pittsburgh: Ediciones Tres Ríos, n.d.

———. "Lipstick Vogue: The Politics of Drag." *Radical America* 22, no. 1 (January–February 1988): 37–42.

———. "Before the Parade Passes By: Latino Queers and National Identity." *Radical America* 24, no. 4 (1990): 15–26.

———. *Erotismo y representación en Julián del Casal*. Amsterdam: Rodopi, 1993.

———. "Julián del Casal and the Queers of Havana." In *¿Entiendes? Queer Readings, Hispanic Writings*, edited by Emilie L. Bergmann and Paul Julian Smith, 92–112. Durham, N.C.: Duke University Press, 1995.

———. "Hellenism and Homophobia in José Enrique Rodó." *Revista de Estudios Hispánicos* 31 (1997): 25–39.

———. "*Modernismo* and Homophobia: Darío and Rodó." In *Sex and Sexuality in Latin America*, edited by Daniel Balderston and Donna J. Guy, 101–17. New York: New York University Press, 1997.

———. "The Queer Theories of Severo Sarduy." In *Between the Self and the Void: Essays in Honor of Severo Sarduy*, edited by Alicia Rivero-Potter, 65–78. Boulder, Colo.: Society of Spanish and Spanish American Studies, 1998.

Montero, Susana A. *La narrativa femenina cubana, 1928–1958*. Havana: Editorial Academia, 1989.

Moreiras, Alberto. "Autobiografía: pensador firmado (Nietzsche y Derrida)." *Anthropos* 29 (December 1991): 129–36.

Moreno Fraginals, Manuel. *El ingenio. Complejo económico social cubano del azúcar.* Vol. 2. Havana: Editorial de Ciencias Sociales, 1978.

Mosse, George L. *Nationalism and Sexuality: Respectability and Abnormal Sexuality in Modern Europe.* New York: Howard Fertig, 1985.

Muñoz, Elías Miguel. *Crazy Love.* Houston: Arte Público Press, 1989.

Murray, Stephen O. *Homosexualities.* Chicago: University of Chicago Press, 2000.

Murray, Stephen O., and Manuel G. Arboleda. "Stigma Transformation and Relexification: *Gay* in Latin America." In *Latin American Male Homosexualities*, edited by Murray, 138–44.

Murray, Stephen O., ed. *Latin American Male Homosexualities.* Albuquerque: University of New Mexico Press, 1995.

Obejas, Achy. *We Came All the Way from Cuba So You Could Dress like This?* Pittsburgh: Cleiss Press, 1994.

Ortiz, Fernando. *Los negros brujos.* Miami: Ediciones Universal, 1973.

Padura Fuentes, Leonardo. "El cazador" (The hunter). Havana: Ediciones Unión, 1991. Reprinted in *El cuerpo inmortal. 20 cuentos eróticos cubanos*, edited by Alberto Garrandés (Havana: Editorial Letras Cubanas, 1997), 56–66.

———. *Máscaras* (Masks). Havana: Ediciones Unión, 1997.

Parker, Andrew, and Mary Russo, Doris Sommer, and Patricia Yaeger, editors. *Nationalisms and Sexualities.* New York: Routledge, 1992.

Paz, Octavio. *Los hijos del limo.* Barcelona: Seix-Barral, 1974.

———. *La otra voz. Poesía y fin de siglo.* Barcelona: Seix Barral, 1990.

Paz, Senel. *El lobo, el bosque y el hombre nuevo.* Mexico City: Ediciones Era, 1991.

———. Interview by the author. Boulder, Colo., 27 March 1994.

Pérez, Louis A, Jr. "Between Baseball and Bullfighting: The Quest for Nationality in Cuba, 1868–1898." *The Journal of American History* 81, no. 2 (September 1994): 493–517.

———. *Cuba: Between Reform and Revolution.* 2d ed. New York: Oxford University Press, 1995.

———. "Identidad y nacionalidad: las raíces del separatismo cubano, 1868–1898." *Revista del Centro de Investigaciones Históricas* 9 (1997): 185–95.

Pérez-Stable, Marifeli. *The Cuban Revolution: Origins, Course, and Legacy.* New York: Oxford University Press, 1993.

Pézard, André. "La langue italianne dans la pensée de Dante." *Cahiers du Sud* 34 (1951): 25–38.

Piedra, José. "Nationalizing Sissies." In *¿Entiendes? Queer Readings, Hispanic Writings*, edited by Emilie L. Bergmann and Paul Julian Smith, 370–409. Durham, N.C.: Duke University Press, 1995.

Piñera, Virgilio. "Emilio Ballagas en persona." *Ciclón* (September 1955): 41–50.

———. *Electra Garrigó.* In *Teatro completo.* Havana: Ediciones R, 1960.

———. "La vida tal cual." *Unión* 3, no. 10 (April–June 1990), 21–36.

Portela Alzola, Ena Lucía. "Dos almas perdidas nadando en una pecera" (Two lost souls swimming in a fishbowl). Havana: Editorial Extramaduros, 1990.

———. "Sombrío despertar del avestruz" (Dark awakening of the ostrich). In

El cuerpo inmortal. 20 cuentos eróticos cubanos, edited by Alberto Garrandés, 113–23. Havana: Editorial Letras Cubanas, 1997.

Pujals, Enrique J. "Carlos Montenegro: de la biografía a la narrativa." Ph.D. diss., Rutgers University, 1978.

Quesada, Gonzalo de. "Nota preliminar." In *Amistad funesta*, by José Martí (Martí, *Obras completas* 18:185–272), 188. Havana: Editorial de Ciencias Sociales, 1975.

Quiroga, José. "Fleshing Out Virgilio Piñera from the Cuban Closet." In *¿Entiendes? Queer Readings, Hispanic Writings*, edited by Emilie L. Bergmann and Paul Julian Smith, 168–80. Durham, N.C.: Duke University Press, 1995.

———. "Homosexualities in the Tropic of Revolution." In *Sex and Sexuality in Latin America*, edited by Daniel Balderston and Donna J. Guy, 133–51. New York: New York University Press, 1997.

———. "Virgilio Piñera: On the Weight of the Insular Flesh." In Molloy, Sylvia, and Robert McKee Irwin, eds. *Hispanisms and Homosexualities*, edited by Sylvia Molloy and Robert McKee Irwin, 269–85. Durham, N.C.: Duke University Press, 1998.

Radclyffe-Hall, Marguerite. *The Well of Loneliness*. Paris: Privately printed, 1928. Reprint, New York: Pocket Books, 1950.

Radhakrishnan, R. "Nationalism, Gender, and the Narrative of Identity." In *Nationalisms and Sexualities*, edited by Andrew Parker, Mary Russo, Doris Sommer, and Patricia Yaeger, 77–95. New York: Routledge, 1992.

Ragland-Sullivan, Ellie. *Jacques Lacan and the Philosophy of Psychoanalysis*. Urbana: University of Illinois Press, 1986.

Ramos, Julio. *Desencuentros de la modernidad en América Latina. Literatura y política en el siglo XIX*. Mexico City: Fondo de Cultura Económica, 1989.

———. "Trópicos de la fundación: poesía y nacionalidad en José Martí." In *Paradojas de la letra*, 153–64. Caracas: Ediciones eXcultura, 1996.

Rivera-Valdés, Sonia. *Las historias prohibidas de Marta Veneranda* (The forbidden stories of Marta Veneranda). Havana: Ministerio de Cultura, Colombia, and Casa de las Américas, Cuba, 1997.

Rodríguez Acosta, Ofelia. *La vida manda* (Life decrees). Madrid: Editorial Biblioteca Rubén Darío, 1929.

———. *En la noche del mundo* (In the night of the world). Havana: La Verónica, 1940.

Rojas, Rafael. *Isla sin fin: Contribución a la crítica del nacionalismo cubano*. Miami: Ediciones Universal, 1998.

Sabas Alomá, Mariblanca. *Feminismo: cuestiones sociales—crítica literaria*. Havana: Editorial Hermes, 1930.

Said, Edward. *The World, the Text, and the Critic*. Cambridge, Mass.: Harvard University Press, 1983.

Salessi, Jorge. "The Argentine Dissemination of Homosexuality, 1890–1914." In *¿Entiendes? Queer Readings, Hispanic Writings*, edited by Emilie L. Bergmann and Paul Julian Smith, 49–91. Durham, N.C.: Duke University Press, 1995.

———. *Médicos maleantes y maricas. Higiene, criminalización y homosexualidad en la construcción de la nación argentina. Buenos Aires: 1871–1914.* Rosario, Argentina: Beatriz Viterbo Editora, 1995.

Santí, Enrico Mario. "*Ismaelillo,* Martí y el modernismo." In *Pensar a José Martí: Notas para un centenario,* 19–50. Boulder, Colo.: Society of Spanish and Spanish-American Studies, 1996.

———. "*Fresa y Chocolate*: The Rhetoric of Cuban Reconciliation." *Modern Language Notes* 113 (1998): 407–25.

Sarduy, Severo. *Gestos* (Gestures). Barcelona: Seix Barral, 1963.

———. *De donde son los cantantes* (Where the singers come from). Mexico City: Editorial Joaquín Mortiz, 1967.

———. *Cobra* (Cobra). Buenos Aires: Editorial Sudamericana, 1972.

———. "Writing/Transvestism." *Review* 9 (fall 1973): 31–33.

———. "Severo Sarduy: Máquina barroca revolucionaria." Interview by Jean-Michel Fossey. In *Severo Sarduy,* by Jorge Aguilar Mora et al. Caracas: Fundamentos, 1976.

———. *La simulación* (The simulation). Caracas: Monte Ávila Editores, 1982.

———. *Colibrí* (Hummingbird). Bogotá: Editorial La Oveja Negra, 1985.

Schulman, Ivan. *Símbolo y color en la obra de José Martí.* Madrid: Gredos, 1970.

Schutte, Ofelia. "La América Latina y la posmodernidad: rupturas y continuidades en el concepto de *nuestra América.*" *Casa de las Américas* 210 (January–February 1998): 46–57.

Sedgwick, Eve Kosofsky. *Epistemology of the Closet.* Berkeley and Los Angeles: University of California Press, 1990.

———. *Tendencies.* Durham, N.C.: Duke University Press, 1993.

Simo, Ana María. "Interview with Ana María Simo." By Ian Daniels. *Torch* (New York). 15 December 1984, 14 January 1985.

Smith, Bruce R. *Homosexual Desire in Shakespeare's England: A Cultural Poetics.* Chicago: University of Chicago Press, 1991.

Smith, Paul. *Discerning the Subject.* Minneapolis: University of Minnesota Press, 1988.

Smith, Paul Julian. *Laws of Desire: Questions of Homosexuality in Spanish Writing and Film.* Oxford: Oxford University Press, 1992.

———. *Vision Machines: Cinema, Literature and Sexuality in Spain and Cuba, 1983–93.* London: Verso, 1996.

———. "Cuban Homosexualities: On the Beach with Néstor Almendros and Reinaldo Arenas." In *Hispanisms and Homosexualities,* edited by Sylvia Molloy and Robert McKee Irwin, 248–68. Durham, N.C.: Duke University Press, 1998.

Sommer, Doris. *Foundational Fictions: The National Romances of Latin America.* Berkeley and Los Angeles: University of California Press, 1991.

Sosa, Enrique. *El carabalí.* Havana: Editorial Letras Cubanas, 1984.

Stoner, Lynn K. *From House to the Streets: The Cuban Women's Movement for Legal Reform, 1898–1940.* Durham, N.C.: Duke University Press, 1991.

Uitti, Karl D. *Linguistics and Literary Theory.* Englewood Cliffs, N.J.: Prentice-Hall, 1969.

Ulloa, Justo. *José Lezama Lima: textos críticos.* Miami: Ediciones Universal, 1979.

Urías, Roberto. "¿Por qué llora Leslie Caron?" (Why is Leslie Caron crying?) Havana: Ediciones Unión, 1994.

Varona, Enrique José. Prologue to *La prostitución en la Ciudad de La Habana*, by Benjamín de Céspedes. Havana: Establecimiento tipográfico O'Reily, Número 9, 1888.

Villanueva-Collado, Alfredo. "Homoerotic, Heteroracial Relationship in the Latin American Naturalist Novel: *Bom-Crioulo* and *Hombres sin mujer.*" *Romance Languages Annual* 7 (1995): 647–52.

Weeks, Jeffrey. *Coming Out: Homosexual Politics in Britain from the Turn of the Nineteenth Century to the Present.* Rev. ed. London: Quartet Books Limited, 1983.

Yarbo-Bejarano, Yvonne. "The Lesbian Body in Latina Cultural Production." In *¿Entiendes? Queer Readings, Hispanic Writings*, edited by Emilie L. Bergmann and Paul Julian Smith, 181–97. Durham, N.C.: Duke University Press, 1995.

Young, Allen. *Gays under the Cuban Revolution.* San Francisco: Grey Fox Press, 1981.

———. "Commentary: 'The Cuban Gulag.' Homophobia and the American Left." *The Advocate* 388 (10 July 1984): 35.

———. "Cuba: Gay as the Sun." In *Out of the Closet: Voices of Gay Liberation*, edited by Karla Young and Allen Young, 206–50. New York: New York University Press, 1992.

Zea, Leopoldo. *El positivismo en México.* Mexico City: Ediciones Studium, 1953.

INDEX

Abelove, Henry, 6n. 12, 165
Abreu, Juan, 105n. 31
Acción por la libertad de expresión de la elección sexual (Action for the freedom of sexual choices) (GALEES), 110
Acosta Pérez, Alberto, 111
active/passive relationships, 30, 32
The Advocate: and Cuban homophobia, 110
Africans, representations of, 30, 35
Aguilar Mora, Jorge, 132n. 8
AIDS (Acquired Immune Deficiency Syndrome), 112n. 51, 129, 140–41, 146, 147, 216, 217
Almaguer, Tomás, 165n. 17
Almendros, Néstor, xixn. 17, 97n. 5, 108, 108n. 41
Alonso, Odette, 111, 170
Álvarez Bravo, Armando, 105n. 31
American: baseball, xviin. 11; capitalism, 102; economic control of Cuba, 41; mass culture, 14–15; modernity, 10–15, 33; neocolonialism, 8, 10–12, 42, 114; popular culture, xviin. 11, 228; preoccupation with masculinity, 10, 211; Republican Party, xvii; utilitarianism, 14–15. *See also* United States
Americanization of Cuba, 12
Amistad funesta (Fatal friendship), xviin.

13, 16–27, 16nn. 13, 14, 22n. 23, 46, 50. *See also* Martí, José
El amor y la prostitución. Réplica a un libro del Dr. Céspedes (Love and prostitution. Answer to a book by Dr. Céspedes) (1889), 32n. 12
Anderson, Benedict, xvin. 7, 3, 219. *See also* imagined communities
El ángel de Sodoma (The angel of Sodom) (1928), xixn. 16, 60, 66–77, 66n. 2, 81, 83
Anka, Paul, 212, 214
annexation: of Cuba, by the United States, 11; and sexuality, 11n. 4
Antequera Amaral, Félix, 220
Antes que anochezca (Before night falls) (1992), xxn. 22, 140–55, 170, 186, 188
antirationalism, xx
Anzaldúa, Gloria, 219
Aragón L'Oria, Alejandro, 111
Arboleda, Manuel G., 206n. 17
Arenas, Reinaldo (1943–90), xiiin. 1, 104, 105, 105n. 31, 108, 109, 140–55, 159, 159n. 4, 169, 170, 186, 187, 188
suicide of, 147
Argüelles, Lourdes, 96n. 3
Ariza, René, 109
art: for art's sake, 167; autonomy of, 70
Asians, and homosexuality in Cuba, 6n. 13, 35